PRINCIPIA ECONOMICA

THEORY AND DECISION LIBRARY

General Editors: W. Leinfellner and G. Eberlein

SERIES A: PHILOSOPHY AND METHODOLOGY OF THE SOCIAL SCIENCES

Scope

This series deals with the foundations, the general methodology and the criteria, goals and purpose of the social sciences. The emphasis in the new Series A will be on well-argued, thoroughly analytical rather than advanced mathematical treatments. In this context, particular attention will be paid to game and decision theory and general philosophical topics from mathematics, psychology and economics, such as game theory, voting and welfare theory, with applications to political science, sociology, law and ethics.

For a list of titles published in this series, see final page.

PRINCIPIA ECONOMICA

by

GEORGES BERNARD

C.N.R.S., Paris

KLUWER ACADEMIC PUBLISHERS

DORDRECHT / BOSTON / LONDON

Library of Congress Cataloging-in-Publication Data

Bernard, Georges.
　　Principia economica / by Georges Bernard.
　　　　p.　cm. -- (Theory and decision library.　Series A, Philosophy
　and methodology of the social sciences)
　　Includes index.
　　ISBN 0-7923-0186-2 (U.S.)
　　1. Economics.　I. Title.　II. Series.
　HB171.B4825　1989
　330--dc19
89-2339

Published by Kluwer Academic Publishers,
P.O. Box 17, 3300 AA Dordrecht, The Netherlands.

Kluwer Academic Publishers incorporates
the publishing programmes of
D. Reidel, Martinus Nijhoff, Dr W. Junk and MTP Press.

Sold and distributed in the U.S.A. and Canada
by Kluwer Academic Publishers Group,
101 Philip Drive, Norwell, MA 02061, U.S.A.

In all other countries, sold and distributed
by Kluwer Academic Publishers,
P.O. Box 322, 3300 AH Dordrecht, The Netherlands.

printed on acid free paper

Printed in the Netherlands

to Stef

TABLE OF CONTENTS

FOREWORD   x

PREFACE   xii

ACKNOWLEDGEMENT   xix

CHAPTER   1. Agents   1

CHAPTER   2. Resources   10

CHAPTER   3. Fields of Forces   17

CHAPTER   4. Relations between Agents. Activity   26

CHAPTER   5. Degrees of Freedom for Agents.
             Alienation and Free Will   36

CHAPTER   6. Choice Criteria. Utility. Resource
             Allocation   44
             Section 1. General   44
             Section 2. Agents' Choices   49

CHAPTER   7. Dimensional Approach   61

CHAPTER   8. Money and Prices   68
             Section 1. Nature and Functions of
             Money   68
             Section 2. Money and Choices of Agents   76
             Section 3. Theory of Prices and of Equilibria 80
             Section 4. Money, Credit and Inflation   84
             Conclusions   88

CHAPTER   9. Elementary Exchange   90

CHAPTER 10. Transfers   100
            Section 1. General Theory of Transfers   100
            Section 2. Different Kinds of PITs
            and PNITs   103

CHAPTER 11. Production and Value Added   111
            Appendix   128

CHAPTER 12. Space and Time in Human Activity   135
            Section 1. Space   136
            Section 2. Time   142

CHAPTER 13. Relations between Agents   153
            Section 1. The VA Distribution   153
            Section 2. The Public Agents   160
            Section 3. Private Individual Consumer
            Agents   164
            Section 4. Saving and Investment in
            Microeconomics   168
            Section 5. Financial and Monetary
            Economy   170
            Section 6. Other Types of Relations
            between Agents   172

CHAPTER 14. Economic Processes   175
            Section 1. Definitions and Notations
            of the Model   175
            Section 2. Presentation of the Model   183
            Section 3. Aggregation   191
            Section 4. Dynamic Interpretation
            and Discussion of the Model   197

SUMMARY AND CONCLUSIONS   204

INDEX   208

FOREWORD

It has already been said, if not written, that progress in knowledge in any domain consists mainly of expressing things that are well known in a different and, if possible, new way. That is the purpose of this book.

In his solitary effort an author is entirely and solely responsible for what he writes, including any mistakes or errors in the text. This is the case here as this book is not a result of a pluridisciplinary effort. It seems to the author that while reflection can be and sometimes is fruitful in a team, the task of bringing to light new ideas or to shed new light on old ones is mostly a solitary exercise. There are many illustrious examples to which, of course, the author does not compare himself: Quesnay, Rousseau, A. Smith, D. Ricardo, Fourier, Walras, Keynes, Freud and many others.

The text contains many analogies between economics and physics. This last 'exact' science has adopted two paradigms in this century: disequilibria are essential and normal states; the dynamics of events, the temporal evolution of states, is *the* explanation of Nature. One could also add a third, the fundamental principles of uncertainty and randomness.

The deterministic models that were current at the end of the last century were, on the contrary, attached to states of equilibrium and were invariant with respect to time as they assumed perfect causality, i.e. a perfect knowledge of the future.

Our approach to economics in this book parallels this progress in the knowledge of Nature. Both the neoclassical and marxist models are deterministic and the main concern of classical models are optimal states of equilibria. In this text we do not consider such states. The models proposed here are: (a) in disequilibrium; (b) not optimal; and (c) essentially fuzzy and uncertain. Fuzziness and uncertainty are, in our opinion, the two main properties of economics.

Our thoughts on economics necessarily intermingle with politics, psychology, sociology, epistemology and the applied natural science called technology. These thoughts are mainly descriptive, but as they endeavour to present the economic paradigm in a different light, they are also normative. More precisely what follows does not try to describe the economic reality that prevails *now* in the West, the East, the North and the South of our planet. It describes the economic sphere as it should be in order to be in step with the rest of human progress and, especially, with our present explanation of Nature. We shall try to describe economy as it begins to emerge in the present evolution of our societies. Thus this description will be normative when read at present but will, I hope, be descriptive for future readers.

The main items to be discussed are: the typologies of agents and of resources; the choices of agents; the relations between agents, between resources and between these two categories of economic objects; utility, exchange and transfer; the influence of space and time on the processes under study; value added, its creation, its distribution and its aggregation; in consequence money, prices, incomes, taxes, macrostates. . .

The book was begun in 1984 but many parts of the text are older. Added to delays in publishing this means that some of the final text may be out of date at the time of its reading. This is one of the reasons why statistics and other quantitative data are seldom used. Andrew Lang's opinion is, moreover, heartily supported by the author: the user of statistics is like a drunkard for whom lampposts are supports, not means of lighting.

PREFACE

Georges Bernard a consacré sa vie à la recherche. Comme plusieurs d'entre nous, après de longues années, il éprouve le besoin légitime de repenser par lui-même ce qu'il a appris de ses nombreux prédécesseurs, et de tenter de surmonter les insatisfactions qu'il a ressenties. Les *PRINCIPIA* que voici me paraissent ainsi marquer une étape importante dans la rénovation de la pensée économique.

C'est par un effort solitaire qu'il espère donner une expression nouvelle de la connaissance économique. Sa tentative est audacieuse et cependant teintée de modestie: il se sent responsable de ses fautes et de ses erreurs. A priori, c'est une grande prétention de ne pas suivre l'enseignement de nos grands maîtres: Smith, Ricardo, Walras, Keynes, pour ne citer que les plus grands.

Cet ouvrage a été mis en chantier en 1984 mais il est le fruit de longues années de réflexions. La formation d'ingénieur de l'auteur permet de comprendre les analogies qu'il découvre entre la physique et l'économique. Précisément la science dite exacte lui a appris que le déséquilibre était à la base de l'intelligence des évènements de la nature. Il est persuadé que les principes d'incertitude, d'aléa, ainsi que ceux de la mécanique quantique, sont essentiels pour comprendre l'économie. Or beaucoup de modèles économiques de la fin de ce siècle continuent au contraire d'être fondés sur l'équilibre. Ils admettent que la causalité parfaite assure une connaissance elle aussi parfaite du futur.

Les modèles régnants s'opposent, mais ils se ressemblent. Le néo-classique et le marxiste sont aussi déterministes l'un que l'autre. Ils ont la prétention d'aboutir à des états optimaux de l'équilibre. A l'inverse, les modèles qui vont être presentés sont des déséquilibres, non-optimaux, essentiellement flous et incertains.

L'auteur affirme que les caractères flou et incertain sont les propriétés fondamentales de l'économie.

C'est dans cet esprit que sont analysées les typologies des agents et des ressources, les relations entre agents et ressources. De ces principes de base découlent les questions traditionnelles touchant la monnaie, les prix, les revenus, les impôts. Ce sont des concepts qui sont analysés: les données quantitatives et les statistiques n'interviennent que rarement.

La partie qui demande le plus d'attention concerne les transferts et la valeur ajoutée. Elle commande l'intelligence de ces *PRINCIPIA*. Après avoir lu et relu Georges Bernard, je me demande si la valeur ajoutée n'est pas à la base de la vocation fondamentale de l'économie. Il s'agit de se demander comment est créée et comment est distribuée la valeur ajoutée.

Ayant défini les prix comme des rapports des flux de monnaie aux flux de ressources réelles, la valeur ajoutée, entité essentiellement nominale, est créée d'après l'auteur par la différence des flux de monnaie qui entrent et qui sortent de l'activité . Par conséquent dans la construction de Walras et de Pareto il n'y a pas de valeur ajoutée puisque par essence l'équilibre réalisé est optimal et assure l'égalité des coûts marginaux et moyens et des prix.

Georges Bernard va plus loin encore dans sa démarche iconoclaste. Il est classique d'appeler transferts les impôts, les prestations sociales directes, l'aide internationale, . . . Ce sont des transactions monétaires non incluses dans les échanges, donc hors de la notion classique de prix. L'auteur les appelle PNIT = Price Non Included Transfers, pour une raison simple. Il propose d'élargir la notion du transfert aux 'transferts inclus dans les prix' (Price Included Transfers = PIT) dont il propose une définition, par la différence entre les prix réels et le vecteur optimal des prix tel qu'il résulte du modèle d'équilibre-optimum de Walras-Pareto.

Les PIT évidemment existent dans les économies réelles: les profits de monopoles en sont un exemple. Et comment ne pas considérer qu'entre 1973 et 1980 le prix du pétrole comprenait d'énormes transferts, lorsqu'il était vendu jusqu'à cinquante fois son coût?

Ainsi, résultat important de la démarche de l'auteur, la valeur ajoutée est créée par des PIT et distribuée par des PNIT. En particulier – cela heurtera bien d'habitudes – la rémunération du travail n'est pas pour l'auteur un achat de ce 'facteur de production' mais est un PNIT dû au même titre que ceux des autres parts de la distribution de la valeur ajoutée.

Cette distribution résulte à tous les niveaux des choix et des résolutions de conflits entre groupes familiaux et sociaux.

Ce qui nous semble nouveau, c'est la distinction entre négociations véritables qui se ramènent aux mécanismes du marché, et les solutions apportées par des manifestations de forces, de pouvoirs et de traditions. En cela les considérations économiques s'allient aux considérations politiques, sociologiques, psychologiques; elles s'insèrent les unes dans les autres. Les citoyens sont aussi acteurs de l'économie. Rappelons que l'activité des agents ordinairement appelée travail n'est pas considérée comme un *input*. C'est le titre donné d'une partie de la valeur ajoutée. En tant que participation à une organisation le travail n'a pas de prix. Ce n'est pas un coût.

Il ne faudrait cependant pas faire à l'auteur la critique de ne pas tenir compte de l'économie de marché. Mais selon une expression originale le marché est pour lui une statistique.

Comment n'être pas frappé par ce qui est répété plusieurs fois avec insistance: les constructions des différentes écoles qui se sont succédé dans l'histoire: ricardienne, marxiste, walrasienne, keynésienne, néo-classique, monétariste, ne sont pas considérées et ne donnent lieu à aucune analyse. C'est bien là où se manifeste cette audace qui, au lieu d'être un scandale, pourrait être regardée comme une supériorité. Plutôt que de s'attrister de ne pas trouver en ces Principes la fameuse distinction classique entre salaires et profits, ne faudrait-il pas s'en réjouir? Il en serait de même du refus des discussions sur la productivité du travail, la maximisation du profit, sur la demande et l'offre d'investissement. En éliminant ces manières de penser, l'auteur s'élève à une vision nouvelle. On pourrait dire qu'il construit une théorie vraiment générale, au dessus de toutes les autres, ce que n'avait pas fait Keynes, malgré le titre de son grand livre.

Voici alors en dernière analyse un modè macro-économique simplifié qui est proposé. Entrent en action quatre agents agrégés: le ménage, la firme, la banque, l'Etat. Un cinquième est mentionné: le monde extérieur, mais il n'intervient pas dans la construction. Notons bien que l'Etat est présent, qu'il n'est pas composante exogène, mais qu'il est nécessaire de l'associer à toute activité. Et rappelons encore qu'il n'est pas tenu compte de la différenciation entre travailleurs, propriétaires, capitalistes et entrepreneurs.

L'idée majeure est maintes fois répétée: la notion d'équilibre n'est pas aplicable à la réalité économique. La croissance est par essence en contradiction avec l'équilibre. Il en est de même de l'inflation et du chômage.

Il faudra nous habituer progressivement à cette vision des choses. J'ai, pour ma part, l'intuition que Georges Bernard est dans la bonne voie. Mais nous sommes tellement imprégnés des idées qu'il combat que beaucoup des nôtres auront une gêne à se rendre à ses arguments.

HENRI GUITTON
de l'Institut

THE ENGLISH TRANSLATION OF PROFESSOR HENRI GUITTON'S PREFACE

Georges Bernard devoted many years of his life to research. As with most of us, he now feels a legitimate need to reformulate what he has learned from his numerous forebears. Through this effort, he endeavours to bridge his dissatisfaction with those teachings. As a result, these *Principia* are, in my opinion, a significant step towards a rejuvenation of economic thought.

Bernard's effort is solitary. He hopes in this way to propose a new formulation of economic knowledge. His is an intrepid endeavour while remaining humble. He claims for himself all mistakes and errors in the text. It is a priori presumptuous not to follow the teachings of our great masters, Smith, Ricardo, Walras and Keynes to quote the greatest only.

Although the writing of the book was begun in 1984, it is the fruit of long years of reflection. An engineer by education, his scientific background allowed Bernard to grasp analogies between physics and economics. Physics taught him about disequilibria as the essence of the natural events. Bernard is persuaded that the concepts of uncertainty and randomness, as well as the principles of quantum mechanics, explaining Nature, are essential to the understanding of economics. Now most current economic models continue to be based on equilibrium and assume perfect causality leading to perfect knowledge of the future.

These current models are antagonistic while remaining alike. Neoclassical and Marxist models are both deterministic. They claim they converge to the optimal state of equilibrium. To the contrary, the models proposed in *Principia* are non-optimal, imbalanced and fundamentally fuzzy and uncertain. Bernard states that fuzziness and uncertainty are essential properties of economic events.

Starting from these propositions, the author analyzes typologies of agents and resources and the relations between these two categories. Next, the traditional problems of money, prices, incomes and taxes are considered. Only concepts are of concern in the text;

quantitative data and statistics are seldom used.

The treatment of transfer and value added requires most attention from the reader. These two concepts govern the intelligence of
Principia. Having read and read again Georges Bernards's text, I
wonder if value added is not the foundation of economics. The
problem is to inquire how VA is created and how it is distributed.
According to the author's view, after having defined prices as ratios
of money to resource flows, the essentially nominal VA is created in
all activities by the difference between the incoming and outgoing
monetary flows. As a consequence, the Walras-Pareto model implies the non-existence of VA as by definition in optimal equilibrium marginal costs, mean costs and prices are all equal.

Bernard goes even further in his iconoclastic approach. It is
traditional to classify as 'transfers' taxes, direct social benefits,
international aid, etc. They are monetary transactions excluded from
exchanges and, as a consequence, outside the classical concept of
price. The author calls such transfers Price Non-Included Transfers
(PNITs) and does so for one simple reason. He proposes to generalize the concept of transfer to Price Included Transfers (PITs)
which he defines by the difference between real prices and the
vector of optimal prices resulting from the Walras-Pareto optimal
equilibrium model. PITs obviously exist in real economies: monopoly profits are a case in point. And how can one avoid considering
oil prices between 1973 and 1980 as including enormous transfers,
when the gap between these prices and costs was a fiftyfold multiple
of cost?

The important result of the author's approach is his statement
that VA is created by PITs and distributed by PNITs. In particular –
this will clash with most customary views – work compensation
(wages and salaries) is, for Bernard, *not* a purchase of this production factor but a PNIT, a claim equal to other claims for parts of VA
distribution. This distribution is the overall result of protracted
choices and negotiations, on all levels, within all agents concerned.

The distinction between negotiations, which in fact are market
mechanisms, and the effects of power and traditional influences,
seems to me to be a new approach. It links economic to political,
psychological and sociological arguments. They are all closely en-
tangled. Citizens are also economic actors. It is recalled that activity

currently called work is *not* considered to be an input. It is a title to a part of VA. Work as participation in an activity has no price and is not a cost.

One will, however, not criticize Bernard for not including market economy in his analysis. By a striking formulation, market is for him a statistic.

A conspicuous fact is to be noted. The author repeatedly distances his approach from the historical sequence of economic schools. Ricardian, Marxist, Walrasian, Keynesian, neoclassical, monetarist models are not analyzed. This boldness could be looked upon not as a scandal but as a superiority. Instead of regretting the absence of the famous classical distinction between wages and profits, why not applaud it? The same should be the case for the refusal to discuss labour productivity, profit maximization and the demand and supply of investment. By eliminating these problems, the author reaches a new vision. His effort could be taken to be a really comprehensive theory. Despite the title of his great work, Keynes did not attain this level.

Finally, a simplified macromodel is built. Four aggregate *Agents* act: the *Household*, the *Firm*, the *Bank* and the *State*. A fifth actor, the outside world is mentioned but not included. Thus, the *State* is present not as an exogenous actor but as an almost trivial economic agent. Remember again that distinctions between workers, owners, capitalists and entrepreneurs are not considered.

The main idea is quite often repeated: the concept of equilibrium is not applicable to economic reality. Growth is, in essence, contradictory to equilibrium. The same is true for inflation and unemployment.

We have to get progressively acquainted with this vision. I feel, for my part, that Georges Bernard is on the right track. We are, however, so pervaded with the ideas he fights against that most of us will shun from surrendering to his arguments.

HENRI GUITTON
de l'Institut

ACKNOWLEDGEMENT

The author wishes to express his deep appreciation for the help he received from: Professor Wilhelm Krelle, who read the typescript and proposed many corrections which improved the quality of the text enormously, and Alex Whyte, who finally 'polished' the English written by a foreigner and thus eliminated quite a number of faults.

The sole responsibility for what follows remains of course with the author.

CHAPTER 1

AGENTS

What do we mean by 'agent'?

The word 'agent' will hereafter mean any person, household, group, local government, firm, association, state or sovereign State, international institution etc., playing a role or, tautologically, acting in human activities on this Earth and now also in space.

In more formal language, an 'agent' is (a) an element of a set and a subset of agents, the last being a partition of these sets and (b) these subsets hereafter called collective agents. All these 'grains' possess structures of great diversity or variety. The set of all agents is defined as human space. This general system, thus defined but by large not described or analyzed, includes a subsystem called the economic sphere.

At this stage, such definitions are sketchy and their clarification is not easy.

Our concern in this first chapter will be with agents. The relations between agents and between agents and other objects of our analysis will be dealt with later.

What defines agents is the fact that they choose. This means that they possess finite sets of criteria. This reality can also be defined by the existence for agents of a *libre arbitre*, i.e. of a number greater than one of exogenous degrees of liberty, synonymous with the fact that the set of choices has more than one element. It is generally assumed that this set is constrained which means that the number of real choices is less than the number of a priori possible choices. We shall elaborate on this point later.

Elementary agents are individuals or persons. Their behaviour, i.e. their choices, depend on the totality of the activity of their brain, the paloencephale as well as the neo-cortex. This activity stems from innate as well as from acquired characters. The psychology, a discipline dealing with human behaviour, and logic and mathematics, formalizing the part of such behaviours defined as rational, are essential for the understanding of economics and politics. People, as agents, are submitted to the influence of the

1

society in which they live and of the environment, which we call
Nature. People are educated in their infancy and youth and, for most,
the learning process continues now throughout each person's life.

Societies and finally humanity are complex sets whose elements
or subsets (also agents) are not only individuals but also groups of
individuals, imbricated by a great variety of modes into a great
variety of collective agents. It is assumed here that in one way or
another these collective agents possess the main character of agents,
the capacity to choose or to decide between elements of the set of
possible choices, under specific constraints and following specific
criteria.

Any society is thus like a Russian doll, only much more complicated than this toy, whose inclusions are linear, i.e. unidimensional. A society can be imagined as a multidimensional Russian
doll. . . Each agent, be it a person or a group, belongs more or less
to, or is an element of several other agents, and all these agents
whether simple or complex, are decision- or, better, choice-mak-
ers. 'Belongs more or less' is an important statement which can be
expressed by writing that sets of agents or collective agents are fuzzy
sets in the sense of the fuzzy set theory.

The fuzziness of the sets and subsets of agents, quantified by the
'factor of belonging', a positive number less than 1, is an essential
feature of the societies. If this factor is equal to 1, the society is
totalitarian and individuals and groups behave like bees in a hive or
ants in an ant-hill. If the factor is 0, the society ceases to exist and
is replaced by perfect anarchy. So the set of factors of belonging can
be used to define the structure of the society, that is its organization.

More formally, let i denote elements (agents) of collective agents
and j such agents and let d_j^i be the factor of belonging of i to j. We
have:

(a) $\Sigma_j d_j^{i^0} \leq N$: an agent i^0 belongs to several agents
$j = 1. \ldots N. \ldots$
If i^0 does not belong to one or more of j, the inequality is strict but
the reverse is not true.

(b) $\Sigma_i d_{j^0}^i \leq I$: agents $i, i = 1. \ldots I. \ldots$ belong to the collective
agent j^0
If some agents i do not belong to j^0, the inequality is strict but the
reverse is not true.

Strict inequalities are common features of human societies. Of course, agents i are most often themselves collective agents.

Social oligopoles and/or classes are 'collective agents', studied in economic theory as coalitions. The term 'class struggle' can be interpreted as a statement that these fuzzy 'collective agents', called classes, are in conflict. These groups however do not 'choose' or decide in quite the same manner as the stuctured collective agents described above.

There are other types of such agents in the groups of sovereign States, such as the European Community or, at the summit, the United Nations. Federal political structures are of the same kind but for their member states the factor of belonging is nearer to 1.

In general agents are vertices of fuzzy graphs. This will be discussed further in Chapter 4.

In the realm of strict economics, individual agents in history have been, and still are, partitioned into blue- and white-collar workers, owners of land, owners of means of production, entrepreneurs, inactive young and old, taxpayers etc. Each of these categories is, in economic theory, aggregated in a 'class', in the formal meaning of this term, by any kind of process. It is an obvious fact that any individual can and does belong to several of these categories so that their aggregation necessarily results in a fuzzy 'collective agent' which may be called a class, as shown above. Beyond the economic domain one can read about the military and the civilians, the elite and the mass, about cliques and lobbies etc. . . .

On a global scale the behaviours or the choices of all kinds of agents belonging to a given society result in what is called civilization, culture, economics, politics, arts, etc. In its total the system is humanity.

A fundamental fact on which we shall elaborate but which is worth mentioning here is that the set of criteria under which choices are made by agents can be and often is of several origins. The simplest example is 'social utility', more formally a collective preference criterion. It has at least three origins. Firstly it can be defined as an aggregation of the utilities of the members, both individual and collective, of the society. Secondly, these elementary utilities can be alienated or delegated to an individual or a group, by any possible procedure. Thus, a representative democracy is a delegation of sets of choices to a Parliament. Thirdly the social utility can be an exogenous attribute of the society as a whole, for instance, the 'national interest'.

Let us briefly comment on the main categories of agents.

To repeat, the elementary category is the person or individual. The simplest and oldest collective agent is the family, more or less extended in history to the ancestry and descent of its present head. This agent, called by today's national accounts economists 'a household', has a head composed by one or two adults of the present generation, the couple. In several ways, defined by tradition and custom, as well as legally it detains the power of choice and possesses the social utility of this agent.

Higher collective agents of this kind existed in history and have survived as tribes, i.e. groups of families or households bound by common rituals and traditions, by what is now called the 'sacred' in contrast to the rationale of contracts or interests. Ethics, morals and religions come under this heading.

In our developed societies there are two main categories of collective agents. The first consists of structural or institutional groups which can also be called political while the second are the spontaneous and/or common interest groups. The first category is a pyramid of at its base a community, then a city, a county, a region, a state, above a sovereign State and then international bodies of all kinds, which in the present outlay are interstate groups.

The second kind of collective agents consists again of two separate types. The first is called the firm. Its aim is to be productive, i.e. to create real goods and services, by means of the input of other real goods and services and of human work. In financial terms, this process results in the creation and distribution of the value added. It is not incorrect to call the value added 'the wealth'. A substantial part of this book will be devoted to this concept, which can and will be used in the analysis of economic activity not only of firms but of all agents.

The collective agent called a firm and/or a shop or a place of work, an industrial or other active site, which are agents different from the firm, can be a set consisting of only one element (a person) or can be a set of many individual and smaller collective agents. The State as well as other structural or institutional groups could also be considered as a firm, since these agents, as just mentioned, also create and distribute goods and services and the value added. In usual economics, however, the term firm defines only such agents who exchange, i.e. buy and sell values such as goods, services or finance.

In short, we shall define firms as all collective and individual agents who deal in inputs and outputs of any kind and we shall entirely dissociate the typology of agents from the typology of relations between them such as division of labour, exchange, gift, transfer, taxes, orders and instructions, information, communication etc.

Actually, two different descriptions of agents can and often do describe the same social objects. A simple example of such partitions and/or imbeddings in the human space has already been mentioned: a person or a household can be an agent in two different categories. He or she is an individual. Or such an agent is a traditional, moral, ethical entity called the family. In usual economics, these agents only consume goods and services and supply labor within the real sphere and they spend or save income in the financial one; but these agents can simultaneously be a firm, such as a farm, a physician, a lawyer, who all create value added, exchange and transfer.

In commercial firms and also in other collective agents the most important but not the only bond or, what we shall call by analogy to physics, the field of forces, which creates the group, is a contract in view of action. Action means making choices according to a set of criteria. Political theory attaches great importance to the concept of contract in the explanation of societies. The same is true in economic theory.

The last category of collective agents depends even more on contractual bonds. These agents are called associations, political parties, labor and professional unions and institutes, scientific societies, churches, universities and schools, all kinds of clubs etc. In some societies they are basically free groupings of people or agents who want to do something together. In other societies they belong to the State's sphere of action. But they all possess the character of agents: they aggregate utilities, i.e. choice criteria or possess exogenous utilities, and make choices. Many of them consume inputs and create outputs, thus creating value added and could be labelled firms, although they may not exchange.

The properties of agents are manifold. We shall distinguish firstly what may be called their demography. We extend this discipline from the consideration of the human population, to which it is customarily devoted, to the population of agents, of all kinds of agents, including societies, States, civilization etc.

Contrary to ordinary demography whose subjects, the human beings, are by definition born, live and die, agents can be mortal, after having been born and having lived, and can also, at least by the horizon of several generations, be immortal. Thus individual agents are of course mortal, since they are human beings. And more often than not, small firms are also mortal, although some firms such as small shops can remain 'alive' much longer than the normal biological lifespan of humans. All political and institutional agents, including States, big firms and contractual groups, churches, societies and cultures in fact most collective agents can be and are considered by the horizon of economics as immortal. This is especially true for States which, once born, never consent to die; this is true of big firms which nowadays, for social reasons, are not allowed to die. Of course, historians write in their works about mortal civilizations, but their time horizon is not ours.

We shall look at the demography of collective agents in later chapters. It is seldom considered in its general scope while it is an important reality. It is obvious that the behaviour of agents, as the behaviour of persons, (i.e. their choices) depends on their lifespan, their age and their sentiment of eternity. For instance the activity of forecasting and planning, a most important economic action, heavily depends on the horizon, the evaluation of the future existence of the agent.

Both mortal and immortal collective agents can be provided with a metabolism. They can possess an autonomous regulation or feedback control, as do living organisms. Cells have a short life while the animal, a structure of cells, has a much longer one. The life of a tree is shorter than the life of the forest which is eternal in comparison. In human societies a family, a club, a tribe, a firm, a village, a city or a nation live longer than the individuals who belong to them.

Of course individuals are something more than cells or trees.

They have brains or, in more ancient terms, a soul. So human collective agents or societies create traditions, beliefs, civilizations and cultures. These are special attributes of collective agents. One can express this special character of collective agents by stating that ideas are social realities.

This is particularly apparent for the two classes of agents situated at the extremes of a scale measuring their size and their complexity: the individuals and the States.

We have written that individuals act, that is choose, according to the activity of their brain. This tautologically states that their choices are subjective. The social influence on the activities of people has always been very strong and is nowadays particularly intense, contributing to the difficulty, analyzed by psychology, of obtaining stability in individual behaviours. The 'insufficiency of control' on this class of agents is translated in economic theory in two ways, represented by two kinds of models. In both, individuals and households consume goods and services and supply an abstract factor called labour.

In the 'open' models, these activities allow people to achieve their personal goals of satisfaction and happiness and their personal aims of accomplishment, mainly by distributing the available time of their life between education and learning, work, leisure, material needs, etc. Economists translate this reality by stating that the choices such agents make tend to maximize their 'utility'. Philosophers agree with this model by asserting that the ultimate aim of the material activity is the satisfaction of individual needs and desires, including the spiritual side of human life. Some religions adopt the same approach while others differ. We may call it a 'libertarian' approach.

It assumes the exogenous character of the supply (offer) of labour. This factor is socially considered as a good or a service of the same kind as other goods and services but is *not* an output of an activity.

In the 'closed' models, individual agents and households (we do not consider here, for simplicity's sake, the distinction between these two kinds of agents) are considered as firms. Their input is the consumption of goods and services and their output is a commodity called labour. Both are endogenous. What could be called value added, but is not counted in the social product, is the spiritual activity, leisure, education, the raising of a family etc. In consequence the criterion of choices in this model is the same as in the open model, namely the maximization of a 'utility'.

The main model of this kind is the one built in the XIXth century by Karl Marx. Adam Smith before him and von Neumann after him have also built closed models. The aptitude of such models to explain reality is hampered by the neglect of subjective choices and of the spiritual side of human life. We call such models, with some exaggeration, totalitarian.

The dichotomy of libertarian or totalitarian approaches to individual agents is closely linked to a similar analysis of the most complex collective agents, the States.

In usual theories the State is an agent of a special quality, as its choices are sovereign thus by definition not constrained. The set of States is truly a libertarian if not an anarchist society. The 'public' consumption as the consumption of the State is called is exogenous and there exists a utility of the State, called social utility, which the State maximizes. So the society of States is less controlled than are those of other agents, and in particular individuals. The evolution of the set of States can be and often is divergent, leading to catastrophes such as wars.

We consider States as collective agents, acting in several spaces, the economic subspace being one of them, and in this space not essentially different from firms.

As stated in the Foreword, we rarely formulate normative opinions. In the present case, however, we prefer the libertarian approach (which is expressed in open models) for the individual agents and the opposite (that is the closed model) for the State. This means that (a) for people labour is never a good but always a part of their activity which contributes to their general wellbeing and utility and (b) States are firms consuming inputs and labour and producing an output of goods and services, which in general are not exchanged, and a value added, the latter being a contribution to the social wealth. We will elaborate on this important matter later in this book and in particular shall propose a variant of both open and closed models. In this variant labour is not a good produced by households (in this respect the model is open). Labour is also never a factor of production, i.e. of the creation of the value added but only a title to its distribution. In this respect our model seems to be new.

Let us add that the problem of the existence or non-existence of markets and in particular the consideration of a labour market is here not essential. In this chapter, as has already been stated, we are concerned with the typology of agents and not with the relations between them.

Last but not least, the fundamental quality of the elements of the set of agents, as of people, is their infinite diversity , the variety of their characters. Agents, as people, are *all* different and *all* unequal. This variety is for agents even more intense than it is for people or in other living creatures. True twins or clones do not exist in the space of agents. Also, by definition, their choice criteria are different, however slightly this may be.

RESOURCES

As this book is about economics, resources are considered here mainly in the light of material activity. Such activity encompasses, or is even founded on the human spirit. Art for instance is also an economic good. The fuzziness of any set of resources, as of any set of agents, is the main character of our present object.

Firstly one can distinguish between material and immaterial resources. An example of such a distinction is the one between hardware and software in DP (data processing) activity. The hardware is composed of cabinets full of electronic components, supplemented by display screens, keyboards, printers, discs and tapes with their drives. The software is an intellectual creation initially represented by symbols on a sheet of paper and eventually stored, i.e. memorized within the hardware. Thus the hardware is a good example of a material resource and the software, although materialized on paper or in the electronic memories (where such materialization is less apparent for traditional minds), is in fact immaterial.

The set of material resources includes all pure consumer goods, such as perishables and food, all kinds of disposable items, all kinds of plant, equipment machines: construction, chemical, raw material processing, earth moving, farm machinery, transport and communication equipment, the whole of urban and rural infrastructure, further what is usually called durable consumer goods such as clothing, domestic appliances and housing. We are not concerned here with the technological niceties of this catalogue and leave it at that, adding only to the list all cultural equipment such as books, audiovisual machines, theater, movie and other similar equipment, monuments and shrines, libraries and museums.

All material resources just listed are artifacts, products of human activity, which are a subset of the set of material resources. Its other subset, originally more important is what carries the generic name of Nature, and what economists call natural resources. They include land, air, water, the biosphere, all components of the crust of the Earth, the electromagnetic spectre and in the near future the resources of space. . . Energy, whose source on Earth is almost exclusively the radiation of the Sun, is one of these resources. We know today that energy is as material as steel or wood.

In economics natural resources have some special qualities that we shall address later and which are closely linked to the next subset of resources generally considered as material although they are nowadays almost entirely physically immaterial, namely what may be called by a generic term of claims or rights, and are generally represented by financial resources. Money, ownership deeds, debts, equity and loans, all physically represented today by pieces of paper but more and more only inscribed in computer memories, are such resources. In economics they are often considered as real or a least as not immaterial, as opposed to say a representation of real physical goods such as a machine or a piece of bread. Financial resources play a big role in our understanding of value, of time, of utility, of prices, of saving and investment while remaining, one must not forget it, only a representation of real objects.

As our above comparison of software and hardware shows, really immaterial resources, which can be most 'valuable', i.e. represented by a large amount of financial resources, are mainly information and knowledge. Historically these resources were exchanged as 'services' such as the advice of a lawyer or cure prescribed by a doctor. As transport and communication as such are immaterial, they were also included in services, together with the services of justice, of police, of the army, of the general administration of societies, although none of these was bought or sold. A finer analysis shows that all these activities essentially use knowledge and information. Transport and communication are today commodities in their own right; only fifty years ago they were not identified as such, although of course they existed. In particular, a finer analysis of transport and communication as economic resources shows that moving physical objects (which defines 'transport') or moving information and knowledge (which defines 'communication') are activities of the same nature as all uses of equipment. Some of the equipment changes the aspect and/or the essence of the physical or spiritual resources involved, i.e. a machine tool, a chemical vessel, a computer; some only 'moves it', i.e. changes its position in space; some transfers spiritual resources in time: books, records, films; some keeps resources, so also transfers them in time: such are housing and office buildings, silos and libraries, warehouses and reserves of raw materials in the earth's crust etc.

All these services imply a cost and thus are a productive activity, since they use inputs to produce them as outputs. Even the most direct communication, the tongue, a tool of acoustic exchange of symbols and ideas, requires time and effort and is thus an output of an input.

We have dwelled on this description in order to be able to apply to the set of resources the reflections which will be proposed in following chapters, mainly with regards to value, to financial assets, to the value added and its creation and distribution, to income, consumption and saving etc.

There exists in the literature other typologies or taxonomies of resources, which are applicable specifically to economic resources, whether exchanged or not.

Firstly one can distinguish between public, merit and private goods.

Public goods are in principle the output of institutional collective agents and are not offered against a price. These are almost every-where public safety and law and order; in our times the administration of justice, i.e. the activity of judges is in general a public good, as are the activities of politicians and administration officials. In many countries education and health care are public goods, also offered, however, as merit or private goods. The transport infrastructures: roads, bridges, waterways, harbours, airports, when such equipment is tollfree, are public goods, as are national forests, parks, reserves. . . The above descriptions are obviously rather fuzzy: a tollfree bridge is a public good; but when one has to pay for its use it ceases to be it. A state or county school is a public good and provides a public service called education. But the same school, when privately owned is a firm selling a private service which is again education. Judges in olden times and nowadays in some societies were paid for each sentence and thus were professionals of the same category as physicians or lawyers.

The category of private goods comprises all items sold and bought, whether on a market or otherwise. One can define this category as the subset of resources which are neither public nor merit.

This last category is an intermediate one. Merit resources are sold and bought as are the private ones, but the conditions of these exchanges: production, prices, delivery terms, quality etc. are 'regulated' by public bodies, i.e. superior collective agents, which set these conditions. The arguments put forward to justify the regulation are, firstly, the existence of monopolies and secondly the public, i.e. collective utility of their fair availability. Examples are numerous. Today they are mainly in the activities of transport, energy, communication, sanitation and health etc.

As is obvious from the above description this first taxonomy is highly conventional if not arbitrary. It closely depends on the layout of the concerned society, its economic and socio-political system. Here are some 'equivalent' public and private resources:

Public	*Private*
Lighthouse	Shipboard radar
Clean air	Air filters and purifiers
Fire Department	Sprinkler systems
Consumer information	Brand-name advertising
Police Department	Alarms, locks, guards, dogs. .

It can be considered that one of the differences between the two main economic systems, the 'socialist' of the Soviet type and the 'capitalist' or market type resides in the taxonomy adopted for existing resources for partition into public, merit and private goods and services.

One can mention here the usual criteria of distinction between public and private resources, called the principles of exclusion and of indivisibility.

The principle of exclusion defines private goods: when a person eats an apple, no one else can eat that apple. The apple is a private good. But when a policeman or a traffic light regulates a road crossing, a motorist who drives through it does not deprive another motorist of this same service. A traffic light is a public good as are the services of the traffic cop.

The principle of indivisibility is another formulation of a similar if not identical reality: an apple can be divided between two people while the services of a traffic light cannot. In other words, public goods cannot, by definition, be the subject of competition between their users or 'customers', contrary to private goods. The principle of indivisibility can thus also be called 'of non-rivalry'.

Contrary to this first taxonomy, the second to which attention is now drawn is a real one, less dependent on the social outlay.

It partitions the set of resources into subsistence, discretionary and deluxe goods (and services).

Subsistence goods are those which are necessary for the immediate vital needs of agents. Applied to individuals, they are and have always been food and shelter. In our present societies many other resources are often considered as of subsistence. They were best summarized by F. D. Roosevelt in the four freedoms: from want, from ignorance, from disease, from fear. The access to education, to work, to leisure, to health, to dignity are today subsistence resources. In some societies they are still unavailable; in others some are missing, even food and shelter.

It is obvious that the concept 'subsistence' is rather elastic. It is however an important factor in the analysis of present human societies as the range of such resources can be taken as a yardstick of the affluence of a society. Such a measure could be the cardinality of the set of resources considered within this society as of subsistence.

The second category of resources is even more associated with affluence. Resources are called discretionary when they are mass produced and in consequence mass marketed without being necessary; that is, not in the category of subsistence goods. It is obvious that such a definition, while being independent from the economic system of a given society, is largely dependent on its cultural, institutional and customary (sacred) structure. And, actually, who shall decide whether a resource is necessary or not?

In developed economies it is generally assumed that 'durable consumer goods' such as domestic appliances, cars, fashionable clothing, leisure goods such as audiovisual products, cameras etc. and all 'beauty' ingredients are discretionary. The definition is, of course, arbitrary and even false as most of the 'durable consumer' items are not for consumption at all but constitute the equipment of individuals and households which increases their productivity in work and in leisure in the same way that any productive equipment does in factories. And in the same way as this last equipment, such resources result from investment which arises from saving. These goods are more or less absent in poor societies.

The third category, of deluxe goods, can be defined by the fact that they are mainly symbols of status and power. They are scarce and very expensive in the labour required to create them and consequently in price.

It is necessary to stress here a fundamental fact. All resources, be they public, merit, private, of subsistence, discretionary or deluxe, are in some sense more or less useful. A measure of their utility can in principle always be attached to all these resources. How can this be done? This is a tricky question which we will try to clarify later in this text. We shall in particular propose to discuss the scale of such utilities, from a large negative to a large positive measure.

The second taxonomy has been established and is used mainly if not exclusively for private goods, i.e. resources exchanged, on markets or otherwise, and used by individuals and households. It is interesting to try to apply this taxonomy to collective agents and to merit and public goods.

Most merit goods, such as energy, transport, communication, education, can be called 'social subsistence resources'. Present societies can only with great difficulty if at all exist without them. Some public goods such as law and order, the administration of police and justice, the general administration, the main infrastructures, the urban services such as sewerage or transit systems or street cleaning can be labelled 'of social subsistence'.

Most collective cultural and artistic resources, such as national theaters, museums, galleries, historic monuments and buildings could be labelled discretionary as could all the other manifestations of the sacred such as pageantry, monarchies when they exist etc.

Public buildings are equipment up to a certain degree of their lavishness while palaces and castles when in current use with their exaggerated pomp could be called collective deluxe resources.

Now what about armies and armaments?

Persons faithful to the present structure of humanity divided among some 160 sovereign States would deem such resources to be of subsistence. The pure rationality distinct from traditions cannot dismiss the possibility that humanity can live and prosper in a different system where national armies and armaments could be considered as discretionary or even deluxe. The problem remains open, at least here. One can only point to an analogy.

In the past, swords or any other individual weapons such as in the XIXth century in the West of North America guns, were indeed subsistence goods for most people. Today in our societies the great majority of us live unarmed. Guns and rifles are sports equipment for some affluent individuals which makes them at least discretionary if not deluxe commodities. What has been the evolution, and progress for individual agents should be possible, in the future, for collective agents.

Coming back to strict economics, two last taxonomies or, here, dichotomies of resources are in current use in economic theory:

- the two 'production factors', capital and labour,
- the distinction between consumption and investment goods.

Both dichotomies have, and have had, important impacts on real economic policies, in both market and planned systems.

In our understanding the first dichotomy concerns abstract model variables which are not resources at all. The second dichotomy is highly conventional. If heavy equipment such as a steel mill or a cargo ship are clearly investment goods, how about cars or typewriters customarily called consumption goods when used by private people or households while accounted for as investment when owned by a firm?

We shall discuss these dichotomies in more detail later when we will dwell on two other abstract pairs of 'resources': proximity and promiscuity and scarcity and abundance.

Finally information has always been and is a prominently valuable resource. It is interesting to see that this 'commodity', even if it is sold and bought on a market, follows the principle of non-exclusion of public goods. It is never 'consumed'. In principle its use by an agent does not deprive another agent of using it so that the principle of non-rivalry applies. But the character of private goods also often applies, when access to information is restricted by its proprietary or secret quality.

CHAPTER 3

FIELDS OF FORCES

In this chapter we shall try to describe the forces that operate in the space-time of human existence and activity. They proceed or derive from fields of cohesion, attraction and repulsion.

In physics there is now no distinction of essence between the matter on which fields act and the energy of which such fields are models. In our realm this seems to be the case as well since 'matter' in our representation are the agents and forces and fields cannot exist without them. In our opinion it is not quite so. Ideas, religions, many social facts do exist and can be considered independently from the agents on which they act.

While in physics the search for the elementary building block of matter-energy is still going on, in socio-economics this element is well defined. It is the individual, the person. Philosophy, biology, medicine, psychology, economics, all study this element (him or her). It is a given, insecable material point in our space-time; a point which, like living cells, is born, lives and dies. This is the individual agent. In the first chapter we have described these agents and also the collective agents whose generic name could be 'organizations'. We are here concerned with the forces which act on all agents and which determine in part their behaviours, i.e. their choices. In a digression which we deem to be necessary but which could be a part of the first chapter, we shall dwell here on the difference between individual and collective agents. There is a dichotomy between these two categories. An individual is a whole, an element who 'internalizes' his or her desires, beliefs, education etc. in his or her behaviours and externalizes these choices in decisions or actions. An organization or a collective agent is on the contrary an entity distinct from such ideas, beliefs, traditions, existing only in the minds of the elements of this collective agent, the people. Of course these beliefs, traditions etc., do influence the choices of the collective agents.

Present day sociology, economics, history or philosophy do not make this distinction between individual and collective agents. For reasons which we shall try to elucidate now, we maintain the distinction. The first argument runs as follows:

Physics or natural sciences that try to understand and explain Nature build 'models' for this purpose. Models are our representation of what Nature is but are never its reality; nor do they influence It in any sense. Nature is totally indifferent to what we say, write or think about It. Of course Man has mightily changed the biosphere but has done so only in the same way as a forest changes the microclimate, without really controlling the change. Unfortunately, if the model of the nuclear winter after the next war, if it happens, represents what will happen, such a statement may not be true.

Individuals are integral parts of Nature. As such, their study by the sciences which are called philosophy, biology, medicine, psychology, genetics etc. are models. These models are distinct from the reality of people and, besides, do not change this reality in any way that is different from the action of engineers on Nature when, for instance, a river is controlled by a dam.

Models of collective agents, i.e. their organizations, have on the contrary the particular virtue of being a part of their reality. They exist as models and are also a part of the reality of these agents, of firms, societies, nations. . . .

The second argument has already been formulated. Contrary to natural sciences where such elements are still searched for, the five billion or so human beings living on this planet are the elementary building blocks of the models of human activity. All collective agents are different sets of these 'elementary particles'.

Sir John Hicks in Value and Capital stresses that: 'Economics is not, in the end, much interested in the behaviours of single individuals. Its concern is with the behaviour of groups. A study of individual demand is only a means to the study of market demand'. (p. 34)

Our approach is less narrow. Agents of all kinds, including individuals, choose and act. Macroeconomics is a method of aggregation of such acts. Instead of only considering markets, a concept moreover subject to controversy, we propose to do so by means of the concept of fields of forces.

Such fields are manifold. As many animal species humans are

social beings. The first attraction field which assembled them was the sheer necessity of subsistence: to procure food, to fight predators and to raise children. Other attraction forces emerged from the unique capacity of the human brain to reason, to correlate, to have a memory, all functions that we can create, in a very crude replica, in computers.

Some superior animals manifest these two forces but on a much smaller scale of intensity or sophistication, since their brains are less developed, that is of a smaller 'computer' capacity.

This specific activity of the human brain created other attraction and repulsion fields. On the side of attraction, one can mention:

- sentiments and subjective feelings such as love, hate, lust for power, from which emerge the family and tribal life, today manifold groups and always wars;
- the anxiety and fear of the future. No animal perceives time and its unidirectional flow as does man. Expressed in dynamics, on the material side the perception of time is the founding stone of economics. Forecasting, expectations, the future of production and trade, on which investment decisions are based, saving, the economics of money and credit, are all fundamentally subject to the variable time.
- on the level of homo faber and not homo sapiens the division of labour, the creation of tools and the specialization of craftsmen and later of the productive activities, command a cohesive social field of forces.

Today all these fields are enhanced to a previously unheard of degree of intensity by the modern techniques of energy, transport and communication.

The repulsion fields are individual and social. The diversity of people living on Earth includes geniuses, criminals, originals, marginals, prophets, anchorites and political leaders. Many of them shun society, repulse it or are rejected by it. Some of these individuals master states and nations and thus become most solitary.

Social repulsion fields proceed from the sentiments against strangers, immigrants, people of other civilizations, customs and external aspects. They cause conflicts and wars and are prominent in the political as well as the economic sphere.

All these fields can be strong or feeble. Their range of action has changed in history. Up to about two hundred years ago, communication and transport capabilities limited the range to small distances. Separate civilizations lived on Earth. Now a unique technological revolution in these two tools made the range of action of many fields extended to the totality of the biosphere.

The concept of a 'World-economy' describes the global field of production and trade. This field is complex. It is a compound of spatial forces, created by geography, the environment, the climate, by transport and communication, of temporal forces represented by money, finance and credit and also by the non-reproducible natural resources. On a lesser scale contract fields: firms, political entities and governments are present as well as other legal and institutional forces. The principle of ownership, which is deeply rooted in the human psyché, whether private or public, can be compared to attraction forces in physics. This analogy can be extended to other socio-economic objects such as the division of labour, organized markets, money and commodity exchanges and all kinds of associations and unions. Last but not least, all spiritual bonds aggregated under the concepts of culture, of civilization, of beliefs and loyalties are also attraction fields.

As in Nature, attraction necessarily coexists with repulsion. Beside those described above, other forces are: (a) the primitive but always present competition for available space and (b) liberties, enhanced by proximity but constrained by promiscuity.

An always present attraction and repulsion field on the individual level but also often active in social life is sex. This is an animal characteristic but also a sublimated human factor, as is power. This last can be compared to mass in Einstein's model of the spacetime continuum where mass locally changes the curvature of the continuum, creating the gravitation field. Power in societies has a similar effect.

Another field or factor in socio-economics, already mentioned, is uncertainty which is similar to but of a different quality than randomness of natural events. Uncertainty is the source of anxiety and of the fear of the future, which is obviously absent in Nature. Moreover, as the French physicist A. Kastler pointed out, in microphysics the quantity of events or objects is in the order of 10^{24} to 10^{25}

while in human affairs it is about 10^8. The fluctuation with respect to the mean is of the order of $n^{-1/2}$, thus about 10^{-12} in physics and 10^{-4} in socio-economics. Thus in macrophysics there is almost certainty of mean results even in total micro-randomness while in human affairs uncertainty produces apparent fluctuations within a population of 10,000 agents.

Kastler's reasoning applies to European societies and is more relevant to smaller collectivities. But even applied to the whole of humanity, in the order of 10^{10}, it shows apparent fluctuations for populations of only 10^5 objects. Moreover uncertainty is perceived by agents within their groups and such groups are much smaller than the above orders of magnitude, perhaps 10^4 or 10^5. Fluctuations are socially much stronger than in Kastler's example.

Fear of the future is an important field of forces in our realm of events. It created what philosophers of history called the sacred in opposition to the contractual or rational. This concept can be enlarged to the whole domain of irrationality or, more precisely, of metarationality in human activity, that is, traditions, beliefs, religions, faiths etc. and also to many aspects of education and, in a sense, to art; in other terms, to all expressions of individual and social perception of themselves and of the world. All these fields are, in general, strong social bonds.

Morals and ethics, the sense of justice, which are important fields of forces, proceed from the conjunction or aggregation of the totality of fields just described. One can for instance define justice as a means of compromising between the forces of cohesion and repulsion, of centrifugal and centripetal fields.

This rather cursory analysis shows another difference between models in natural and in social sciences, at least in the present state of both.

The natural sciences are almost fully formalized, that is shaped into a formally logic, mathematical thinking. Newton's Law of gravitation, Ohm's Law in electricity, Gibb's and Carnot's Laws in thermodynamics, Maxwell's equations of the electromagnetic fields, Einstein's tensor representation of the spacetime continuum are such models of increasing sophistication. Modern thermodynamics of disequilibria, quantum mechanics, the cosmology of the Big Bang studying the first fractions of a second after the 'Beginning', are contemporary examples of these models, going beyond our common sense. This is conspicuously broken in the eleven-dimensional Universal now on the agenda of physicists. If in life sciences mathematics is less prominent this is only due to its enormous intricacy which is difficult to formalize.

There is nothing similar in social sciences. Common sense is still the fundamental yardstick. If mathematics is extensively used in economics, the experimental check, the main tool of the scientific method, is lacking here. Its surrogate, applied statistics or econometrics, can verify formalized models with only a great fuzziness, due to unsufficient data and also to Kastler's fluctuation proposition. In consequence, in natural sciences predictions can be of great accuracy and of very small uncertainty while this is impossible in social sciences. The result is that pertinent models in this latter domain are mostly still formulated in literary, i.e. approximate terms.

We conclude this chapter by some concrete illustrations alleviating the abstractness of the above.

'Governments are primarily institutional arrangements that sell protection, security and justice to its constituents'. (Bruno S. Frey)

Two opposed meanings of the word 'justice' coexist in economics. Liberals say that justice requires redistribution of wealth tending to the equality of the quality of life while conservatives argue that justice entitles everybody to the fruits of his activity. A. McIntyre states that these two ideas, of justice as fair distribution or justice as fair acquisition are mutually incompatible. The first proposition stumbles on the question: 'who shall decide what is a fair distribution?' and the second one implies exploitation of man by man. As Marx has put it, justice N° 1 is 'to each according to his needs' and justice N° 2 is 'to each according to his merits'. And he proposed a solution for the reconciliation of both. Present reality has shown that his remedy was perhaps worse than the contradiction.

In fact the mixture of the sacred and of the rational in the socio-economic fields of forces creates compromise solutions such as the existing, although not numerous, 'mixed' democracies, which are acceptable.

One can describe a very crude picture of a feedback between economics, considered as being governed by rationality within its

theory, and socio-politics, in all societies a mixture of such rationality and of the metarational sphere of social attractions and repul-
sions (as sketched above) by the diagram shown in Figure 3.1 (from
Bruno S. Frey, Theorie Demokratischer Wirtschaftspolitik, *Kyklos*,
31, 1978)

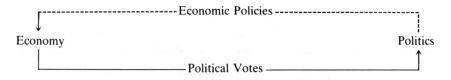

Figure 3.1

Voters elect a government which acts by its policy on the economy.
If the citizens accept the resulting situation they re-elect the incum-
bent governing bodies. The diagram shows the economic sovereignty of the economic agent which is complementary to the
political sovereignty of the citizen.

Of course this is not the sole feedback in social life. A fundamental one is what I called elsewhere the relation or function of élite-
people. Opinions of the élite condition and influence those of
people at large by means of all the media of communication. When
the people were illiterate, this medium was essentially the Church.
Books, brochures, then newspapers and magazines served this
purpose when people started reading in numbers. Such was and is
voice broadcasting and is today the very powerful tool of television.
Political and economic communication which is sometimes called
propaganda and is the advertising, uses all these tools and deeply
influences or duplicates the dashed line as well as the full line in the
above diagram.

Nor is the full line of the vote the only one by which people
influence the élite. At all times the opinions of the former changed
those of the latter; nowadays the continuous polling of the 'public
opinion' has enhanced the intensity of this graph. Such a relation
also exists through the markets especially those of the 'communication goods'. Publishers and networks are firms which sell, by
means of newspapers, books, or the electromagnetic spectre, the
information which must be bought literally or figuratively by 'cus-

tomers'. Thus people at large influence the élite which produces all these 'goods'. There is an immaterial or cultural mutual feedback between the governed and the governing in all realms of the lifes of individuals and societies and in all socio-political and economic systems.

A good example of such complex and, as we shall see, unstable feedback is the one of peace or war in the present world. This is conspicuous in the successive phases of 'cold war' and 'détente' in the relations between the two superpowers, the USA and the USSR.

To describe a possible evolution let us start with the situation where the US government, well informed on facts and issues, wants to come to a settlement of differences with the USSR. It starts to slow down the expenses on armaments and at the same time to try to influence its public opinion in the same direction: doves are prompted to air their ideas and hawks are, to a measure, silenced. Thus both the economic or material and the cultural or immaterial relations between the people and the élite, in the direction élite to people, work for peace. Now the situation changes and the governing élite starts to anticipate a possible danger of confrontation. It tries to reverse its influence on people, increases the armament effort, hawks are listened to and doves are silenced. But public opinion opposes this trend and when it finally changes and gets hawkish, the crisis has subsided and, in the minds and choices of the élite, East-West cooperation is again on the agenda. Again, the mood of people is in the opposite direction. The same instability, probably of lesser intensity, due to the difference in overall freedoms, surely exists in the USSR.

A second example of the feedback between the élite and the people, more restricted in its scale but better formalized is the relation between the marketing and sales effort and the production and turnover in business activities. This feedback is enhanced or disrupted by finance (loan or equity financing or other credit operations) which allow a change in the intensity of the interaction or coupling, to use an electrical term.

The monetary economy is a powerful tool of action on the economic processes, and can either stabilize or unbalance these processes. A careful analysis of this effect will be developed in subsequent chapters. It can be stated here that not only the rational or formalized parameters play a role but also the metarational, subjective ones, which are more difficult to grasp. This is especially true with regard to money and credit, globally the finance, where time and the future are of prime importance. The modern theory of 'rational' expectations is an example of a surrogate endeavouring to circumvent these subjective variables.

Our examples show that an essential feature of the fields of forces in human societies is the instability of their effects. Instability can lead to catastrophes, wars, revolutions, economic crises and slumps . . .

In applications of nuclear fission, stability is necessary when this natural event is used for heat generation. The instability of the chain reaction leads when not constrained to an instantaneous release of energy, an atomic bomb explosion. The stability of the fission reaction in a power reactor is 'artificial' which means that the inherent instability of the reaction is controlled and restrained by means of a regulating device.

The same applies to human activities in general and to economics in particular. Their evolution, inherently unstable, must be controlled by regulatory devices. This necessity is the main thread of our present effort.

CHAPTER 4

RELATIONS BETWEEN AGENTS. ACTIVITY

One can imagine humanity in its overall generality as a very complex graph. Its vertices are the agents, its arcs are activities. The intensity of any activity can be quantified by a measure on the arc representing it.

Any activity, be it production, exchange, gift or transfer, knowledge, information, justice, command, constraint or war, can be represented in this manner.

In a point of a time, such a graph exists and represents the 'state of the world'. It is a function of time and is essentially dynamic or diachronic. In time, not only intensities vary but vertices and arcs appear and disappear.

Moreover the graphs are connected in time; there exists a relation $G(t_i) \, RG(t_j)$. This means that if $t_i > t_j$, the future graph $G(t_i)$ is connected to the less future, present or past graph $G(t_j)$. This is obvious and expresses the essence of history as a science. If $t_i < t_j$, the relation is less obvious. How can the present state of the world, for instance $G(t_0)$, where t_0 is the present time point, depend on a future state $G(t)$? This relation however is fundamental in human activity. It represents the influence of the prediction or forecasting of the future on present choices. In narrow economics it accounts for all decisions on investment. In narrow politics it evaluates future power centers for guidance on present action. In applied science it is the discipline called technological forecasting. In philosophy it analyzes and/or describes the fate of civilizations and the dynamics of the sacred: of traditions, beliefs, cultures, moral and ethical principles etc. All these partial models G can be of great pertinence for the consideration of the whole of the graph as defined here.

Partial synchronic models or subgraphs are also positive contributions to the analysis of the relations between agents. For instance the representation of the production and exchange as formalized by W. Leontieff in the input-output tables was a great advance in economics.

It is obvious that in the relation $G(t_i)RG(t_j)$, when $t_i < t_j$ if t_j is in the future, the graph $G(t_j)$ it is not what will really exist at t_j but its prediction or forecast.

Instead of the topology of the graph G the human activity (the relations between agents) is often formalized by analytic models of the general systems theory. This does not change the approach.

Coming back to economics, Leontieff's model is a refinement of the principle of the taxonomy of activities. When Marx divided the industry into two parts: (A) capital goods, and (B) consumer goods, Leontieff divided the production into nearly 600 sectors. In fact all such partitions are fuzzy or, more precisely, conventional. For instance an electric bulb will be a capital good in a factory and will be depreciated in its accounts while in a household it is a consumption. Moreover nearly all activities or sectors produce both capital and consumer goods, more precisely final and intermediate commodities and very little of all these activities' output consists of a single real product or service. We will come to this point in more detail later.

Another fact that has an important influence on relations between agents and on other topics discussed in this book, is uncertainty. It has been touched upon in the preceding chapter and will be considered again later.

The diachronic evolution of the graph G can, in abstracto, be due to three kinds of variables:

- deterministic or logic variables. These would be possible if G was formalized and if a general causality was established. Such an ideal dynamics is closely linked to
- voluntary or chosen evolution. This second dynamics is the theoretical model of planned societies. Actually only some parts of the general graph G can be planned, essentially those pertaining to material activities; for instance, centralized plans in socialist States or strategic planning of big firms, on investment and/or marketing.

These two kinds of the dynamics of the graph G are submitted to a good deal of

- uncertainty of the future. This is the third set of variables of the dynamics of G.

Formal models of G are thus mixtures of some determinism, some choices or voluntary planning and some representations of uncertainty, by means of the probability theory. The influence of uncertainty on the variables and/or results of causality and planning is often called 'risk'.

Some important questions arise. Does the dynamics of G possess a metabolism, something similar to the homeostase of living organisms? Does human activity as expressed in relations between agents include some feedback or some regulatory devices which influence its dynamics? In other terms, does this dynamics, which necessarily manifests fluctuations, for instance as estimated by A. Kastler's reasoning, spontaneously control them? In even shorter terms: is the dynamics stable?

There is of course no clear and unequivocal answer to these fundamental questions. Whole libraries exist where historians, sociologists, philosophers, economists study the problem, for short, medium, long and very long time periods. Theories of cycles of different frequencies have been proposed. Our questions amount to asking whether such cycles are or are not convergent or are at least of a stable amplitude.

Karl Marx has asserted the instability of the main economic system of his and our time, which is currently called capitalist. The marxists proclaim that this system will evolve into a new one, called socialist and which is understood to be capable of stability.

Whatever the case, the majority of interested people do question the spontaneous stability of 'G'. J. Lesourne calls the cause the 'insufficiency of control'. All politicians and, in particular, all planners proclaim their ability to enhance the regulatory devices so as to master the fluctuations. Controlling economic fluctuations such as inflation, unemployment, the imbalances between monetary zones is an everyday topic of discussion.

The state of the dynamics of the graph G is subject not only to the three kinds of variables listed above but also to two others:

- the cultural, spiritual, ethical, religious, synthetically metarational processes within the individual and collective agents. The sense of justice belongs to this category.
- the progress of knowledge, synthetically the rationality in the

relations between agents, including the evolution of technologies which act on Nature, this last concept including humanity itself.

The resulting global dynamics seems to be essentially divergent in the trend and in the fluctuations and requires exogenous regulatory devices. These devices have always existed and still exist, although they can today be considered as insufficient within both realms of metarationality and of rationality.

In a different dichotomy one can observe a first domain which could be labelled spontaneous or free (even if it is not). This is the sphere of production, exchanges and transfers, communication and education. These activities or relations between agents do exist even if they are not constrained. They result in markets, i.e. in aggregations of choices. Markets regulate such activities.

The second domain is the one of organizations i.e. essentially of collective agents. Their existence implies the existence of constraints on the choices of all agents. The constraints are expressions of the regulatory devices of the graph G and govern its dynamics. An essential fact which has been often mentioned is the fuzziness of all sets. If this fuzziness is small, in the limit nonexistent, the system G is rigid, totalitarian, as are the societies of ants or bees. If the fuzziness is high, G represents anarchy, a Brownian agitation.

Economics in our approach is a particular subset of the graph G. This subset can be partitioned into two subsets, those of production and of exchange. I shall distinguish two further partitions, those of transfers and of organizations.

Moreover, economics does not only deal with relations between real agents, individuals or organized groups but also between 'imaginary' or abstract ones, such as labour, capital, sector, national economy etc. This set of abstract agents results from aggregations of real agents more or less well defined. It is generally called macroeconomics. When reminded of the analogy to macrophysics, one shall not forget the reasoning of A. Kastler on the difference between the two as regards their fluctuations.

Macroeconomics results from the aggregation on resources, for instance raw materials, food, manufactured goods, services, or on agents, such as capitalists, landowners, entrepreneurs and workers in the work of Walras. Such virtual agents, contrary to real ones, cannot choose. They are spiritual creations of economists which allow them to build models. Similar kinds of virtual abstract agents also exist in the minds of historians, politicians, sociologists and are known as ethnics, tribes, nations, religions etc.

In our opinion, a better description or model of the human activity, that is of the vertices and arcs of the graph G, is the consideration of

(a) individual and collective real agents. The second category is the one of organizations, more or less tight, such as firms, communities, local structures, states, churches, associations of all kinds etc.

(b) the set of their possible choices

(c) the set of their constraints on such choices

(d) the set of their criteria of choices

Categories (b), (c), and (d) are attributes defining agents and different for each of them.

One can try to aggregate the above sets. The aggregations create what exists under the terms of economic, historical, social and political sciences where agents are replaced by classes or categories, as discussed in this book. Transfers, exchanges, production, consumption and saving, investment and development give birth to normative and positive theories, such as Walras' or Marx' economics, socialism and capitalism, the theory of public choices, of public finance, of war and peace etc.

It is appropriate to return here to the consideration of the set of resources. Besides the real or physical resources and besides the services, some relations between agents can be considered as resources. Such are claims and rights. This domain includes the whole of the monetary economy, all scarcities and satisfactions, the intellectual property such as royalties, patents and copyrights, the works of art, the goodwill, even the sense of beauty. All consist in relations between agents. We shall discuss the problem of immaterial resources in more detail in connection with the concept of money (largely analyzed for centuries) and the concept of utility (of much younger background).

When examining the relations between agents, other concepts emerge which are older than either money or utility. The first is competition and, at its extreme, conflicts or fights between agents. Many wars, aiming at the destruction of some agents by other agents, are exacerbated relations between them. The neoclassical economic theory considers competition, i.e. a fight or at least a conflict between many agents, limited in intensity by legal and ethical constraints, to be beneficial, that is to have a 'good' effect. Perfect competition is the optimal state in this theory, although implying ruthless elimination of the feeble by the strong. It is dialectically contradictory to its definition, as it asserts that a conflict generates harmony . . .

In the real world perfect competition does not exist. The relations between agents, be they economic or otherwise are oligopoles, monopoles and monopsones or proceed, in an another extreme theoretical idea, from overall planning. This last outlay is by its essence an endeavour to rationalize, even to formalize the general system or graph G, as described at the beginning of this chapter. Now the existence and the behaviours of the vertices of G, in space and in time, as of the arcs, their relations, cannot be only rational. Any plan or any logical approach to G can only be a model, a simplified picture of its reality.

The second important concept pertaining to relations between agents is the one of equity or justice. It is closely linked but yet different from ethics. This last concept is exclusively normative while one can try to establish an absolute or formal notion of justice, independent from any 'value'. For instance Marx' proposal of a definition of an equitable distribution: 'to everybody according to his needs', is descriptive. In the reality of human affairs justice is an elusive criterion of choice, a fuzzy quality of relations between agents and is largely subjective. To quote an important effort, J. Rawls' theory of justice is essentially a conventional model.

The third concept of interest is that of efficiency. It can be considered as belonging to the criteria of choices, as can also be equity. The criterion of efficiency says that one should choose such action or establish such relation between agents which requires the least expense of available resources for the 'greatest result' or 'happiness'. When applied to the global system G or to a subsystem belonging to G, one can consider on the contrary the efficiency to be not a criterion of choice but expressing a quality of relations between agents.

Last but not least the relations between agents are influenced if not determined by a temporal evolution whose generic name could be 'progress'. This dynamic event, while closely linked to the graph G is in a way exogenous in that it is a distinct system currently called knowledge. This is of course a personal opinon. Many authors and thinkers consider this sphere of the activity of our brains to depend on the overall evolution of the system G, to be even a part of it. The difference of opinion remains an open question.

To summarize and also to simplify, that is to truncate, one can assume that the part of the system G called distribution is influenced by the concept of justice; the part called production is governed by efficiency and the part called progress, not only in physical technologies but also in organization, that is the structure of G, by knowledge. In other terms, the main economic process is the creation and subsequent partition or distribution of the value added. This process is governed by the three concepts of justice, of efficiency and of progress. As always in human affairs they often collide. Life is the result of trade-offs between these three concepts.

It is my permanent aim, in this book, to avoid, as far as possible, normative or prescriptive views, the value judgments. I shall, however, conclude this chapter on relations between agents by some personal views on the essence of such judgments, on the concept of value. This term has been and continues to be in frequent use in economics and in other social sciences too. One can hold this use to be often inappropriate or, at least, in need of some clarification.

The outstanding case is the 'value added' "VA" in economics. Its creation and distribution is the monetary representation of the productive process. We shall see later that creation of VA is a 'Price Included Transfer' (a PIT) while the distribution of VA is a 'Price Not Included Transfer' (a PNIT). Neither 'satisfaction' nor 'well-being' nor 'happiness' are choice criteria acting in this dual process, stemming from relations between agents. These preference functionals are subjective qualities, for people, of resources. The quantification of such criteria is called utility. Economic choice criteria of collective agents active in production (of firms) pertain on the contrary exclusively to the creation and the distribution of 'value added' and not to the resources used, which are of no 'utility' to them.

It can be seen from this example that 'value' must be distinguished from 'satisfaction', 'well-being' and 'happiness' and also from 'utility'. Moreover, morals, equity, ethics create value judgments which per se have nothing to do with these four concepts.

Other uses of the word 'value' are common in economic theories. It seems not inappropriate to recall here some of these uses. By doing so, we shall again repeat in different terms what has just been stated.

Economic 'values' were best defined by Karl Marx who continued the quest of his predecessors, Adam Smith and David Ricardo.

The *exchange value* of Marx is for me what stems from production, in most cases the global cost of a unit of product or 'merchandise'. The product which has an 'exchange value' for the producer does not have any utility for him. This 'exchange value' enables a producer to create a value added, thus allowing the subsequent partition of this wealth-increment between the income of the participants in the production and a saving. The exchange value originates in exchanges, as its name says, but, as is seldom clarified, mainly in exchanges between firms. It can be considered to be what is called today the prices of intermediate activity.

The *usage value* measures the utility in view of consumption as we shall see in detail later.

The *surplus value* stems from the general transformation theorem of Marx which links production, i.e. in the present terms the value added creation, to consumption, rendered possible by value added distribution. The surplus value is, in today's terms, only a part of this distribution of value added between incomes and savings. It is in part a share of the total distributed income and in part a saving. We shall analyze the whole problem in detail in Chapters 11 and 13.

It is clear that the marxist terminology and its resulting doctrine are the cause and effect of a confusion. This historic confusion was and is due to the fact that Marx mixed up production and consumption, which are distinct and are represented by distinct processes of the creation and distribution of the value added. Both processes utilize monetary exchange. But in production this exchange serves the division of labour while consumption is the final utilization of only a subpart of a part of the value added which are incomes. The usage value which operates in this final process is defined independently of exchanges.

Thus self-consumption in primitive societies and in some present rural economies can be analyzed by usage values not exchanged. The commodities self-consumed have only a virtual exchange value. Only when such commodities appear on markets or are otherwise exchanged do they integrate the division of labour between producers.

The labour theory of (exchange) value which was established at the time when the creation of commodities and subsequently of the value added required a mostly muscular effort, is today completely outdated, as production is now only very seldom due to 'labour'.

The above has of course nothing to do with the rules by which value added is distributed among the participants in production. This is the case for instance for the level of wages per hour compensating for this time of presence at the site of production.

The same is true for the marginal theory of value which for instance connects the level of wages to a marginal 'labour productivity'. It is only one of such rules of distribution of the value added and has nothing to do with the concept of value.

In his writings K. Marx mixed all this purely objective reasoning, due to his immense genius, with value judgments stemming from equity and ethics (exploitation of man by man . . .).

One can express the above in different terms by stating firstly that to speak of the utility of the elementary exchange has no meaning since the concept of utility is attached to only one agent (see Chapter 9). The exchange where two agents cooperate cannot have a utility unless interpersonal comparisons of utility are assumed to be possible or a social utility is assumed to be an exogenous datum.

Secondly, and to the contrary, the production of a specified productive individual or collective agent is a real sum game, its 'utility' positive or negative being expressed by the VA created. For instance, pollution is a negative sum game. It remains that in our view the 'values' of the games of production and of exchange are fundamentally different from their 'utilities'.

Besides production and exchange, progress and transfers

whether mandatory or voluntary play important roles in economic processes.

Let us cite as a conclusion Immanuel Kant who defined value as what is done in spite of natural preferences (he wrote: inclinations) in order to follow the categorical imperative. And he defined utility as the result of action, whether accomplished by inclination or by duty, with pleasure or by obligation.

The citation conspicuously shows the existence of progress not only in natural but also in social sciences.

CHAPTER 5

DEGREES OF FREEDOM FOR AGENTS. ALIENATION AND FREE WILL

As put forward in the preceding chapter, human activity or the relations between agents can be described by four sets of: agents, their possible choices, constraints on such choices and criteria of choices. A fifth, described in Chapter 2 is the set of resources.

We shall here further analyze the possible choices and the constraints on choices while the criteria of choices will be dealt with in Chapter 6.

The set of constraints on the set of possible choices defines in our approach the degrees of freedom available to any agent.

As a matter of principle, our analysis not only encompasses individuals but the whole set of agents as described in Chapter 1. We treat them all in the same way, as entities which choose and act.

Such an approach is, to our knowledge, seldom found in the literature. The important ethical, moral and political domain of liberties is usually treated mainly on the level of people. Economic freedoms are treated in the same way. When collective liberties are examined, such as the freedom to associate and to publish, they are immediately referred to the individuals who can use such liberties. General or political philosophy is concerned with internal freedoms and/or ideologies. It studies models of societies where personal freedoms, such as the practice of a religion, are guaranteed.

It is of course true that the final aim of any and all human activity, of which the material side is only a part, can be assumed to be but not always is the freedom or more precisely the happiness of people. The means of achieving this aim are, however, of several kinds. In particular, collective and individual liberties often collide in real societies. We shall consider this particular point later and shall restrict the present inquiry to the two sets of possible choices and of constraints on these choices.

They are both attached to each agent, be he collective or a person and are both subsystems of the graph G, depending not only on the agent concerned but also on spatial and temporal circumstances. In other words the two sets vary according to the agent concerned, to time, location and other circumstances in which they are considered.

The link between the two sets can be formalized by a multiple mapping of the set of constraints into the set of possible choices. We can define the 'free will' of an agent as the subset or partition of the set of possible choices complementary to the subset subject of the mapping. Let $P\,(a, l, t)$ be the set of possible choices of an agent a at a place l at time t and let $C\,(a, l, t)$ be the set of constraints on these choices with $C \xrightarrow{f} P$ the mapping of C into P. The complement $\mathscr{C}\,(P \xrightarrow{f} C)$ is the freewill of agent a located at l at time t. It measures the degree of freedom of this agent. Absolute freedom is the state in which the mapping f is nil and the complement $\mathscr{C} = P$. This is a limit state, not attainable in reality.

Actually humans are social persons and live in groups or societies which in turn belong to higher levels of the structure of humanity. So, eons ago, a first constraint was formulated by the slogan 'the liberty of a person ends where begins the liberty of another person'. We generalize this saying by stating that it is valid for *all* agents, as defined in Chapter 1. In economics this principle plays a big role in market regulation as well as in planning. In fact all relations between agents, be they production, exchange or transfer should follow it. In politics, besides the usual political freedoms discussed in the literature and mentioned hereafter, a good example is the present highest level of collective agents, the nation-states. These agents, by definition of their claim to be 'sovereign', should only possess a small if any constraint of this type. The difficulties of our time may generally be attributed to the collision of the principle of sovereignty with this first general constraint on the possible choices of *all* agents. We shall return to this point and state that a second obvious and general constraint on the set of possible choices of any agent is the fact that humanity is a part of Nature or more precisely, of the biosphere of the spaceship Earth. This second constraint is of course closely linked with the first. When humanoïds started to form small packs of a few families of hunters and gatherers in the savannahs and forests of East Africa, the first constraint of life in society started to be active on a very small scale while the second was exogenous, i.e. did not depend on the activity of these beings, but proceeded from their needs for food, shelter and their fight against predators. As human history proceeded, the second constraint started in its turn to be increasingly dependent on what humanity did. We assist in our time to a quantitative explosion of our population while our need for all kinds or resources increases many times. The impact of the existence of humans on the biosphere has in only about 200 years been multiplied by several orders of magnitude. The second constraint is now a big problem for all of us. Not only is the available space on emerged land on Earth beginning to be limited but pollution, climatic changes, desertification and deforestation, all express the growing importance of this constraint, resulting in a shrinkage of our freedoms.

As we pursue our analysis we shall not discriminate between individual and collective agents, contrary to usual practice. Readers are invited to clarify for themselves the constraints that are applicable to the various categories of agents.

Ethical, social, moral, political and economic constraints on the set of possible choices of an agent are manifold. Some of these constraints are defined a contrario be specifying the positive liberties as inscribed in constitutions, bills of rights, ordinary laws, it being understood that such liberties are the only ones allowed in orderly societies of people and collective bodies, all other being prohibited. Thus political freedoms are defined as (a) a citizen has at his or her disposal, if he or she is entitled to it, several choices for the selection of who is to represent him or her in local, regional or national political bodies; and (b) he or she is free to travel, to work, to spend as he or she wishes his or her free time, to set up and raise a family, to be a member of any kind of association with lawful aims, itself free to manifest its existence and to act. This means that he or she is *not* free to choose to kill or to steal, *not* free to stop the traffic without sufficient reason, *not* free to walk undressed on the street, *not* free to pollute a stream or discard trash in a public place, *not* free to form an association with a criminal object etc.

One can see from these examples that such constraints mainly result from valid laws and regulations and also proceed from traditions or conventions if not religious canons or social taboos.

A modern kind of a positive freedom results from the right to health or at least to life. Illness and age are restrictions on the set of possible choices, as is childhood. This last however is natural and transient. Thus nowadays medical care is socialized even in under-developed societies. While relaxing these restrictions it also creates new ones such as constraints on travel liberties by quarantines and mandatory vaccinations. These sets of constraints are due to the same social choices as the protection of clean air and water, constraints that are closely linked to economic freedoms.

The main economic freedoms consist in the availability of several choices of work, of activity (profession, trade etc.), of travel, of settling in a place, of manifold goods and services being offered. Thus well stocked shelves in a supermarket, the supply and availability of a great variety of goods and services, and also a sufficient income that permits the choice between these goods, once the subsistence necessities are satisfied, are prerequisites of economic freedoms. In our systems where incomes are linked to work, the right to work or to full employment can be considered as a condition of economic freedom.

It has been inscribed in constitutions and is often asserted that the right to ownership is one of the requisites of economic freedoms or, better formulated, is an enhancement of the degree of freewill at the disposal of agents. In our opinion it should be included in the list of freedoms of individual agents described above but should be qualified when collective agents are considered. The existence of (a) shareholders in firms, be they private or public bodies, including the State, (b) the members in associations, (c) the principle of government for the people by the people (who are 'owners' of the society), while certainly democratic and useful, are all constraints on possible choices of all such collective agents rather than enlargements of their freedoms.

The economic process of the division of labour which is a fundamental relation between productive agents, is a constraint on possible choices of these agents. When a final product of any kind depends on cooperation or intermediate exchange between those who participate in its production, each of these agents is obviously restricted in his possible choices. One could resolve this dialectic by an optimization program: obtain the maximum freedom, i.e. the smallest set of constraints on choices under the condition of efficiency. In other terms the division of labour could be optimized, that is, to be the most efficient under the constraint of a maximum of freewill of each and all participants. It is not at all certain that this program can be satisfied by the sole means of prices.

It is a fact that the really 'free' people are selfsufficient farmers. Some religious communities in North America are examples of such degenerate programs, where the constraints of maximum freewill seems to be strong but efficiency is low and indeed the set of non-economic freedoms is mostly very small, due to the existence of strict moral, ethical, religious and customary rules and taboos.

In today's developed economies the same dilemma is concretely expressed in the two main available systems. Where is the set of freewill the largest? Under massive unemployment but high efficiency of the division of labour in market economies or under mandatory job distribution but low efficiency in planned societies? The formalization of these programs in a better way than in the present world would maybe improve our understanding of and eventually solve the optimization task, of course restricted here to economic choices.

One can link this problem to another economic freedom currently inscribed in constitutions and laws, the right to strike, to stop an activity by concerted and organized union action or otherwise. Here again the dialectic could be between this freedom and the effects of the disruption of useful activities providing public goods of transport, energy, security etc. This dilemma often results in constraints on possible choices of agents.

Cultural freedoms are closely linked to economic ones. The availability, i.e. the possibility of choosing between such cultural activities as plays, movies, TV channels, books, magazines and papers, sports etc. which are freely created by people that are capable of this creation, once the material and educational needs are satisfied, are the conditions of free people, that is of individual agents whose constraints on the set of possible choices are relatively small. It is a fact that wealth relaxes the constraints on freedoms and poverty increases them. These freedoms, as all others, are moreover constrained by codes of conduct materialized by penal and civil laws, by the orderly management of urban and rural space, of land, sea and air transport, of the electromagnetic spectre. And all these social constraints are influenced if not established by a particular constraint resulting from the dominance of the governed by the governing, within the overall set of agents, both collective and individual. This is the phenomenon of power. When the relation of dominance is strong, liberties suffer which means that the set of constraints on the set of possible choices of dependent agents increases in size and scope. The limit is dictatorship and totalitarianism. As the saying goes, the best government is the smallest. . .

Power is a restriction on the set of possible choices of the governed by enlarging this set for the governing. One can state that the governing feed their sets of possible choices on the sets of choices of the governed. In other words the existence of power in human societies bears on all sets of constraints on possible choices, external and internal.

Actually our description of the constraints on sets of possible choices is incomplete. Besides all the extended external limitations on freedoms a person possesses a subset of internal ones. This subset expresses what the people believe in, what he or she thinks and feels. In a similar manner, a society is constrained or, in a sense, defined by a set of constraints on its choices. This set can taken to be the culture of the society, what one may call its collective soul. Even firms are distinguished by their 'esprit de maison'.

One could submit that internal freedoms are unconstrained because thought and sentiment never infringe on the freedoms of others and, as thought and sentiment are not actions, they cannot trespass laws and constitutions. This is not so. Firstly the internal and external liberties are connected by the drive, the desire and even the necessity of communicating, which demands the freedom of publication, of meeting other people, of transmitting and broadcasting information and culture. And the exercise of these freedoms can infringe on the internal and external freedoms of others and thus demands the respect of some constraints on the internal freedoms of agents, be they individuals or groups.

Secondly, the thoughts and sentiments of a person are in all circumstances constrained by his or her beliefs, by what he or she assumes to be truths. Such constraints established by education and social conditioning are always present in variable intensity. A totalitarian, religious, or 'fundamentalist' society works towards the uniformity of the beliefs and the behaviours of its members, who are, in consequence, deprived of a vector of possible choices and are not free, without any physical coercion. In fact any revealed truth, any belief or faith is a restriction on the set of possible choices. One limit here is a total internal and external anarchy, the opposite is Orwell's thought police.

The above is an example of our positive or descriptive approach to facts, without any normative value judgments. Of course, in many instances the internal constraints on possible choices can be, and are, the most valuable side of personalities.

Collective agents are also constrained on their set of possible choices by internal rules of behaviour. They are mostly of an institutional kind and more material. Thus the budget constraint is a standard restriction on management, i.e. on current choices of firms. Nor are ethical arguments negligible.

To this description of the various sets of constraints on possible choices one could add that the activity of choosing results in the future states of the system, in the dynamics of the graph G. Now the future is in its essence uncertain, as it does not yet exist at the time of choice. This uncertainty introduces into the set of constraints on possible choices a singular one which is expressed in the models of the theory of decision when they try to describe, to analyze and to normalize the activity of choosing 'in the presence of uncertainty'.

We only mention here this important point and shall deal with it in more detail in the next chapter, which is on the criteria of choices. In conclusion of the present chapter two more points seem to be in order.

Firstly, for any agent be he a person or a group, the sets of possible choices and of constraints on them are both continuously modified by the relation between the elite and the mass. This relation plays an affective part in economic, political, social, cultural realms of life and is currently called advertising, marketing, political propaganda, the activity of religious bodies etc. In fact it goes much deeper than these tools of the government of minds and permeates the whole material and spiritual activity. It is what could also be called either culture or spiritual alienation, in contrast to the material alienation in economic activity.

Secondly the analysis of choices dealt with here can be an object of an inquiry as objective (i.e. as scientific) as possible. Traditionally choices have been an 'artistic' activity and, as such, not submitted to an inquiry of this kind. This was due, at least in our opinion, to ignorance and, as is often the case – see for instance the history of medical 'art', today a science – this ignorance was proclaimed a virtue. Our analysis of freewill, a subject of great effort in philosophy, by means of the two sets of possible choices and of constraints on them, is in this respect iconoclastic. It infringes on sacred tradition. We shall plunge even deeper into this crime in the next chapter.

CHAPTER 6

CHOICE CRITERIA. UTILITY. RESOURCE ALLOCATION

SECTION 1. GENERAL

In Chapter 4 on relations between agents and on activity we listed three attributes of agents: their sets of possible choices, of constraints on these choices and of criteria of choices. In Chapter 5 we proposed descriptions of the first two sets; in this chapter we shall deal with the third one, that of criteria of choices.

Chapter 4 was concluded by some remarks on the concept of value in relation to the concepts of exchange and of utility. It seems necessary to start our analysis of the criteria of choices with some elaboration on this point. The matter will not be exhausted here and will be discussed again in Chapter 7 which is on dimensionalities in social sciences, in particular in economics.

A more comprehensive analysis of the problem must enlarge its scope beyond the two concepts of value and utility to money, prices and uncertainty and risk.

Firstly what do we mean by the word 'utility'? We assume its significance to be restricted to the quantification of preferences. To state: 'The utility of A is greater than the utility of B' is tautologically equivalent to stating: 'A is preferred to B'. The meaning of the word 'quantification' is extended here to either a cardinal measure of the utility or only to an ordinal ranking of choices.

A first consequence of this definition is that utility in its generality can be taken as the criterion of choices. In fact it is a complex criterion, a set of criteria. In the most common example it is currently assumed that individual agents 'maximize their utility under the constraint of their budget'. According to our definition, this is tautologically equivalent stating that these agents choose or will choose between possible choices the one they prefer. It is obvious that this choice, called here 'maximization of utility' is an aggregation of criteria. For instance it is composed, in a still unknown manner, of preferences for consumption of food, the use of clothing, fun and art, for saving etc.

The activity, in its general sense, is a vector of very high dimension and utility is a means to reduce this dimensionality to *one*. This enables economists to claim that individual agents maximize such an index of preference, as some of them call utility. This is an important fact. As we shall repeat later and elaborate, in economics as in all social sciences our representations of the reality lead to building 'reducers of dimensionality'. In physics such reducers are either non-dimensional numbers as Reynolds, Mach or Froude numbers in fluid mechanics or absolute constants such as the velocity of electromagnetic propagation in vacuum, Planck's constant etc. In our discipline corresponding entities are the three concepts of utility, money or prices, and, as proposed by A. Smith, D. Ricardo, K. Marx and others, labour.

In economics the elementary criteria of choice or 'utilities' can be easy cardinal measures, such as physical measures of quantities or amounts of money. They can also be intangible moral, ethical, cultural, or animal drives, such as love and hatred, the sense of good and evil, of equity, of beauty. . .

They can be material facts not easily measurable, such as efficiency. They can be the exogenous factor of uncertainty, the randomness of events, for instance in forecasting the future and the results of present choices, more generally in passed and present activity. This last and important item, the uncertainty, is spatial, temporal and/or of unique or repeated events.

That is enough for the time being about utility. Let us now turn our attention to value. This is a more difficult problem. G. Debreu has built a theory of value, by starting with a definition which is as follows: 'the value of an action a with respect to a price system p is the vector product $p \cdot a$'.

Our endeavour is to consider the concept of value as distinct from those of utility, of money (i.e. of prices), of uncertainty and of such criteria of choices as equilibrium or optimum. Moreover we shall try to define the concept of value with respect but 'outside' the set of agents or their possible choices and constraints on these choices. The concepts of commodities, of prices, of producers and consumers and of savers are in consequence used here in a manner which is quite different from that used in the current theories of value.

What then is value? The answer is difficult. It is certainly not only the vector product $p \cdot a$ which assumes its dependence on money.

One possible approach is that value is a specific attribute of resources, while utility is an attribute of agents and the two other reducers of dimensionality, labour and money, are concepts related to activity, i.e. the action of agents on resources. Elaborating on these definitions, it can be assumed that value is an objective attribute, since what concerns resources cannot depend on a specified agent, i.e. be subjective, while labour and money are, in our opinion, (as we will see later) subjective or objective and utility is of course subjective.

The elusiveness of the concept of value is now clear. It cannot be quantified without using the reducers of dimensionality: utility, money, labour. It nevertheless exists and is distinct from these three concepts. It is, for instance independent of, or invariant with respect to, scarcity and abundance, two events pertaining to resources and influencing utilities, prices and effort (labour).

One often finds in the literature a current definition of value as 'the utility of certain gains of losses' while utility is defined as preferences on distributions of probability. This implies that value is a subjective quantification of resources, pertaining to a specified agent. Operations on such 'values' cannot be the subject of a general theory.

A more subtle example of the distinction between value, utility, scarcity and price is Catherine in the story Arthur Koestler narrates in his 'Art of Creation' (p. 403 of the paperback edition). This lady was given a drawing from Picasso's classical period. She took it to be a copy and hung it in the staircase of her house. An art amateur visited her and asserted that the drawing was an original. It was immediately placed over the mantelpiece in the drawing room. In fact only an expert with a good magnifying lens, if not better equipped, could tell if it was really an original work by Picasso. Koestler asked Catherine why, since the quality of the picture did not change, her attitude toward it did change. He analyzes in detail the possible answers to this question, stating for instance that the origin and rarity value of the object did not alter its qualities and should not alter the purely aesthetic value-judgments based on these qualities. Translating into our language what Koestler writes on almost two pages of his book, the value of the picture remained the same whether it was a good copy or an original. Its price on the market, as a unique and rare work of art, would of course enormously increase if it was recognized as such. We shall analyze in detail in Chapter 9 what this last sentence means. It seems appropriate to mention only that such a high price would express the utility for a prospective buyer of an original drawing by Picasso as compared to *his* utility of the sum of money with which he will have to part in order to acquire the picture and *not* to the utility of the picture to the seller, Catherine. While rationally her utility should not change if only the aesthetic value judgment had to be considered, it did in fact change as snobbish feelings, an anticipation of the wealth represented by its possible price, the pleasure of ownership and finally the 'utility' of uncertainty, i.e. risk aversion or risk love intervened.

Is 'value' then the amount of the resource, whatever this means? This seems to be the least unsatisfactory or the best possible answer to the question 'what is value' if by 'amount' we understand not only the physical quantity, for instance mass, when it exists, but also immaterial 'quantities' such as information and all qualities of the resource, which can of course be immaterial also, such as doctor's prescription or beauty, as in Koestler's example. Money and labour, if assumed to be resources, possess a value that is distinct from their utility or their price. These values are objective, i.e. independent of agents.

In many circumstances to which we now come value as just defined is a criterion of choice. In such circumstances preferences, i.e. utility, are not pertinent.

This point will be clarified somewhat in the next section which deals with the criteria of choice according to the categories of agents to which they are attributed. This means that we shall successively discuss the criteria of choices of individuals, households, firms, political bodies, these last starting with cities and counties up to States and also associations, clubs, churches, ethnic groups and tribes etc. Current economics considers such criteria for (a) individuals and households, (b) firms and (c) governments both local and central. For (a) and (b) the discipline is called microeconomics and for (c) it is macroeconomics, with regard to policy and public choices, or sometimes political economy as it used to be called in the past. Macroeconomics is essentially concerned with the action of public agents on other agents, according to some set of criteria, while public choice concerns in essence, as the term implies, the choices of public agents as regards their own activity. This means in economics their consumption, saving and investment, in our approach their creation and distribution of their value added.

A general remark of some significance is to be made here.

Choices, governed by their criteria, can be of vital importance to any agent. For instance the choices of a profession or trade, of a career, of a life companion are decisive for an individual, as is today the choice of couples to have children, and, on the other end of the scale the choice for a nation between peace or war. Business management consists of current everyday choices, many of them of little importance, but also on long term investment and other decisions that will have a bearing on the life or death of these agents. In general the importance of choices increases or at least their impact on other agents increases with the cardinal of the set of agents called a collective agent. The choices of people are a fluctuating agitation that could be compared to the brownian motion of molecules in a gas. The choices of a big firm has consequences for many other agents, and the economic policy of a government strongly influences the activity of all members of the society that such agent governs. If this agent is a superpower it can change the life of all the agents composing humanity. In other terms, often used in the quarrel between the proponents of market and planned economies, in the former's perfect model the choices of an agent are of no importance and can never lead to be social or political mistakes while the choices of planners in a socialist society can lead to disasters, as Poland has shown in the Seventies. The importance of a 'good' or 'rational' manipulation of criteria of choices increases when we scan the scale of agents in their increasing size; the gravity of the consequences of choices increases when their centralization at higher levels gains in intensity.

This being so what are the criteria of choices of the different kinds of agents? We shall scan the answer without of course being exhaustive.

One can settle the point in a single sentence: *all* agents choose according to their preferences, i.e. choose the action that maximizes their utility. But such a statement is a tautology as we have shown and, besides, must be clarified especially with respect to the meaning of the word utility in different circumstances.

SECTION 2.   AGENTS' CHOICES

Individual Agents

What people decide has been extensively researched, discussed and written about in ethics, philosophy, utility theory, economics. . .
We shall make two remarks at the start. Firstly the choices in individual agents are by definition subjective, depending on the agent at the time, place, mood etc. of that person. Choices of other agents can be 'objective', i.e. accepted, chosen and valued by many agents of different types at different times and locations, or can remain subjective.

The second remark is that utility as defined by us is in our opinion distinct from any 'value judgment', be it ethical, moral, social political or material. Such judgments are something else. We consider them in the following as elements of the sets of criteria of choices and not as the utility which is an aggregation or dimensionality reduction of these sets.

Standard economic models of personal utility are to two types. The first type proceeds from the theory of consumption and demand. The reducer of dimensionality is money and uncertainty is not considered. The main parameter, on which the whole of the neo-classical economic theory is built is the marginal utility of money and of real resources including time and labour. This model is also used for the choices of people as aggregated in the theory of equilibria. The main paradigm is the consideration of a 'bundle of goods', i.e. of sets of distinct means of satisfaction of needs or preferences, at given prices. One of the bundles is chosen, for which the total monetary outlay is at most the available income and which is preferred from all possible choices of the available bundles.

Two points are obvious in this approach. Firstly this 'theory of consumer demand' as it is called, dispenses from measuring the utility of the bundle, thus remaining only ordinal. One can assert that this is only an illusion. The availability of the bundle is represented, in given prices, by a quantity of money; the marginal utility of money, at this point of wealth of the person concerned is, for this person, a cardinal measure whose integration will deliver, up to a constant, a cardinal utility of this wealth equal to the cardinal utility of the bundle. In current theory such reasoning is called the 'indirect marginal utility' of a commodity when a variation of the utility of the representative quantity of money is caused by a change in the quantity of this commodity in the bundle. Similar formal procedures study the optimal bundle by proving that marginal utilities of all commodities are proportional, at the choice of the consumer which he prefers between all available choices, to the prices of all commodities. From this result it is immediate to equate the marginal utility of any item to the utility of an amount of money, the product of the proportionality constant by the price of the item. Now, secondly, this result has sense only if the commodities are divisible, even provided with a continuous measure.

We reiterate that our approach is: individual agents as all agents choose by means of a set of criteria. This set includes a subset of resources. Each of the elements of this subset is a criterion of choice. Current economic theory reduces the cardinality of this subset by means of money at given prices considered as exogenous. But money itself is one of these elements and an important one as it is the tool of the reduction of the cardinality of the subset, in the model and in the reality. And in real life the economic subset of the criteria of choices is only a part, although in many cases a predominant part, of the total set of criteria of choices of individual agents. The sense of good and evil, love, hatred, the lust for power, envy. . . the choices of other agents inducing status seeking, all these criteria must be included. And the complementary subset to the subset of economic criteria cannot be dimensionally reduced by means of money, at least not by the simple means of the use of prices. The utility on the other hand, even if this measure is not additive, can be taken as a general reducer of the dimensionality of the whole set of criteria. In other words, in a given situation the agent makes the choice that has the highest overall 'index of preference', by whatever means such a quantification (i.e. the utility of the choice) is obtained. If this approach is adopted *all* elementary criteria, be they material or ethical, moral, aesthetic, etc. can be dimesionally reduced to one.

The second model, used in economics and elsewhere, of the choices of all agents, in particular the individuals, is based on uncertainty. Choices result in consequences by definition situated in the future. And the future is in essence uncertain. So this approach seems in its principle to be a pertinent model and a correct representation of the real world.

The current method for formalizing the utilities of uncertain events is the analysis of bets, of the insurance industry, of the speculation and of investment in uncertain economic activities etc. The theory thus often deals with money and with financial assets, as does the first model. But money as a reducer of the dimensionality of the set of criteria is here not a prima / tool. The fact that in general the marginal utility of gains decreases with increasing gains, which is a general quality of the availability of any resource, in the first model also, has now an important bearing on the analysis of the criteria of choice between uncertain events. As losses are as important as gains and as their marginal (dis)utility is generally increasing, its limit being no-availability or, in common language, ruin or death, the marginal utility of results is an important variable.

Uncertainty is, as well known, quantified by the concept of probability. The utility of uncertain results, i.e. the criterion of choice between such results depends obviously on these results and on their probability of obtaining. The current model of the measure of this utility is the 'expected utility', i.e. the mathematical expectation of the probability distribution of the utilities of these results. The model is obviously ambiguous. The words 'the utilities of these results' are tautological to 'the agent expresses preferences between these results' and thus assume that such preferences do exist in the uncertain state of obtaining *one* result. Now these preferences are of course different from the preferences in the comparison between such results if *all of them* were certain to obtain.

This very short and crude summary of the theory of choices in uncertainty corresponds to an extensive mathematical literature and numerous congresses and symposia which have not as yet proposed a satisfactory solution to the difficulty.

Collective Agents

We shall restrict our analysis to three kinds of collective agents: households or families, productive firms and governments or, more precisely, public bodies of all kinds.

In current theory families are treated in the same way as individuals. This is here an excessive simplification. As for any other collective agent their utility or their quantification of preference, by a single character or number, of their set of the criteria of choices stems from two distinct sources: (a) the consideration of all sets of criteria of choices of the individual member of the family, which is an aggregation of utilities or the endogenous social utility; and (b) the family's own set of criteria. The elements of set (b) are, for instance, the necessary saving, the provision of housing, of raising and educating children, the care of the aged and what is called familiar atmosphere: love and kindness, the cultural needs, prestige and social status etc. The reduction in dimensionality of this set results in turn in a quantification known as the social utility of the family.

The family cell, the elementary collective agent, is treated in closed economic macromodels as a productive firm: its output is the labour of its active adult members (in the recent past of the male head of the family), its input is the homework of its members (essentially of the housewife) and the consumption of the family. Labour and consumption are in this model goods exchanged on markets.

The reality is at present more complex than this simple model. For reasons that will appear later I would propose to consider a household as an elementary public body and to define such collective agents by the fact that, whatever their scope and size, they make their choices by means of an aggregation of endogenous and exogenous social utilities. This 'mixture' is a dimensional reduction to one of the set of criteria of the agents both individual and collective, who are the elements or subsets of the collective agent considered, combined with this collective agent's own set of criteria. We shall come later to the methods by which the reduction in dimesionality can be achieved. It is in general neither money nor uncertainty nor personal satisfaction of needs and desires, at least in the main.

Before doing so, and for reasons that will become apparent, we shall now discuss the set of the criteria of the productive agents called firms. This problem is one of the most dissected in economics. The present neoclassical school has inherited from its ancestors a simple answer: firms are profit maximizing agents and 'utility' as operated upon in the theory of consumption and demand has nothing to do with their behaviour.

This answer is, in our opinion, much too simple, in all senses of the word 'simple', to be good model of the present reality. We shall propose in this book a detailed analysis of the behaviours of productive agents and, to begin with this task, elaborate on two concise remarks.

The first remark is related to the second part of the current answer as formulated above. The negation of the use of the concept of utility in the consideration of the criteria of choices of firms expresses an important truth of real economic life. The factors of production (i.e. the real input in the productive processes) and the products of these processes (i.e. their real output) have no utility for the firm and are not elements of their set of criteria of choices. Let it be more clear: the technology of the productive process is of course closely concerned with real inputs and outputs and such technology has an impact on the set of economic and other criteria of choices. It is closely linked to the set of criteria but inputs and outputs as such do not intervene.

The proposition as just spelled out must be illustrated by concrete examples.

A car rolling off the assembly line, a ton of steel in a mill, a drug for the owner of a drugstore, the prescription for a physician, a pencil for its manufacturer have no (direct) utility for these agents. Similarly, cardboard for packaging products or parts bought from suppliers have no utility for the firm which procures these items for its productive needs. The statement 'have no utility' means that the agent 'firm' does not express preferences over these real resources excepted as regards the technology of the production and their prices. The choice criterion of the firm is, in classical economic models its profit and, in most of the present real world, a set of multiple criteria whose main element is the value added.

In other terms the prices and qualities of input and output are of importance: prices play an essential role in the creation of the value added and the qualities and necessary quantities of inputs enable the process of production to be realized while the qualities of outputs and their prices allow the products to be sold. But these criteria of choices are not subjective preferences. Moreover the marginal 'utilities' of monetary flows of a firm are constant, as they are registered in accounts where every cent has the same importance. Finally the technological needs of production, in quantity and quality as well as the physical output of products cannot use the concept of starvation or satiation and the corresponding limit values of 'marginal utilities' of these resources. It is also in this sense that the criteria of firms are of a different nature from those of people.

To repeat, the current economic theory expresses these facts by building all its content on the paradigm of two simple criteria of choices: consumers maximize their utility under their budget constraint while firms maximize their profit. We have analyzed the first part of this sentence and shall now consider the second part.

We have shown that the 'utility maximization of consumers' is a reduction to one of the dimensionality of the set of criteria which can be of high cardinality.

It is now widely accepted that the criteria of choice of firms which in management science are sometimes called strategies and sometimes objectives are not unique. Their set, which can also be of high cardinality, has spatial and temporal elementary criteria, among them a concept currently called profit.

We shall restrict our analysis to the material subset of this set and not bother about its immaterial elements such as ethical and meta-rational criteria, which of course exist. For the time being we shall also put aside from the set of criteria two important temporal ones, investment and uncertainty.

The statement about the absence of a direct utility for firms of the real resources (goods and services) that they process can now be simply formulated by enouncing that the material subset of criteria of choices of firms is expressed in monetary units (even if the firm is engaged in barter) and that this subset consists of (a) maximizing the value added created and (b) realizing optimal partition of this value added. These objectives are expressed by means of accounting techniques implying a constant marginal utility of money.

Thus the material subset of the criteria of choices for firms can be partitioned into two subsubsets: those criteria which result in maximizing the value added and those by which an optimum of the partition of the maximum value added is achieved.

The first subsubset can be tentatively described as follows:

- maximize the prices of products. The constraints are the action of competitors, of the government, the tools are monopolies, advertising, marketing and sales efforts.
- maximize the quality of products in order to enlarge sales.
- minimize the prices of inputs. This in general depends only marginally on the firm considered except as regards the competition between suppliers and of course monopsones.
- essentially, increase the efficiency of the production process. This criterion is expressed by the maximum of real output for a given real input or a minimum of real input for a given real output. In itself it is a complex requirement, where economics, science, psychology, engineering and finance meet.

We shall study these points in detail in the following chapters; here they are only listed.

The second subset of the set of criteria of choice for firms is how to optimize the distribution of value added once it is created.

Here again only a very rough description is presented. Value added is in any productive activity divided in two: distributed income and retained income or saving.

Distributed income goes to:

(1) individual agents who work in the firm. It is called wages in current economics.

(2) other individual or collective agents who in the legal setup of the economy are entitled to such distribution. This part is currently called in its bulk dividends or a share of profits.

(3) the State (this includes all public bodies) entitled to such distribution in any possible way. This part is currently called taxes.

Retained income is the sum of :

(4) the depreciation allowance.

(5) the net cash flow after taxes and dividend, currently called the net saving of the firm while including a part of what is currently called the net profit. It is immediate that the resolution of the problem of optimization of such a partition of the value added is of very great involvement and complexity. It can be approached only by the general system theory.

In current economics the problem is simplified by including those parts of the value added (VA) numbered (1), (3) and (4) in the inputs or costs and calling the sum of parts (2) and (5) 'the profit'. The criterion of choice is thus reduced to maximization of (2) + (5).

This simplification was justified in the past and remains so in all cases where the firm is owned by a 'capitalist' free to decide alone on the partition of the VA into its five parts. It is nowadays only seldom the reality.

Almost all neoclassical as well as marxist models, be they micro or macroeconomic, are derived from this simplification which is usually expressed in two quite strong hypotheses: consumers (i.e. wage income bearers) maximize their utility and do not save, firms or capitalists or entrepreneurs maximize their profit which represents their consumption and the saving necessary to finance the gross investment.

Our endeavour is to go beyond such a simple if not simplistic assumption.

Two remarks are in order before we close this section:

(i) the definitions used here are conventional and often arbitrary, as are most concepts of economics. What really are positions (1) to (5)? None is exempt from fuzziness which, however, we cannot examine further here. What are inputs and outputs? There will never be an universal consensus for any of these concepts. How should we treat the distinction between the nominal and the real VA? This last quite important question raises the point of the role of money, i.e. of prices in the economics of firms, and of their criteria of choices.

(ii) linked to this last point, we have omitted from our description of criteria of choices of productive firms the economics of finance and credit. This is intentional for two reasons: (a) for the sake of simplicity and (b) because we put such transactions under the heading of transfers studied in Chapter 10. Transfer is, in our opinion, a very important feature of relations between agents, today mainly embodied in the complex structure of public and private finance. Just to show the conventional character of the partition of the VA into its five parts as we have done above, position (3), the part of the State is often taken to be a transfer; some national accounts in the past have even included the position (1), the wage expense as well as remaining distribution income into transfers. One can hold the opinion that the entire partition of the VA is transfers, if it leaves the firm. We do so in the following.

Public Agents

This last category of collective agents is currently distinguished from the others by the assumption that its criteria of choice, even its sets of choices and of constraints on choices differ from those of 'private' agents, individuals, households, associations and firms. The distinction has its roots in the past. Public agents are the main subject of history; they were and often remain embodied in powerful persons whose choices commanded the behaviours of other members of society and controlled their lives and the life of the society or State itself. The sovereignty or, in modern formulation, the political will is the word describing the main quality of public agents. A greater or a smaller part of this concept is always present in the essence of all such agents.

The present and, one can hope, future evolution however makes the State and the other public 'hands' more and more economic collective agents similar to other members of societies living on this Earth. National accounts collect data on the VA created by the activity of the State and include it in the domestic product, as is done for all other contributions to the wealth created by the toil of people and, today, of machines. One can consider it as a paradox that the household, the oldest and smallest of the 'public' agents is not included in this category of agents. It is worthwhile mentioning that its VA, stemming in most cases from the activity of the housewife is not included in the social product. For a long time the same has been true for activities of public bodies, in particular of the State.

Our endeavour is to systemize and to clarify the principles of economics, here of the criteria of choices of public agents. The questions arises: are the material criteria of public agents the same as those of firms, i.e. maximization of the VA and optimization of its partition or do public agents act as people, i.e. maximize a social utility? The same question while clearly answered in the current economic theory which assumes the second alternative also arises for households. And the answer is almost the same for public agents and for households; moreover, one can at this stage generalize the answer for firms also.

The criteria of choices of public bodies *and* of households are twofold:

(a) material, expressed in the maximization of the VA and optimization of its distribution. This for public bodies is currently growth, economic and social policies, income distribution and other macroobjectives. The tools of these actions, following choices, is public finance, the monetary and budgetary policies. On the level of households this corresponds to the budgeting of available income.

(b) political, spiritual and structural. This is mostly the realm of the sacred, of the traditional, of the institutional and also of the affective, the aesthetic, generally embraced by the term 'irrational'. It could be more appropriately called 'metarational'.

Both classes of criteria are of course closely linked. The description of the feedback between economy and politics as proposed in Chapter 3. illustrates this link. We will brieflly elaborate on this description by a somewhat deeper look into Figure 3.1.

All agents are active in economy. In consequence the vertex 'economy' should be better called 'society' or 'agents'. The vertex 'politics' on the other hand includes only two categories of agents, the public agents and the citizens or voters, i.e. a subset of individual agents that however do not choose as such. There is here a significant distinction between households and people, i.e. individual members of the society.

Now the plain arc of the graph represents not only political votes but all kinds of action by all agents on politics, including votes and also lobbies, communication and information, all kinds of informal and formal influences and, last but not least, the markets, i.e. the aggregated economic choices.

The dashed line represents not only economic policies but also all kinds of informal and formal influence such as, for instance, TV talks by politicians.

Thus the plain arc is an overall representation of the aggregation of choices while the dashed line represents the feedback of politics on economy. In a more specific light the dashed line can be taken as representing the maximization of the aggregated VA, i.e. of the economic growth and of its distribution on the choices of all agents. This is what is commonly called economic policy.

To recall, the VA is by definition equivalent either to the difference between the receipts and outlays of an agent or to the sum of the distributed and retained (saved) income of an agent.

We apply the first definition to households. Their VA is equal to their savings. Thus the material or, more precisely, the monetary criterion of choices is their saved income: the receipt of households is their total income and their outlays are what they spend. There is, as for all agents, a difficulty in this definition. Since the outlays of a household consist not only in its current consumption but also in all its real investment, one must rely on a convention. The current one is that households maximize their utility, a criterion equivalent to the optimization of the distribution of the VA by a firm. The utility criterion applies not only to the current consumption but also to services of real investments: cars, housing, furniture, appliances, clothing etc., usually called durable consumer goods. The two main criteria of households are (a) the utility of what it obtains by what it spends (of the bundle of commodities bought, in current terms)and (b) its saving, i.e. its financial investment. This current description shows the similarity of household's and a firm's two main criteria of choices: maximize the VA and optimize its distribution.

We propose to apply the second definition of the VA to public agents and state that it is equal to their distributed income plus their savings. Their distributed income is the sum of salaries and wages paid out by such agents and the most of their tranfers; their saving is in current life quite often negative: public agents borrow the savings of other agents by what is called deficit financing. The same is at first glance also true of firms, as the savings of people and households are represented by financial investments in firms, by public bonds or by cash holdings. In fact public agents and firms both save but their expenses either current or on real capital are in general superior to their receipts or revenue and the balance is either borrowed, is a loan investment of net lenders or is an equity investment, legally a purchase of share of ownership in a firm. We can here only state an ambiguity in the determination of the VA created by an activity of management and transfer of savings, which is the object of a special type of a firm called a financial institution. A comprehensive theory of transfers is required to study this activity. This will be the subject of Chapter 10. A precise theory of real investment that is of the utilization of savings is also needed. This will be dealt with in Chapter 11. It is essential that these theories be dynamic as time is here a prime variable. One can add that what is currently called 'consumer credit', a part of the activity of financial institutions, creates the same ambiguity in the definition of the VA of households.

The second definition of the VA is of course, we repeat, equivalent to the first: the receipts of public bodies are called revenue in the treatises on public finance and the outlays are called public consumption in national accounts including all wages and some transfers i.e. the income they distribute. One can summarize the distinction between firms and public bodies as wells as households as follows: in public bodies and in families in general the preferences of their members are solidary and convergent, although conflicts arise from divergent beliefs and ideas, that is within the realm of the sacred. These conflicts have in the past been causes of religious wars; they are now tolerated and compatible with peaceful social life. That is why democracy, the government of the people by the people for the people is a possible if seldom attained goal. In firms, on the contrary, the interests of their members are naturally in conflict as they have to divide between them the results of their activity. The will of the majority is in such circumstances not acceptable by the minority. This is a difficulty which Marx has called the class struggle. It can be asserted that the conflict for the distribution of the VA occurs today mainly within the realm of the rational. This situation renders economic democracy a very difficult proposition.

CHAPTER 7

DIMENSIONAL APPROACH

Professor De Jong states in the preface of his book on the 'Dimensional Analysis for Economists' [1] 'that the use of dimensional analysis, a branch of mathematics of a simple type' in economics has, up to his effort, not been systematically tried. It is true that one only seldom if at all meets in the economic literature with applications of the Clerk-Maxwell and Buckingham theorems. In our opinion this is due to two difficulties, the second one being redhibitory.

Firstly economic data are seldom measured with sufficient accuracy and robustness to make applications of these theorems not dangerously hazardous. Secondly, in addition to the quantitative aspect of their measure the economic objects possess qualities that are absent in physics where the Clerk-Maxwell and Buckingham theorems are applicable. Moreover the subjective valuation is fundamental in exchange as we shall see in detail in Chapter 9 and the exchange is a paramount phenomenon in economics.

In their current approach economists bypass the two difficulties by conventional assumptions such as those used in the theory of indices and in general in the theory of aggregation. A good example of this approach is given by Professor De Jong. He assumes that in the Fisher's equality $MV = PT$ the vector of goods, called the 'product' or the 'trade volume', T, is reduced to a scalar (R) which he calls the 'real dimension', the vector of financial objects is reduced to scalar (M), the 'money volume', and the vector of prices to a scalar (P), the 'general price level'. If (P) can be obtained by operating on indices, (M) and (R) are purely heuristic concepts.

We consider that such macroeconomics is far too arbitrary and jumps over several stages of reasoning, for instance in assuming prices as given. Different goods and services as well as money are all distinct objects whose attributes are their quantities and qualities. The cardinality of the sets of these objects cannot be correctly reduced in any other way than by the use of what we call 'reducers of cardinality': money itself but also utility, labour and value. Of these four only money is easily quantified, hence the importance of the concept of prices and of the value added. All four are important in the correct analysis of economic phenomena and should be treated on an equal footing.

In only one aspect can standard dimensional analysis be used in economics and this is in the distinction between stocks and flows. Flows are economic objects per unit of time and their dimension is QT^{-1}, heterogeneous to Q, the dimension of stocks. A famous example of the confusion between stocks and flows is Marx' proof of the existence of the surplus value (see [2] and [3]). A reference to the distinction between stocks and flows can be found in [4] where the late Luigi Solari utilized it for the analysis of semi-aggregated choice functions.

In this chapter we are briefly going over the existing paradigms of the four dimensionality reducers to which one can add a fifth: 'capital'.

Let us first deal with value. This was discussed in Chapter 6 where the elusive character of this concept was shown. It was stated that value is, by definition, attached to a resource and as such should be objective, i.e. the same whatever the agents are.

Bearing this fact in mind, Adam Smith and his followers, the most prominent among them being Karl Marx, proposed the labour theory of value. The universal (dimensionality reducer) called value of a resource has been correlated to, or assumed to be equal to, the 'amount of social labour necessary to produce a resource', 'the value of any article is the amount of labour socially necessary for its production.' (Capital, I, 39)

Now dimensionally this proposition is inconsistent: the dimension of value, whatever it is, is *not* the dimension of labour and stating that both are equal is equivalent to comparing pounds and inches.

Moreover, and all supporters of the labour theory of value were and are aware of the difficulty, value stems not only from production but also from the use of resources. But here it is obviously subjective and closely linked to utility. Marx bridged the difficulty by proposing the concepts of the exchange value based on labour and, in fact, strange to the final exchange or trade and of the usage value based on utility: 'the utility of a thing makes its use value; lastly nothing can have value without being an object of utility'

(Capital, I, 35). Walras and other supporters of classical and neo-classical theories proposed to generalize this last approach and assumed that value stems only from the marginal utility of resources or, with a greater generality, from their scarcity. In our dimensional approach Walras' theory is also inconsistent. Whatever are the dimensions of value and utility, they are different so that it is again the same as comparing pounds and inches. And in this light scarcity, per se an objective attribute of a resource, can produce value only in conjunction with specified agents, turning value into a subjective concept, i.e. the utility.

The obvious conclusion of these remarks is that in the final analysis economic theories, be they marxian, keynesian or primitive walrasian only have a meaning if labour, value, scarcity and utility are distinct attributes.

Scarcity is not, by its nature, a reducer of dimensionality. Value and utility, the first an objective attribute of resources, the second a subjective one, are such reducers but are quite difficult to quantify if money is not used. These two concepts were also discussed in Chapter 6.

I would suggest that we consider utility as dimensionless and not use for instance the 'utiles' so as not to decide in the dispute between ordinal and cardinal concepts of utility. Two difficulties remain: (a) the aggregation (or the reduction in dimensionality) by means of the utility is only relative to a specified agent and (b) the utilities of distinct resources are in general not additive as comp-lementarity and substituability play a part. Of course the 'specified agent' can be an individual, any collective agent or the society itself. We shall discuss this further in Chapters 8 and 9.

As far as value is concerned the labour theory is a semantic device which, by substituting the concept of labour for the concept of value should allow resources to be aggregated, i.e. reduce the dimen-sionality of their set. It is obvious that this device comes up against numerous and important obstacles. The most apparent one is how to measure the many kinds and qualities of labour. Can it be done by the time spent at the 'place of work'? Such a proposition is dimensionally inconsistent since work does not possess the dimen-sion of time, a well defined, easily measured and most important factor in economics as in all human and natural processes.

Karl Marx seems to have been the first to build a model to bypass this and other difficulties by analyzing what I call the partition of value added (VA). His partition is in two parts: the hourly wages of 'workers' and the 'profits' of the owners of the means of production, called capitalists.

But: (i) the real input of 'labour' into productive activity is today quite a complex process, which is mainly technological and intellectual. The outlay of muscular energy by people has almost vanished in firms and remains important only in primitive farming in poor countries and in some handling operations in these regions; (ii) the monetary valuation and the distribution of the VA created by an activity is also a complex socio-economico-political process in which the will of the owners of the means of production, totally sovereign, i.e. void of constraints on possible choices in the thought and at the time of Marx is at present one of the arguments of negotiations and currently not the most important. May it be recalled that the important factors in the choices for the partition of the VA are today (a) the necessities of gross investment, (b) the distribution of fair incomes between those agents who, in their manifold capacities and talents, participate in the activity and contribute to its success, (c) the necessities of the financial market and the credit management in economics where such markets exist and finally (d) the needs of the State.

To these criteria of choices for the partition of VA one must add a most important one which, in business theory and practice, comes under the heading of marketing, purchasing and pricing policies. These policies lead to a measure in monetary units of the VA created. Only when this is done i.e. when production is made possible by the availability of factors and the VA is created by the sale of the products, can VA be distributed among all titles to such a distribution. To do so, one must use money, the most important and the only operational dimensionality reducer, to the analysis of which we devote the next Chapter 8.

The theorem that the 'value of any article is equal to the amount of labour socially necessary for its production' which the followers of Marx believe they have perfected, in particular with regard to the objection of manifold kinds of actual 'work', by adding the adjective 'abstract' before 'labour' is, in my opinion, not at all an operational dimensionality reducer besides lacking in its great abstraction of any power of conviction. The transformation theorem of K. Marx by which such abstract labour is linked to money and prices indicates to me that the activity of the creation of the VA has nothing to do with its distribution, i.e. possible exploitation, and only marginally with labour. Further details on this are given in Chapter 6 above and Chapter 13 below.

We conclude the present chapter by insisting on the necessity of dimensional consistency in economics, so strongly required in physics. We recall the famous inconsistency in Marx' analysis quoted above in references [2] and [3]. A more common case is the usual formalization of production functions currently written $Y = f(K, L)$. In this scripture the output Y and the labour L are flows, the amounts of these aggregates divided by time. On the contrary K is a stock of means of production, an atemporal amount of this aggregate. For instance to make the Cobb-Douglas function $Y = AK^a L^{1-a}$ homogeneous would require for A the dimension of $yt^{-a}k^{-a}l^{a-l}$, where y, k, l are the dimensions of Y, K, L. If Y, K, L were expressed in money, the dimension t^{-a} would be required for A . . . .

To show how the dimensional approach makes inconsistencies and contradictions apparent, let us quote the statement of Michio Morishima (in [5], page 73): 'price and value are dimensionally different: the former is measured in terms of money or some other commodity taken as numéraire, the latter in terms of labour-time . . . Therefore a rigorous treatment of the transformation theorem is possible only by normalizing prices so that they are dimensionally identical with values' . . .

Professor Morishima, an outstanding analyst of economic theories explicits in this way but does not resolve the inconsistencies and the contradictions by comparing the heterogeneous concepts of 'price' which is the result of exchanges, with value, an attribute of a resource, with labour, a human activity and lastly with time, a physical fact, and neglecting that main factor, the 'utility' or preference functional.

The XIXth century economics was in our opinion essentially

scalar. Marx tried to go beyond this simplicity. We should now try
to analyze some vectorial economic theories by considering the four
'dimensions' of value, money, utility and labour.

Up to now we have dealt with the high cardinality of the sets of
agents and of resources. It seems appropriate to recall here the
important problem of the cardinality of the sets of criteria of
choices. The different categories of agents have developed three
classes of methods of reduction of such cardinalities. Firstly, for
choices in uncertainty, a fairly important and common case, a very
simple paradigm is taught. It is what is called the expected utility
rule, i.e. the weighted average of the utilities of possible outcomes,
the weights being the probability of obtaining an outcome. We only
mention this rule here without entering into its justification. Secondly, collective agents reduce the cardinality of their sets of criteria
by mainly two classes of methods. The first is applied in political
bodies. The aim is to be able to 'govern' such bodies, i.e. to choose
and to act. 'Gouverner c'est choisir' is a saying in France. The
theoretical model is democracy, i.e. the vote of all capable members
of these collective agents either to decide, for instance by a majority
rule, directly on issues or to elect representatives who will do so in
the same manner. It has been well known since Condorcet and more
recently by the Arrow impossibility theorem, that this method of
reducing the cardinality of the sets of criteria of choice of the
citizens cannot be formally consistent if it does not operate in the
case of a dictatorship when the criterion of *one* of the members of
the society is the tool of reduction to one of the dimension of the set
of criteria of *all* elements of such an agent. More on this subject can
be found in libraries on political science dealing with theories of
voting and/or public choices.

The second class of methods of reducing the cardinality of the sets
of criteria to one is in use in productive collective agents, that is
firms. These methods are taught by what is called management
science. They are very imperfect as historically firms were dic-
tatorships of owners and excluded all other members of these
agents from expressing choices. The present tendency is to include
all members of firms in the processes of choice. The procedures in
use are as yet rather fluid for the reason that the majority rule is not
applicable in economic life, essentially in the two functions of

creation and partition of the VA and on markets. The same is true for the smallest collective agent, the family, where voting is seldom the best method for reaching decisions, that is, reducing the set of criteria to one element.

It must be recalled that any aggregation of data, expressed here by the reduction of the cardinality of sets of objects, reduces the amount of information available. This is the mandatory price to be paid for the possibility of operation on such sets.

REFERENCES

[1] F. J. de Jong, *Dimensional Analysis for Economists*, North Holland, 1967.
[2] N. Georgescu-Roegen, Mathematical Proofs of the Breakdown of Capitalism, *Econometrica* **30**, April, 1960.
[3] G. Bernard, Quelques réflexions sur les modèles de croissance, *Econometrica* **31**, Jan-Apr., 1963.
[4] L. Solari, *Théorie des choix et fonctions de consommation semi-agrégées*, Droz,1973.
[5] M. Morishima, *Marx's Economics*, Cambridge University Press, 1973.

CHAPTER 8

MONEY AND PRICES

In this chapter we take up the fundamental object of material activity, namely money. We shall not rewrite the enormous literature on the subject nor attempt to be exhaustive. Following the purpose of the book we shall try to explicate some 'principia' and do so in four sections:

(1) The nature and functions of money
(2) Money and choices of agents
(3) Applications of (1) and (2) to the theory of prices and of equilibria
(4) Money, Credit and Inflation.

SECTION 1. NATURE AND FUNCTIONS OF MONEY

Defining money is no simple matter. The easiest way is to elude the problem and state that 'money is what money does'. A similar more precise but only partial answer is the assertion that 'money is whatever is generally accepted in exchange'.

Economists and politicians have for many years attempted to go beyond these two tautologies. Three attributes of money are found in the literature:

– it is a standard of value
– it is a general medium of exchange
– it is a repository of value.

We will elaborate on and somewhat qualify these three definitions of money and supplement them with six additional ones. Before doing so it is useful to briefly recall the history of money.

It started with the exchanges of resources between agents. This barter was a cumbersome procedure, linked with religious rituals. Very soon one of the resources became what economists call a numéraire, a material resource 'generally accepted in exchange' which very soon evolved into the most convenient one, pieces of stable metal which eventually became coins of gold, silver and copper alloys. These objects had an 'exchange value', initially without any interference by individuals or institutions wielding power in societies. But very soon again priests and/or sovereign rulers did interfere by 'coining money', i.e. attaching a mandatory exchange value to such coins and often cheating their holders by decreasing the mass of precious metals in alloys utilized for coining.

Up to quite recent times, in fact up to 1914, in modern economies, the gold and silver bullion, a physical resource shaped into coins, remained a part of the monetary volume (an economic aggregate quite unknown at the time). In fact bullion was losing its importance long before the first world war. Knut Wicksell detected this evolution in the second half of the XIXth century. At that time, contrary to what happened in the XVIth century after the Spanish conquest of Central and South America, the massive arrival of new gold from the West of the United States, from South Africa and from Russia did not kindle inflation. Gold started at the end of XIXth century to be more and more a commodity and all that this new gold did was to entirely eliminate silver as a numéraire.

This evolution is now complete. Today in most countries money is no longer a numéraire but a certificate of debt, a CD, an IOU, issued by the society on itself. In fact money is not a debt but a claim of its holder on society. This present reality is a development of the old usage by private bankers to issue receipts as a representation of a deposit with them of real resources of any kind, including bullion and thus create an instrument of spatial displacement of 'value'. These CD's were exchanged for what they represented by correspondents of the issuer at the destinations of the travels of their holders and dispensed such holders from the often cumbersome and dangerous transport of real resources in kind. At this stage of the development of monetary economy the final exchange extinguished the debt of the banker who was of course compensated for his service by an interest or commission on the deal. But progressively the CD's ceased to be presented for exchange and became objects of monetary trade, i.e. they became money in our modern sense. This private money was eventually replaced by public money of the same nature issued by a central or State bank. It now represents, as stated above, the debt of the society to its holder who can exchange it at any time and in any place against real resources created by the activity of the members of the society, that is, its economic agents, or against similar CD's valid in other societies. This money is now called 'fiduciary' currency which is supplemented by a return of private money of a different kind from the medieval CD's, as it is represented by data stored in the memories of the computers of banks, labelled in units of public money. It is called 'scriptural' currency and in all countries is closely monitored by the State or the Central Bank. This second kind of currency at the end of our century is progressively replacing all other kinds in particular by the use of credit cards, the 'plastic' money.

Whatever the kind of money, Henry Thornton's saying in 1802 that: 'Money of every kind is an order for goods' is always valid. Money represents for its holder, an individual or a collective agent, the liberty to obtain in exchange for it all the resources he needs or desires. These IOU's bear no interest in their original shape. But if there is a rise in prices which value resources in terms of money, such an evolution is obviously equivalent to a negative interest rate of money. If prices fall the interest rate of money is positive. The appreciation or depreciation of money either quick or slow depends on the evolution of the real economy and, of course, on the volume of money issued in a given society and on its velocity of circulation. In the present world where all currencies are interrelated by real and financial trades the inflation or deflation in any economy also depends on the evolution of all other economies.

This brief recall of trivial facts allows us to discuss the three current attributes of money as found in the literature.

Firstly, it is asserted that money is a standard of value. This definition is not convincing. The value is a very fuzzy and difficult concept, as already shown. Is it objective or subjective, pertaining to an agent? We have proposed for value an objective definition attached to resources . . . Does this first definition of money mean that value is measured by means of money? In his last book, on the 'Economics of Industrial Society' Michio Morishima attempts to be more precise. He writes 'the price of a good A expresses the amount of money which is of the same value as one unit of A'. This sentence seems to mean that the value of one unit of A is measured by the value of a certain amount of money, called the price of A. Now Morishima's proposition is arbitrary and at discrepancy with reality.

It pertains to the act of exchange of money M against a resource A. As we shall show in the next chapter exchanging a volume x of A against a volume m of M results from comparisons of the utilities to the exchangers of the volumes x and m. The price m/x is only a result of secondary importance in the reasoning of the act of exchange. And utility and value are different concepts as we have shown in Chapter 6 and shall discuss again below. Of course one can identify by definition utility and value. But this will only be a convention.

In other terms the function of money as a measure of value which seems to be simple and self-explanatory is, in fact, linked to the very complicated subject of prices where utilities of money and real resources are put in relation. The problem of prices will be dealt with in more detail in Section 3 of this chapter and further in Chapters 9 and 13. One can only mention here that prices allow money to play its many functions.

Secondly, money is asserted to be a general medium of exchange. This is quite obvious in the present world. Even if trade is reduced (complicated, not simplified) to barter, the volumes of resources exchanged are, with some rare exceptions, compared by means of prices, i.e. by volumes of money. As is well known, in theory Say's identity is equivalent to barter while money allows not to respect it. Prices, i.e. the ratios of the volumes of money to the volumes of resources exchanged, are prominent parameters of economic activity, not more. See more on this elsewhere in the book.

Thirdly, money is deemed to be a repository of value. Such an assertion is largely wanting. How can money be a repository? The relation of money to value is at least a difficult proposition.

We propose to formulate otherwise this third definition of what money is. Since money is a general medium of exchange which results in prices, one can assume that by means of prices money represents real resources or, more precisely, their availability. While the main attribute of a resource is to be localized in time and space and its transport may be cumbersome or impossible, money, its representation, allows an easy and convenient method of displacing the 'value' of resources in time and space. It is in this sense that money is a repository of value.

In this third role money is nowadays supplemented or even

almost replaced by a most involved credit economy, which is also called financial trade. The documentary credit displaces money in space; lending and borrowing funds, and, at the maturity of loans, operating in the opposite sense, is displacing money in time. One must mention that in the financial economy the spatial and temporal transfers of 'value' are closely linked with the 'storage' of this value currently called 'saving' and with the existence of capital whatever this word means. The interest rate plays an important role here. It is often called the 'price of money'. We will not use this term in reference to money markets as price is a ratio between an amount of money and an amount of a resource, while the rate of interest is a discount of the future, closely linked with uncertainty and is a price only if uncertainty or its evaluation and, of course, money itself is considered as a resource. We do not agree with this last point.

Such are the three current definitions of money. We propose six more of its attributes:

4. Money allows an easy and convenient way of valuing, more precisely assessing how wealth is created by the activity of agents and how this wealth once created is divided among its beneficiaries. Technically, money allows the VA created in the activity to be measured and then divided between distributed incomes of all kinds, and savings. Thus at a microlevel money is the tool of social relations in activity and, at a macrolevel, more or less reliably measures the total wealth created by society in a period: the sum total of VAs created by all agents, members of society, is the social product. The realm of the creation and distribution of VA is also a seat of many transfers for which money is nowadays almost exclusively used in contrast to the past. We devote Chapter 10 to this matter.

The creation and distribution of VA is in our opinion the most important, the sole fundamental economic event. It is a flow in which prices resulting from exchanges of the input and the output of real resources have a specific importance in the creation of VA while wages, profits, transfers, financing etc. equally play their role in the distribution of this VA as created. Of course our approach is only a model which differs from the current models of the usual micro- and macroeconomics. Chapters 11 and 13 will deal with the matter in more detail.

5. This fourth role of money results in its important fifth role as

the tool of the management of savings and of their use, the investment. The creation of savings is threefold, as will be discussed later: from the direct partition of the VA created between distributed incomes and saving, from the partition of distributed incomes between consumption and free saving and from public choices within public budgets. The price structure also plays an important role so money is here again the main tool. In usual language and in real life the savings create the financial capital and the financial markets when they exist. But, by the manifold quality of money, these markets of savings are linked with the current activity of the creation and distribution of VA in such a close way that one cannot clearly distinguish between what in America are called flow markets and what are called asset markets, separate both from public finance and policies of taxation and expense. Similarly, in the early XIXth century English and Scottish financiers could not settle the quarrel between the banking school concerned, in our present parlance, with the management of savings, and the currency school concerned with the creation and distributon of the VA. In other terms it is quite difficult to distinguish between (a) the circulating money, at the service of exchanges and of the creation and distibution of the VA, and (b) the savings money or financial capital, at the service of investment.

6. These five attributes of money result in a sixth: the concept of money shares with the concepts of value, of utility and labour the function of a reducer of the cardinality (of the heterogeneity) of the sets of resources, of choices, of constraints on choices and of criteria of choices. All four reducers are rather difficult to manipulate and they deliver only fuzzy results. But money seems to be the only one that is able to reduce to one the dimensions of these sets by a cardinal universal measure, through the use of prices. That is why for instance neoclassical economics essentially founded on money is better understood than the marxist theory which attempts to reduce the cardinality of economic sets by the use of labour. In fact prices are as difficult to manipulate as utility or labour . . . It remains that utility is subjective and its aggregation doubtful while labour and value are quite fuzzy concepts. Only an amount of money M available at time t and location l is a simple measure of the wealth or activity of any agent, be it an individual or a firm or a State, even if

this measure utilizes a 'rubber' unit.

7. In a first conclusion which is the seventh attribute of money one can state that money has been and continues to be a powerful instrument for the progress of global productivity of the material activity and of efficiency in all activities.

Barter was and remains a cumbersome device of exchange while money has brought a great improvement to its technique. More specific and less discussed in the literature is the role of money in the measurement and subsequent distribution of the VA. For this task primitive economies used transfers in kind, which were quite inefficient, as were such operations in the Greek, Roman, Chinese and other civilizations, based on slavery and on all kinds of discriminations in personal statutes. Money existed but was used almost exclusively for trade while VA was distributed mainly in kind. The same was true for feudal societies where the distribution as well as the creation of VA remained in kind.

In parallel with the first industrial revolution money became the exclusive tool of these activities. The classical capitalist system of wages and profits introduced a great increase in the productivity of the management of VA. We experience today a further improvement in the monetary economy by the substitution for material money of data stored in the memories of computers. The process is going on. At the time of this writing we live in a great revolution in the financial aspect of the world economy. This is due to the very low cost, compared to the recent past, of transporting, storing and processing great volumes of information and, at the same time and by the same means, to a total instantaneity, on the human scale, of all these immaterial exchanges which may be defined by the concept of communication and data processing. The present communication revolution acts also of course in all other domains of the economic and other human activities. This present manipulation of money makes it, as is the case in its other roles, a factor of productivity.

Moreover throughout all human history money enhanced a fundamental source of productivity called 'division of labour', which is understood to be the cooperation of economic agents in splitting in successive stages the transformation of primary natural resources into finished goods and services. These 'exchanges' in older times mostly effected in kind now utilize a very intricate spatial and temporal structure of product and commodity prices as opposed to final prices of consumer goods and services. Without money this structure would have been impossible and in consequence the very existence of our highly refined and efficient 'division of labour' would also have been impossible. We shall deal extensively with this particular role of prices, i.e. of money, after analyzing their formation.

8. Money is a powerful tool of freedom. The availability of money obviously enlarges the set of choices of any agent and relaxes the constraints on these choices. For people this role of money enhances the current concept of freedom and of free societies. Affluent societies are more free than the poor ones. For firms, affluence gives more market power and a larger set of other choices. For local authorities and states sound budgets and their surpluses mean less dependence on central government's grants and controls. For nation-states the same is true with respect to international financial institutions and the more powerful members of the world community. No other reducers of dimensionality such as value, utility, labour play this role.

9. A last, at least in this reckoning, function of money is its power of illusion and dream. The monetary illusion is an important phenomenon in fiscal and other financial matters. One can also place under this heading the role of money in gambling and in the never ending fight of human souls and behaviours against uncertainty, especially with respect to the future. This role of money is not unimportant. Any choice of any agent, be it economic or of any other kind always includes a bit of a gamble against the uncertainty of its result. Even in the 'perfect' societies of dreamers, as, for instance, the final communism where according to Karl Marx there will exist no merchandise, no value, no money, no prices and no wages, as the society will be ruled by the principle: 'from everybody according to his abilities to everybody according to his needs', money will be needed to play games and participate in lotteries . . .

Of course one shall consider these nine functions of money only in their totality. They are distinguished here as models only. Our exercise approximates the complicated and involved reality and thus help us to understand it better.

As a conclusion to this section it seems obvious that money is eminently useful. The academic quarrels about the direct utility of money seem to this author void of substance. Considering only the nine attributes discussed here it is apparent that this direct utility of money is quite evident. We shall see that this is also the case in the technical meaning of the concept of utility.

Money in its eighth attribute is not only a private good, as would be concluded considering that its possession increases the set of choices of its holder and has, in this respect, the quality of exclusion. Money can also be considered as a public good as (a) it satisfies a common interest of the members of the society, (b) it is in this capacity, for instance in measuring and distributing the VA, non-exclusive and (c) the control of money is to a large extent delegated to the State. But money is not an ordinary public good because it does not impose on agents any apparent costs such as taxes, if we exclude inflation, while ordinary public goods are financed by the public revenue.

SECTION 2.   MONEY AND THE CHOICES OF AGENTS

This section is about the role of money with respect to the three sets of choices, of the constraints on these choices and of the criteria of choices of the agents, as described in Chapter 4. As already mentioned, money has the eminent role of a reducer of dimensionality of all of these three sets. This is its sixth attribute.

2.1. For individual agents the elements of the set of choices are 'bundles' of commodities. For collective agents called firms the elements are activities, products, investments, factor inputs, market shares and for many of them prices. For collective agents called public bodies, such as governments, the elements are those of macroeconomic aggregates and mainly the budgetary and monetary policies, which act on the elements of national accounts such as the social product, the price level, employment, consumption and investment, balances of trade and payments, and regional differences. In all these cases the sets of choices are completed by intangible elements of many kinds; for instance, for individual agents these are aesthetic feelings, religious creeds, love and hate, for all agents traditions and usual behaviours, power and status, for public agents their sources such as elections . . .

The purpose of social sciences and, in particular, of economics is to describe or prescribe the operations of agents on their sets of choices. The task can only be achieved if these sets are specified and, as far as is feasible, quantified. Money is the powerful and unique tool of such a quantification by reducing the cardinality of the sets of choices by means of prices for individual and private collective agents, and in macroeconomics by aggregating the resulting monetary amounts. Prices given for an agent are a vector which he maps on the set of his choices, a matrix, to obtain a product vector of quantified choices. When the agent can choose prices too, the matrix of choices is to be multiplied by the matrix of prices to obtain a quantified picture of the set of choices. This reduction of the cardinality of the set of choices does not in general allow actual choices to be made.

2.2. To do so, constraints on choices must in turn be specified and quantified. For individual agents (which we identify here with households) the main constraint seems straightforward enough: it is in the period the available amount of money, i.e. the sum of current disposable income and of possible consumer credit, corrected by the net balance of saving. But both saving and taking up credit are elements of the set of choices, so the set of constraints is not disjoint from the set of choices. This is true for all agents. For collective private agents (firms) the sets of constraints have more elements: accounts or financial statements, technological possibilities of production, availability of factors of inputs, human skills and motivations, the market situation etc. As far as is feasible, the cardinality of such sets is reduced by means of imputed (shadow) or actual prices, either given or elements of the set of choices, that is by means of money. Here, too, the set of constraints is relaxed or tightened by the credit activity, i.e. the relation between saving, expense and revenue within the activity, essentially expressed in money and thus closely linked to the set of choices since this last relation is subject to a rather free choice of the agent.

For collective public agents their material constraints as expressed in money should be quite similar to those of collective private agents. This is not so since the budgetary constraint is more easily relaxed by 'deficits' for the main public agents, the governments. The money, as IOU's on the society, brings for the agents who manage and control the monetary volume (this was called 'printing money' up to about the middle of this century) a relaxation of the budget constraint. For other public agents, such as agencies or local bodies who today do not issue money, the constraints on choices are more similar to those of firms. Banks and other financial institutions are hybrid collective agents who create money and thus possess this supplementary degree of freedom. For this reason they are under tight control of the central banks, issuers of the 'high power' money.

The simple budget constraint is of course not the unique element of the set of constraints of collective agents. For governments the measures of macroeconomic aggregates listed above are such elements. Most of them are expressed or have to be quantified in monetary terms.

2.3. The third set in which money plays a significant role is that of the criteria of choices. The quantifications in money which result in the reduction of the cardinality of the set of choices by means of prices is the paramount choice criterion for all agents. This criterion is so important in economic and other choices that quite often all other criteria which however always exist and have an influence on decisions are neglected. The monetary criterion is extremely simple and straightforward: the choice that obtains the greatest amount of money available for the choice maker is taken.

The consequences of this reality for different kinds of agents are important. For individual agents, i.e. households it is assumed in economics that their preferences, i.e. their criteria of choices, are quantified by means of the concept of utility. Utility is a reducer of the cardinality of these sets. An obvious problem arises, that of the utility of money i.e. of how the preferences are expressed when the set of choices and constraints on choices is reduced to the scalar of an amount of money.

It is widely accepted and verified by actual behaviours that in such circumstances the marginal utility of money decreases with its increasing availability. Richard and Peggy Musgrave in their book on public finance ([1], p. 204) quote the results of Koichi Mera reported in QJE, August 1969. This author correlated the available income to the utility of one additional dollar and obtained a smooth decreasing relation starting at an index of 8.51 for an income of $1,000 to an index of 0.003 for an income of $200,000. Of course such a relation is subjective, i.e. pertains to a specified agent. It is widely assumed however that its shape is in general valid for all agents.

In this author's opinion this is in general not true. For public bodies and for firms the marginal utility of money is invariant. These agents create and distribute wealth measured by the VA and do so by measuring the VA and its allotments to agents entitled by means of the accounting theory and practices. Now in accounting the 'marginal utility' of money is constant: a cent has the same importance as a million dollars. Thus the volume of wages, the amount of profit, the depreciation allowance, the budget of education or of defense are amounts of money in a period (flows) whose 'marginal utility' is a constant. In the opinion of this author at least, a fundamental distinction is to be made as regards utility of money for households or people and for collective agents. For the former this utility is an expression of preference and its derivative is decreasing; for the latter it is an arithmetic or linear measure of the VA and of its parts, whose derivative is a constant. One can illustrate this difference by two statements: (a) the differences in the role of money as a criterion of choices for individuals and for collective agents show that value and money are quite distinct concepts. The definition by Morishima as quoted in the first section of this chapter cannot be accepted; and (b) the famous reasoning by K. Marx about consumption represented by the exchange AMA' (A a commodity, M money) and about production represented by MAM' is a premonition by a genius of the distinction just presented: AMA' is the expression of the utilities of commodities in an exchange between consumers: the utility of A' is greater than the utility of A, so the exchange takes place; MAM' is the creation of the VA measured by the difference $M' - M$. The first defines for Marx the 'usage value', often associated by his interpreters to utility while the second defines the 'exchange value', similarly compared to cost and price.

Let us conclude this section by two statements related to the distinction between the individual and collective agents with regard to the role of money:

- individual agents manifest irrational expectations about money, called the monetary illusion. They subjectively consider money as a physical commodity of a constant character and, especially by virtue of its variable marginal utility, do not correctly evaluate its depreciation (the inflation) and/or the fiscal burden. This is not so for collective agents who by virtue of precise accounting procedures are generally 'rational' in their expectations.
- on a macroscale money is a important factor or criterion of choice when the society is atomistic or libertarian. If its structures are more rigid, for instance when unions, corporations or big financial institutions control prices, incomes and markets or when a totalitarian government controls the creation and the allotment of the VA, money loses some of its importance. Thus in primitive economies money was less important than in present free market economies of strong competition. It has lost some of its importance in socialist systems.

SECTION 3.   THEORY OF PRICES AND OF EQUILIBRIA

The theory of prices will result from what is written in Sections 1 and 2 above and from what will be formalized in the next chapter. If one is to complete this theory then to the four concepts of value, of utility, of labour and of money one must add a fifth, the scarcity of resources. This fifth concept plays no role in reducing the cardinality of the five economic sets. It is fundamental only in the theory of prices.

Price has two origins. One resides in the process of creation and of distribution of the VA, by 'monetarizing' inputs, outputs and, in consequence, the VA itself. This is done by accounting procedures. In the current economic language this origin of prices is described as costs in the chain of production. We say that the VA cannot be expressed in money unless the monetary valuation of the output is superior to the monetary valuation of the input. Both valuations are made by means of prices. This origin of prices has to do with scarcity but has close links with the division of activities between agents, usually called the division of labour.

On the contrary when utilities govern the exchange of money

against resources, scarcity plays a fundamental role in the formation of prices. We shall see in the next chapter how this works in an elementary exchange. On the macrolevel, scarcity is expressed in the aggregate demand and costs in the aggregate supply. Both meet on the market when it exists. Prices stemming from this macro-process are often considered as being social data, exogenous to exchange. In our opinion this attribute of prices is mainly due to the two fundamental phenomena of economic activity, namely the creation and the distribution of the VA and the division of labour, which both define the essence of societies on the material side.

But what is scarcity? It is a concept distinct from value and from utility yet it acts on both. Here are some cases of these distinctions. A glass of water for a thirsty person is of great utility to him whether it is scarce or abundant; its value in the current sense is negligible; when this person is satiated, his utility vanishes while the 'value' or the scarcity of the glass of water does not change. A particular shell on a beach is unique and very scarce but its value or its utility to a particular person are normally zero. A stamp of 1860 is very scarce, of great price and maybe of great value to a particular person but what is its utility to the person who pays a high price for it? etc. etc.

Thus prices, scarcity, utility and value are distinct concepts whose relations are manifold and, in general, strong. Value, in particular, is very difficult to clarify, as we have already shown. Marx' proposal to define economic value by socially necessary labour is not convincing. Further utility, as shown in the above examples, is something distinct from price, scarcity or value. It is incorrect to take marginal utilities or linear transforms of marginal utilities as a means of reducing the dimensionality of economic sets; it is even more incorrect to use for this purpose relative prices equal to marginal substitution rates.

On the theoretical level Walras' statement that: 'the total of all material and immaterial things capable of having a price because they are scarce, i.e. useful and limited in availability, is the social wealth. Thus pure economics is the theory of social wealth' must in consequence and in our view be qualified. Firstly this statement is static and apparently confuses stocks and flows. Secondly, Walras' definition of prices as only representing scarcities is incomplete as prices also stem from costs and transfers. We would reword this statement as follows: 'the sum total of VA's created in a society is the increment of the social wealth quantified by means of prices'.

We have just mentioned transfers which brings us to a concept seldom if ever found in the literature on prices while playing a big role in their formation. We call it Price Included Transfers (PITs). Their intensity depends not only on costs and scarcities but also on the market power of the agents who exchange, on social and political constraints and, in pure macroeconomics, on price elasticities of demand and supply. All these influences are interdependent. As will be shown in Section 4 of this chapter and in more detail in Chapters 10 and 14, the PITs are zero only in the state of perfect competitive equilibrium of neoclassical theory or zero *mehrwert* in a marxist approach. We shall show that the VA, i.e. any new wealth created can exist in monetary terms if and only if PIT's are present. This result is fundamentally at variance from current economics which has been developed for at least two centuries and taught up to the present. At this stage we shall only touch upon this discrepancy while an important part of it will be analyzed in detail later when the creation and distribution of the VA and the elementary exchange are analyzed.

One must mention here the commodity markets where prices often wildly fluctuate. Such fluctuations are currently explained by scarcities and gluts. This is the case for metals, for agricultural products, for crude oil etc. The reality, for this author at least, seems to be that scarcities and gluts in these activities are only a smokescreen hiding gambling and essentially fluctuations of PITs, of transfers of wealth between the losers and the winners of the game, not only in pure speculations but also in the national and international division of stages of activities, commonly called division of labour. Of course the wealth transferred in the game is the VA created in economies.

L. Walras defined political economy as a 'theory of price definition in absolutely perfect competition' while G. Debreu formulated the starting stage of his formal theory of value as follows: 'the two central problems of this theory are . . . the explication of the role of prices in an optimal state of an economy.' I take a different start in this book. I am not, at this stage, interested in such market structures as perfect competition, a duopole, oligopole or monopole.

Prices for me stem, as stated, from costs and from demand (scarcity). They are established in exchanges where either utilities or costs but not both play a role. The most important, basic economic events are the creation and distribution of VA which exists if price included transfers exist. This utterance is equivalent to stating that economy is *not* in an optimal state nor in equilibrium. Our model is thus antinomic to neoclassical models such as Walras' or Debreu's. Their models assume a given production and a given creation and distribution of incomes. Agents are not differenciated as holders of initial exogenous wealth or income. In this last respect it is worthwhile to mention here, before elaborating on this point later, that one of the consequences of our approach, in deviation from these current models, is that *all* distributed incomes are considered as parts of the global distribution of VA. Thus 'wages' are *not* costs nor prices of labour which is *not a good*, a resource or a merchandise but only a *title* to a part in the distribution of VA, identical to all other titles to other parts of this distribution. In our model the creation and distribution of VA is *the* exogenous activity from which prices and real macrostates derive. The sets of agents are specified, their choices are exogenous and are governed by the three sets analyzed in Chapter 3 to 6. The analysis starting from the creation and distribution of VA is antinomic to all current models not only of Walras and Debreu but also of Keynes, Patinkin and Marx. In particular *all* models are negated which link the wage level to micro or macroequilibria, to marginal productivity of labour, to elasticities of substitution, to marginal cost pricing, to unemployment and to levels of subsistence and to exploitation. We shall not deal with equilibria, optimal growth, golden paths etc. but shall remain interested in the stabilities of evolutions, whether they are divergent or convergent. Putty-putty or putty-clay models, the 'rate of profit' etc., are not prominent variables here, as must now be clear to all interested readers.

The macro approach to the role of money is twofold. The management of the volume of money existing in society (in a monetary zone) is governed by its creation or emission, primarily by the public institution empowered by law to act to this end (almost everywhere the central bank). The credit of the central bank is theoretically unlimited, in fact constrained by law and/or by political choices of a monetary policy. So the volume of the high power or central money is formally exogenous. The volume of secondary, commercial bank money is on the contrary endogenous since it is constrained by the necessity of balancing accounts of such banks, by the credit regulations established by the government and/or by the central bank and, last but not least, by the available saving provided by its three sources: the undistributed part of the VA, the free saving of the holders of incomes and the public budgetary saving.

A second approach to the role of money in macroeconomics has been largely discussed in the literature, under the heading of the quarrel between those who thought money to be neutral and those who asserted it to be active. In the neoclassical models money could be eliminated which means that these models deal with barter and use money only as a convenience, assuming prices to be given as do present day socialist economies. In all such situations money is neutral. But real market economies are not represented by such models. The creation of VA requires a structure of product and commodities prices expressing the existence of PITs and of the division of labour. These prices depend on the monetary volume. The existence of VA which only has meaning in nominal terms implies that money must be active. Walras thought that money is active only because of the existence of savings, interest rate etc. In other terms, in his opinion, only the use of money as a means of transfer of value in time made it active. In our opinion this 'active' quality of money is not only due to the existence of savings but also to the creation of VA and of the *whole* of its distribution which is the source of *all* incomes, including public revenue and which includes also a part of the savings, made of the undistributed part of the VA created.

SECTION 4.   MONEY, CREDIT AND INFLATION

As stated above we do not label the interest rate as the price of money. It seems appropriate to explain what we mean by this opinion.

Money is defined here (and elsewhere too) as a claim on the society or its debt certificate: an IOU. This claim does not imply any price in the sense of an exchange of an amount of money against an amount of real resource. Only savings, whatever their use, for instance for current exchanges against resources such as equipment, are in relation to interest rates. Money possesses the attribute of an interest rate only in its third role as a means of transfer of value in the time dimension. The credit economy which is defined here as the economics of savings is the only one in which interest rates play a role.

Now prices fluctuate and in particular depend on the volume of money present in the economy. If they rise, (the evolution called inflation) all holders of monetary assets 'pay' an interest rate on such holdings equal to the inflation rate; if prices fall, all holders receive a 'payment' of positive interest rate. The agent who receives 'payments' in inflation or pays them out in deflation is the society itself. In other terms and in accordance with our definitions of money all debtors increase their real wealth in inflation while all creditors suffer losses; the reverse is true in deflation. In still other terms the burden of a debt increases when inflation ceases or is reversed. Finally when prices fall one can get more resources for the same amount of money detained and on the macrolevel the debt of the society to the holders of money increases when measured in real resources. For this simple reason falling price level has negative if not catastrophic effects in macroeconomics while inflation, when it is moderate, makes the task of governments less strenuous.

As money in the credit economy transfers value in time, the 'nominal' interest rate on credit operations is the sum of the 'price' of the uncertainty of the future or, put more simply, the price of time, an essential economic resource, and of this just discussed virtual 'interest rate' stemming from the variation of the global price level. The first element of this sum is currently called the real interest rate.

An important remark which is rarely found in the literature can be made here. The money in the credit economy creates by means of interest rates transfers of values within the current economic flows. Each time an agent pays an interest rate to another agent an amount of wealth is transferred from the former to the latter. This transfer has just been described with regard to the variation of the price level where it is in a sense virtual or implicit. It really exists for all interest payments made within the credit economy. Banks and other financial institutions collect a part of the product, i.e. of the VA by means of interest payments. The same is true for relations between collective agents called States, economies, monetary zones, etc.

In the primary distribution of VA within firms or other agents creating it interest payments are a part of this distribution. For consumer credit and for public loans subscribed by people these payments are not a part of the distribution of VA but of an utilization of incomes which is a secondary distribution of the product. We shall examine this problem in detail in Chapter 13.

It follows that the credit economy or the financial sector of the economic activity has a powerful effect on the final distribution of VA. Its complex processes tend, in general, to limit the real income distributed to agents entitled to it by their activity in the creation of VA. This is obvious since interest payments are a part of the final distribution of VA whatever processes are active in the economy including, as shown above, inflation due for instance to monetary creation. This fact is an argument in favour of the consideration of money as being active.

We shall now indulge in some technicalities. The current economic reasoning on the balance between the demand for credit and its supply equates the demand for gross investment and for financing public deficits to the supply equal to the gross saving. This reasoning assumes that investment and saving both depend on interest rate, in an opposite sense, the result being an equilibrium rate.

This is not entirely correct. The supply of credit must include the variation of the volume of money which acts as a transfer of value in time, in the same way as saving. Thus in past but not so distant times the budgetary deficits were financed by printing paper money while today more sophisticated ways of increasing the monetary volume are used to this end, as a supplement to straight borrowing. D. Ricardo's equivalence theorem stating that rational agents offset the present budget deficit by the future tax burden needed to redeem government bonds now financing this deficit should be completed by the 'rational expectations' of the virtual interest rate shown above, which discounts the effect of the variation of the monetary volume. Any credit today, and a deficit is such a credit, is a transfer of real wealth, the goods of Thornton in the quotation of

Section 1 of this chapter, from the future agents who will create it to the present ones. More precisely not only the monetary volume but also its velocity of circulation bears on the economic dynamics. The product MV in the Cambridge identity expresses the volume of the 'debt' in circulation in a period, as a representation of the volume of available real resources. If the former volume exceeds the latter, prices rise i.e. the 'debt' carries a negative interest; in the opposite case the debt carries a positive interest.

One can briefly formalize this reasoning. In a period let G be the public deficit, S the total saving, dM the positive variation of the monetary volume (in fact MV), I the real investment and E the external net balance of payments. Then one has:

$$S - dM = G + I + E$$

and the total spatio-temporal transfer in the period is

$$T = S - dM - I = G + E$$

G is financed by borrowing in any kind of assets within or without the economy. The transfer T is temporal from the future to the present period. The part of the domestic debt variation plays a role in the variation of the domestic interest rate while the part of foreign debt variation (by the processes of exchange markets) varies the domestic monetary volume. The external deficit or surplus is by itself a spatial transfer effected within the trade accounts and also within the world financial markets.

This is not however the whole picture. The role of money, in its widest definition, is not only financing investment or public deficits, as in the above equalities but also primarily paying for consumption. Prices, incomes and savings depend directly or indirectly on the supply of real resources as well as on the monetary volume and on the final demand. The links between these aggregates are a good example of a bidirectional causality: if the monetary volume increases, the supply of money increases and in the current reasoning where the nominal interest rate is its price this rate should decline. But the increase of M induces inflation if and only if it is unbalanced, too high with respect to the increase in the supply of real resources. If inflation occurs, the price of money should increase with all other prices, i.e. the nominal interest rate should increase, in contradiction to our just stated reasoning. One could submit that the *real* interest rate should decline in this situation. This is however quite dubious since the real interest rate is the real price of time depending on forecasts of the uncertain future and *not* on the present relation between the supply of money and of real resources. In other terms one has:

$$i_n = i + i_r$$

where i_n is the nominal and i_r the real interest rates and i the inflation. If M increases above the supply of real resources, i increases and i_n will increase too unless i_r decreases at least to compensate for the increase of i. This result is quite dubious. The nominal interest rate does not decrease in inflation as would be the case if it were the price of money whose supply increases but to the other hand generally increases. The contrary occurs in deflation.

This in a nutshell is our presentation of the monetarist, supply side and rational expectations philosophy.

Of course, as previously stated in this chapter and repeated many times in the book all such models simplify and thus truncate the complex reality by specifying functions, relations and items in order to be able to present plausible and understandable descriptions. The models are never the reality. In this reality trade, production, creation and distribution of the VA and financial and budgetary activities and policies are intimately intermingled.

CONCLUSIONS

1. One could summarize all that is written up to the present in a system language. Economics deals with a twice dimensional world. We find on one side four dimensionality reducers: money, value, utility and labour and the other side four abstract spaces: uncertainty, freedom, time, physical space. The graph of relations between these eight items is complex. Any of the eight concepts has links with all the other. Economic dynamics, as physics, evolves in a space-time continuum in most cases studied in the discrete mode. In physics the continuum is structured by energy, i.e. fields of forces. In economics one could submit that choices and for most of them utility are fields whose dynamics is expressed by money or, to state

it more precisely, money is their model.

2. The paramount importance of money requires what exists in all societies: a strict control by decision makers of the monetary economy. Moreover the representation of resources by means of money is simple and homogeneous. For these two reasons one could hold an opinion at variance to the usual one, namely that it is quite possible to include finance in the sector managed in a centralized mode without a significant loss of overall efficiency. In fact in many developed economies the financial power is highly concentrated.

On the contrary, a centralized or planified real economy sector is necessarily very inefficient. This is obviously due to the high cardinality of the set of real resources so that any adjustment of requirements to offers, by any conscious process, is an impossible task.

The difficulty of such a dual system lies of course in the interface between the two sectors. In the current economic discipline this point is stressed with respect to the relation between saving and investment, besides mentioning difficulties in the satisfaction of individual needs and desires in the possible absence of markets. We submit that the difficulty is even greater in the processes of the creation and distribution of VA.

The world is at present confronted with this difficulty, translated in daily economics by inflation and unemployment in market economies and by scarcities, inefficiency and lack of liberty in planified economies.

REFERENCE

[1] R. A. Musgrave and P. B. Musgrave, *Public Finance in Theory and Practice*, McGraw Hill, 1973. Paperback Student Edition.

CHAPTER 9

ELEMENTARY EXCHANGE

The literature on elementary exchange is rich and the case has interested people for eons. Today's teaching starts mainly with reference to Edgeworth and his box. F. Hayek deals with the matter in his 'catallaxy'.

We shall first propose a simple model and then show how the problem is intricate when real exchanges are analyzed. Our model is in essence a rather heuristic translation of the principle of Nash equilibrium and has of course much to do with bilateral monopoly.

Two agents exchange a certain amount of a real resource against a certain amount of money. Why does each of them choose to do so? My purpose in seeking an answer to the question is not to recall the results of anthropologists such as Malinowski or Margaret Mead who have studied gifts and exchanges in primitive societies but is just to show how money and utility explain at its primary foundation the economic activity.

The two agents exchange for a simple reason: by doing so they both increase their utilities. This language is tautologically equivalent to the statement that for one of the two, whom I shall call the buyer, the sum of money he gives to the other one, whom I shall call the seller, is of less utility *to him* than the resource he receives in exchange from the seller. The contrary is true for the seller: the resource he gives to the buyer is of less utility *to him* than the sum of money he receives in exchange from the buyer. In a still other equivalent statement, the buyer prefers the amount of resource received to the sum of money given away and the seller has the opposite preference. One can mention here – we shall come back to the point later – that the aim of all 'sales efforts' such as advertising and in general marketing is to change the structure of preferences of the buyer.

Economists would object to what has just been formulated saying that in real life the ratio of the amount of money to the amount of resource exchanged, what they and people at large call the price of the resource, is in many circumstances exogenous to the exchange.

Even if the seller or the buyer do have some leeway to choose the price, the constraints on its possible variation are strong. So the price should be the main variable in the reasoning on elementary exchange, as is the case in 99 per cent of the existing literature. In this author's opinion by focusing for centuries the interest of the economic inquiry on prices as social data, given to the agents in perfect competition and not considering their origin (which is an exchange of a sum of money against an amount of resource) economics has missed an important aspect of its content.

If it were assumed that the utility of money and of the resource exchanged were proportional to the amounts of each of the two (an assumption equivalent to the statement that their marginal utilities are constant), once the buyer preferred the resource to money and the seller money to the resource, they would exchange unlimited amounts of each. The result is paradoxical and the question arises of how to resolve the paradox. The answer is straightforward and of great importance to the understanding of the concepts called money, resource and utility.

The marginal utility of money and of the resource decreases with increasing amounts exchanged and these utilities of small increments are *different* for money and for any resource and also for *different* agents. Thus the amounts exchanged increase up to the point at which the disutility for the buyer of giving away an increment of the sum of money exactly compensates the utility of obtaining the increment of the amount of the resource. The opposite occurs for the seller.

It is easy to formalize this result which is found, expressed in different ways in all manuals and treatises on economics within the theories of the core, of the Nash equilibrium and in the Edgeworth box, the fixed point, the auctioneer etc.

Let u_{rb} be the utility of the resource exchanged, *to the buyer*, let u_{rs} be the same, *to the seller*, let u_{mb} be the utility of money, *to the buyer* and let u_{ms} be the same, *to the seller*. The exchange takes place if $u_{rb} > u_{mb}$ and $u_{rs} < u_{ms}$. It is assumed that all marginal utilities are positive and decreasing: $\dot{u} > 0$, $\ddot{u} < 0$ but the values of these derivatives for a given value of arguments r and m are different for the buyer and for the seller.

The quantity exchanged is *not* defined by equalities $u_{rb} = u_{mb}$

and/or $u_{rs} = u_{ms}$ as is often found in the literature but by *either* $\dot{u}_{rb}$ $= \dot{u}_{mb}$ *or* $\dot{u}_{rs} = \dot{u}_{ms}$.

The analysis of these situations is rather intricate. In current economics one can study a strict duopole, a bilateral monopole, a perfect market etc. We shall deal with the matter in a different way.

Figures 9.1 and 9.2 illustrate the exchange when no assumption whatsoever is made about possible situations. The buyer increases the amounts exchanged up to the point m_b^e, r_b^e at which point he stops buying at the price $p_b^e = m_b^e : r_b^e$. The seller offers to sell up to the amounts m_s^e, r_s^e which define a price $p_s^e = m_s^e : r_s^e$. In Figure 9.1 $m_b^e < m_s^e$, $r_b^e < r_s^e$. Figure 9.2 shows the opposite situation. At this stage nothing can be asserted about the relation between p_s^e and p_b^e. The only result here is a definition of a 'seller's surplus' in Figure 9.1 which is the area of the hatched triangle between the seller's marginal utilities curves. This surplus is virtual and would only exist if the buyer continued to buy beyond his interest at the point m_b^e, r_b^e. Similarly on Figure 9.2 the hatched triangle between the buyer's marginal utilities curves is the buyer's surplus, which is also virtual since it would only exist if the seller agreed to sell beyond his interest, beyond the amounts r_s^e, m_s^e.

These virtual surpluses are measured in utilities: the hatched areas are $\int \dot{u}_{ms}\, dm - \int \dot{u}_{rs}\, dr$ in the case of the seller's surplus and $\int \dot{u}_{rb} dr - \int \dot{u}_{mb} dm$ in the case of the buyer's surplus. They are heterogeneous to the current consumer and producer surpluses found in the literature which are quantified in money.

If we make the plausible but at this stage gratuitous assumption that $p_b < p_s$ in Figure 9.1 and $p_b > p_s$ in Figure 9.2, it follows that the buyer pays a price higher than either the seller in the first case would be inclined to receive or he himself in the second case would be inclined to pay.

How can this presentation be connected to the usual demand and supply curves and to the price elasticities of supply and demand?

Demand functions are relative to buyers. But such a function does not exist for a given buyer in given circumstances. For him there only exists a point r_b^e, m_b^e up to which he is willing to buy. The usual demand curve expresses the state of the market where many buyers want to buy. Each of them possesses a different set of utility functions as represented for two different buyers in Figures 9.1 and

9.2. The same is valid for the sellers. For any seller in given circumstances there exists a point r_s^e, m_s^e up to which he is willing to sell. Each of them possesses a different set of utility functions as represented for two different sellers in Figures 9.1 and 9.2.

Thus demand and supply functions are aggregates of points r_b^e, m_b^e, r_s^e, m_s^e at which exchanges take place, drawn in coordinates r, p. Price elasticities are derivatives of logarithms of these functions; so, in our opinion, this approach cannot be applied to elementary transactions.

Our simple model which, by the way, clarifies a correct definition of virtual surpluses, is of course only a model. Real exchanges are more intricate. We shall now go beyond this simple model and consider the following cases:

(a) The prices are given for one or both of the agents. The second subcase is the case of perfect competition, the first subcase occurs for buyers from monopolies and sellers to monopsones.

(b) The seller is a productive agent producing or distributing the resource and the buyer is an individual agent labelled a household or a consumer. This case happens when people go shopping at commercial outlets or at producers directly.

(c) Both the buyer and the seller are collective agents. This is what is called in national accounts the intermediary trade and is also the case in foreign trade. Such trades are performed either by transactions on all kinds of commodity markets or by direct exchanges. In the former case prices are often given. The exchange (procurement and sales) of public agents is assimilated to this case.

(d) The buyers are collective agents and the sellers are households. If labour is considered as a merchandise this is the general case for salaried employment and for its compensation called wages. We do not include in this case the sales of professional services to firms since we assume professionals to be firms even if they are one person.

(e) Finally for all these cases one must distinguish between exchanges for money of divisible or undivisible resources, both either tangible or intangible. The simple model of elementary exchange presented here assumes perfect divisibility of resources bought and sold, as is money.

The fundamental point in all these cases is the fact that while for

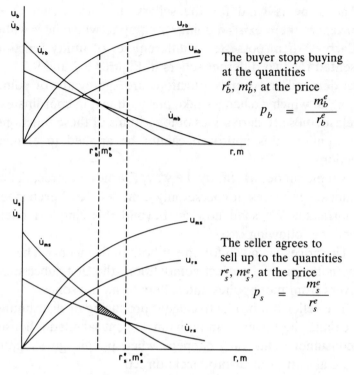

The buyer stops buying
at the quantities
r_b^e, m_b^e, at the price

$$P_b = \frac{m_b^e}{r_b^e}$$

The seller agrees to
sell up to the quantities
r_s^e, m_s^e, at the price

$$P_s = \frac{m_s^e}{r_s^e}$$

The area of the hatched triangle is the virtual seller's surplus.

Figure 9.1   Elementary exchange. First case.

households or private persons the resources exchanged possess
utility in the sense of a subjective preference structure, this must be
highly qualified in the case of collective agents. For such agents both
the resources produced and exchanged and the money do not in
general have this attribute. The objective of their activity is the
creation and distribution of the VA, nothing else. The resources
which are the physical side of this activity have no utility for them:
for a pencil manufacturing firm pencils have no utility; gasoline has
no utility for a refinery etc . . .

What governs the choices of collective agents, i.e. their decisions
to exchange are the monetary flows for factors and products, the
outlays and the receipts. This reality is (mis)represented in current
economic models by consideration of production functions,
budgets, costs and prices, wages and profits etc., where the creation

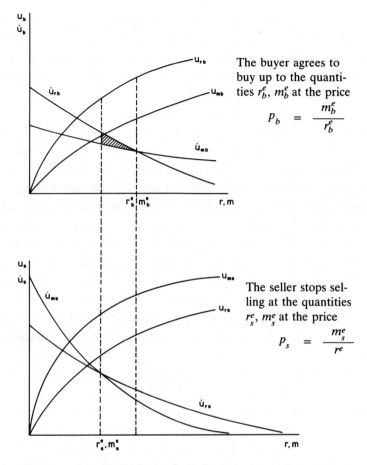

The buyer agrees to buy up to the quantities r_b^e, m_b^e at the price

$$p_b = \frac{m_b^e}{r_b^e}$$

The seller stops selling at the quantities r_s^e, m_s^e at the price

$$p_s = \frac{m_s^e}{r^e}$$

The area of the hatched triangle is the virtual buyer's surplus.

Figure 9.2 Elementary exchange. Second case.

and distribution of the VA is blurred by failing to clearly separate the exchanges, the transfers, the criteria of distribution of the VA etc.

The dichotomy between the criteria of choices, which are here the decisions to exchange, between the individual and collective agents is expressed in current economics by the assumption that people maximize their utility and firms maximize their profits. This is highly unsatisfactory, as we try to show in this book and in particular in this chapter. If people in elementary exchange do use their preferences as criteria of choices, the criteria for collective agents are neither preferences nor a part of the distribution of the VA called profits but the whole of the activity of creation and distribution of this VA. This is an intricate set of criteria of choices where feedbacks are manifold and good models difficult to build. Such models are and were the contents of the 'science' of economics.

We shall now go over the five cases of exchange.

(1) Prices are given. The amount of money given away by the buyer and received by the seller is $m = pr$ where p is the given price, r the amount of the resource and m the amount of money exchanged. According to Figures 9.1 and 9.2 the limits up to which the buyer buys are r_b^e and $m_b^e = pr_b^e$ and to which the seller sells r_s^e and $m_s^e = pr_s^e$. These limits are still determined by the equality of the marginal utilities of money and of the resource but now only result in the quantities of the resource bought and sold. If $r_b^e < r_s^e$ there is a virtual seller's surplus (Figure 9.1 top and bottom); the buyer stops buying while the seller still wants to sell at the given price. If $r_b^e > r_s^e$ there is a virtual buyer's surplus (Figure 9.2); the seller stops selling while the buyer still wants to buy at the given price.

(2) If for one or both of the agents prices are not given and the agents have control over them their behaviours will be governed by some relation $m = f(r)$ instead of the linear relation $m = pr$ as in (1) above. This is currently written as $r = g(p) = g(m/r)$. It is, for instance, widely assumed that the quantity purchased r is a decreasing function of its price p and the quantity sold is an increasing function of its price. In reality such functions g possess arguments other than the price only. Assuming however their specification in price only, Figures 9.1 and 9.2 are valid under the assumption that if the scale of r on the abscissa axis is arbitrary, the scale of m results from the mapping $m = f(r)$. Of course the precise analysis of the case will be more complex and will include the whole of the current imperfect competition theory. We shall not enter into this matter.

(3) The seller is an agent creating and distributing VA. This is a better definition of case (b) above. Within the results of (1) and (2) Figures 9.1 (top) and 9.2 (top) are valid while Figures 9.1 (below) and 9.2 (below) now have the shape of Figure 9.3. The marginal utility of money for the seller is constant and his utility of the resource sold is nil; his marginal utility is of course zero as well. So

the intersection of marginal utilities of the seller is rejected to infinity. The meaning of this result is that the criterion of utility for the seller is inappropriate; he would sell any quantity in order to increase the VA created. His limit is firstly his physical production possibility called his capacity and secondly the fact that he will sell as long as the receipts obtained from the sales will cover his outlays. We formulate this last criterion by stating that the seller will be active (will sell) as long as he creates some VA.

(4) Both the seller and the buyer are VA creating agents. This is the case of intermediary trade.

If exchanges are performed on commodity or financial markets prices are given but fluctuating. Only the criteria of VA creation govern choices and not utilities of resources. It is necessary to include uncertainty and risk behaviours as they are inherent to the activities of such markets. The resources are here only tools with no utility of their own; only money plays a role. One can assume that in speculative activity on commodity markets the marginal utility of money is not constant but decreases as for households (see Section 3 of Chapter 8).

If the transactions considered are for the procurement of raw materials or semi-products for the needs of production only the creation of VA governs the choices and the exchanges. The quantities bought are those necessary for production while money outlays are defined and limited by the necessity of obtaining a positive VA. In current economics this criterion is called profit maximization but nowadays such motivation is a very partial one. In a nutshell, in intermediary trade both buyers and sellers are businessmen.

(5) Indivisible resources. In all previous cases it has been implicitly assumed that resources are as divisible as money. By the way, this last quality of money can be said to be its tenth attribute (see Chapter 8, Section 1). This quality of money is of very high convenience when compared to real resources often available only in given sizes or in sizeable units such as machines or buildings.

In principle the above analysis applies within the results of (1) and (2) above with only one change. In Figures 9.1, 9.2 and 9.3 the utility functions of resources no longer exist since utility is no longer a more or less continuous function of a continuous argument of amounts of resources. Figures 9.1 and 9.2 are replaced by Figure 9.4

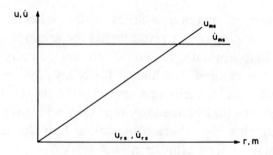

Figure 9.3 The seller is a firm.

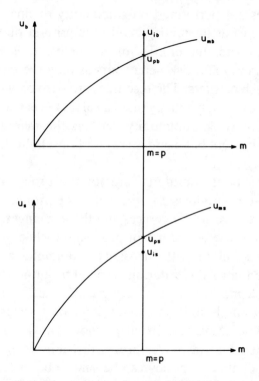

Figure 9.4 Elementary exchange of indivisible resources

where only the utility of money is represented. Let us assume that the item i to be exchanged has a 'price' p. This means that in order to obtain one such item one must give up an amount of money equal to p. One cannot speak of p as a ratio of the amount of money to the 'amount' of resource exchanged.

The utility of the item to the buyer is $u_{ib} > u_{pb}$ and for the seller is

$u_{is} < u_{ps}$. If the two agents contemplate to exchange n items instead of one, the utility of these items to the buyers will certainly be less, except in some special cases, than the utility of the first item multiplied by their number. So in most cases for n items the utility u_{nib} will be less than the utility u_{Mb} where M is the amount of money necessary to buy n items. The buyer will stop buying.

The seller, assuming he is not a firm, will probably be willing to sell all the items in his possession since very rapidly the disutility of holding them will prevail over all the other criteria of choice and in any case be largely inferior to the utility of receiving M.

This case, where indivisible resources are exchanged between 'consumer' agents is marginal if not unrealistic, beyond at least a small number of items. Exchanges of indivisible resources between collective agents are mostly governed by the criteria of investment, as a part of the problem of the creation of VA. Chapter 13 deals with this matter.

At the end of this chapter it is worthwhile mentioning that most exchanges imply costs which somewhat distort the results that are shown above. These costs are born either by the sellers or by the buyers, according to particular circumstances. We do not enter into an inquiry of this reality. One can find it in the literature.

CHAPTER 10

TRANSFERS

In the two preceding chapters we discussed money, prices, and exchange. A further fundamental economic process is that of transfers.

Transfers in our understanding are not barter nor the creation and the distribution of VA in kind as mentioned in Chapter 8, Section 1 on the history of money. Transfers are defined here as transactions different from exchange. The latter is a two-person game: there is a buyer and a seller who increase their utility by exchanging. In transfer there are also two agents, but in this case one agent obtains an amount of money and thus increases his utility while the other gives away this amount without directly obtaining anything. So one can define transfers as transactions in which the utility of one of the two agents involved decreases.

This definition has a direct consequence: the agent whose utility decreases does not make a free choice; he is obliged either by a legal title or otherwise to surrender the transfer. For instance in those transfers between private and public agents that are labelled taxes, the direct utility of the former decreases and of course they are not free to refuse such a transaction i.e. to refuse to pay taxes.

It is not always so: the head of a family distributing his income makes voluntary transfers to his children and sometimes also to his parents and does not feel that his utility is decreasing. And all prices include transfers, as we shall show. So the above definition is unsufficient. It is even more so if our view, presented in the following chapters, is accepted namely that the creation and the distribution of value added consists of transfers.

SECTION 1. GENERAL THEORY OF TRANSFERS

Economics has been and is mainly concerned with production and trade whereas transfers, dealt only marginally within the discipline, have been and remain of great importance in the material activity of agents. In History the relations between slaves and their owners, vassals and lords, kings and subjects were and between States and their citizens remain relations of transfer and only marginally or partially of trade.

It seems to this author to be necessary to generalize the above proposed definition of transfers. In an apparent contradiction to the content of Chapter 9 on exchange, and to this definition, I propose to include in the concept of transfers what I call Price Included Transfers (PITs) while the standard type as defined above, for instance direct taxation, will be called Price Not Included Transfers (PNITs) ([1]).

The concept of PITs seems antinomic to exchange, a sale and a buy which defines a price. It is however obvious that PITs do exist. We shall moreover try to prove that transfers of this kind are the essence of the creation of VA; and they play a great role in trade and in financial economy.

As in any scientific inquiry into reality, always full of contradictions such as this apparent one, the first step is to state or to assume some measure on the proposed concept of PITs. To begin with it is necessary to define the zero or PIT-free state. This seems easy by reference to current macroeconomic models. In market economies one can define a PIT-free state by the Walras–Pareto equilibrium price vector. In the neo-classical marginalist macroeconomics we possess formal proof that such an equilibrium is an optimal state in which marginal costs equal average costs and both equal prices. This last result seems to be a good practical definition of the non-existence of PITs.

It is however well known that this state is full of contradictions or at least is distant from reality. In order to be able to formally establish the existence and the optimality of the Walras–Pareto equilibrium the axioms assumed are quite strong. They are:

- non increasing returns to scale in production
- perfect competition and complete information of all agents i.e. total market transparency
- all consuming agents maximizing their utility under the constraint of their budget
- all producing agents maximizing their profits
- free price formation on all markets

- non existence of PNITs, i.e. non existence of the State and of investment
- no externalities
- a perfect divisibility of activities and commodities, formally continuity and differentiability of production and utility functions.
- In fact and in our language, inexistence of VA.

The proof obtained under these axioms states a posteriori that profits, a part of transfers arising from production are zero in the optimal state, in contradiction with the assumed behaviour of producers.

Although modern mathematical economics endeavours to generalize the equilibrium theory by relaxing its axiomatics, by including increasing returns to scale, social utility, 'rationing' i.e. gaps in volume and price vectors and by introducing in the models the State and the investment and internalizing externalities, these developments have as yet not provided a satisfactory picture of the reality.

We take a different approach. While keeping in mind the purely formal equilibrium model, we propose to quantify PITs by the difference between costs and prices, the former *not* including any component of the VA. The proposal amounts to consider VA as a PIT: Value Added is a Price Included Transfer.

Our proposal is far-reaching and will raise controversy. Chapter 13 is devoted to its discussion.

One can attempt to define PITs in the marxist approach and in the real economies based on this approach, at least in theory. In these economies prices are mostly administered, i.e. fixed by a planning authority which also plans the volumes of production and the considerable PITs and the PNITs present. The zero-PIT state seems here to exist when value, as defined by the marxist model, is equal to price.

The marxist exchange value is measured by the total socially needed labour included in the commodity, so one can assume that when this value is equal to the usage value and to the price there is no PIT in the latter. In other terms if constant and variable capital were equal to value, i.e. the mehrwert be zero, the economy would be in the ideal state of price = value, exchange value = usage value and PIT $= 0$. Whether this theoretical state is identical to the Walras–Pareto optimum and both price vectors are equal remains an open question.

Our proposal differs from both marxist and neo-classical proposals. In both models work is considered as a merchandise bought and sold on a market and as a factor of production while its compensation is a cost. We consider work as a title to a part in the distribution of VA, identical to other titles such as a tax liability or the ownership of shares. . . .

SECTION 2. DIFFERENT KINDS OF PITs AND PNITs

Land Rents

The land rent is the historical PIT analyzed by early economists. When one reads A. Smith, D. Ricardo or K. Marx, the above statement does not clearly appear. The difficulty is due to the fact that costs and transfers are closely mixed up in the total rent paid to the landlord.

In all types of economy the price of a product is more or less independent of the costs of a particular production unit. Thus in agriculture the price, whether formed on a market or fixed by an authority is valid not for one production unit, (a given farm) but for a defined region or a physical market in which there exist and/or participate different farms with different costs. The original land rent was deemed to stem from different qualities of soil which are more or less fertile. In the presence of a unique price of produce the rent increased with the relative fertility of a particular piece of land and decreased to zero on the marginal one. Below this fertility land was left untilled. In reality the total land rent includes a part of the distribution of VA resulting from the title of ownership of the landlord.

Productivity Rents

In our present language the land rent is a particular kind of productivity rents of any factor of production, existing in all activities which are aggregates of many different production units making the same products under different conditions. The productivity rent has

been a big headache for marxists since it attacks the consistency of
the axiom of objective value equal to the labour socially needed to
produce the commodity. So they invented the abstract labour. This
seems to us an unnecessary complication. Productivity expresses the
relation of output to input and is naturally widely scattered within
the set of different production units in a given economy. Since prices
are less dispersed within this economy or are often even unique,
transportation costs allowed for, the productivity rents are an obvious reality. They are parts of PITs within the prices.

Productivity rents are the driving force of market economies. The
PITs generated collect savings of firms, constituting a part of total
social savings which are subsequently invested in the same or other
activities of higher productivity rent. Thus activities are born, live
and die in a manner similar to the biological processes, their 'vital
force' being the PITs due not only to productivity rents as this
chapter will show.

Market Control

If prices are free the PITs, which are usually and erroneously called
profits, can be increased not by better productivity but by market
control, i.e. manipulation of supply and prices in the presence of the
market demand. An example of such a process is a monopoly or a
cartel or even any real market structure excluding, of course,
perfect competition. The price elasticity of demand plays a big role
here. PITs can be high when this elasticity is low; this is the case, for
instance, of energy supply. When elasticity is high, it is the most
effective check to the exaggeration of PITs, for instance of the rates
of turnover taxes. In the production sector the elasticity of substitution is an important factor. It limits the PITs unless a monopoly of
all substituable resources exists.

Market control rents exist within many trades in variable intensity,
for instance for taxi-drivers, hairdressers, plumbers, physicians,
chartered accountants etc. Farmers benefit from such rents. Very
often the power struggle for the distribution of VA between agents
who manage savings and agents who receive incomes, and also
within this last category, are described as rents. This description is
for instance found in the literature dealing with the activities of

unionized labour, of manufacturers associations and similar lobbies. In our opinion the social and economic activity consisting in the distribution of VA is in a different category since such a distribution consists of PNITs while rents are PITs.

All rents, and perhaps especially market control rents, are important politically. A formalized theory has been built for correlating elections of politicians with sectorial market control rents obtained by these politicians for their constituencies.

Terms of Trade

PITs appear within transactions. They are often well represented by the terms of trade. Two examples can help to clarify the point.

The first example is the structure of the relative prices of raw materials and manufactured goods. Since raw materials were, until only very recently, the main export item of poorer economies and manufactured goods were exported mainly by the richer ones. This structure was closely linked to international aid, i.e. to PNITs between economies. If the prices within the trade between the two types of economies exceeded costs by a wide margin, exporters enjoyed large PITs. Thus exporters of crude oil collected enormous PITs during the Seventies and for the first half of the Eighties. Exporters of finished goods and of armaments also collected such PITs.

These realities of international trade have for many years been formulated by the concept of the terms of trade. The formulation is rather unhappy as terms of trade which are ratios of prices, encompass costs and PITs not separately but in total. This fact distorts the results of models of comparative advantage and limits the validity of connected theorems.

The second example concerns the trade within economies. The most important case is the relation between agriculture and other activities, that is of 'terms of trade' between rural and urban spaces. In substance PITs are necessary here if less productive agricultural activities are to be protected from death due to higher productivity rents elsewhere. The problem of adequate PITs, i.e. of adequate terms of trade between agriculture and other sectors has not as yet been solved. Absurdities such as destroying valuable crops, warehousing enormous volumes of produce, limiting acreage on fertile land and introducing great negative PITs in order to sell produce at bargain prices are examples of the difficulty of the problem. The present American, Russian and European agricultural policies are an excellent illustration of manifold manipulations of PITs within the relation between agriculture and the rest of economic activity. PNITs are of course also largely used.

Private Finance

The money credit economy generates widespread PITs. Similar to other prices, interest rates carry transfers. As in prices PITs in interest rates help to regulate money markets (when these exist) and the general economic activity, especially investment.

Public Finance

The public finance is an important realm of transfers. Revenue and expense are mixtures of exchanges and of transfers, the latter gaining in importance nowadays in our welfare state economies. Direct taxation is a PNIT depending more on the distribution of VA than on its creation. Straight subsidies and 'tax expenditures' when they concern direct taxes are also PNITs. Indirect taxation such as the value added tax (VAT), the subsidizing within prices for instance of transit fares, of housing rents, of food, of raw agricultural produce etc. are on the contrary PITs. Controlled prices, public rates, the prices of merit goods include PITs set often following extra-economic criteria. For instance, the prices of alcoholic beverages and of tobacco include high PITs not only for economic or fiscal reasons but also to protect public health. Such PITs can accrue either to the State or to private hands. In this last case difficult problems arise when, for instance, noxious and illegal drug production and consumption generate very high PITs to the benefit of the underworld which by this process collects a private indirect taxation of a vice.

In other cases, on the contrary, the regulation, i.e. the assessment of PITs, tends to promote consumption while limiting privately accrued VA. This is the case of telephone networks, of public utilities, of land transportation etc. As in any policy, the difficulty is to be consistent and rational when confronted with the complexity of real life. Thus for political and social reasons obsolete activities are not allowed to die. On one side resources are pumped into these activities by subsidies (i.e. PNITs), resulting in PITs to the users. On the other side indirect taxes are levied on competitive, i.e. more productive activities, generating high PITs in the prices of their products. These PITs flow into the public budgets. The global result is a distorted resource allocation and a waste of available product. PITs are in such situations the apparent picture of the underlying lack of efficiency.

In Europe and elsewhere the heavy subsidization of railways on the one side and the heavy taxation on road traffic on the other are examples of such situation. Taxing telephones and subsidizing mail is another example. Many agricultural policies mentioned above reveal the same pattern. In the domain of energy the coal, oil, primary nuclear materials markets show the same interplay of taxes and subsidies, of PITs and PNITs.

The public finance is thus closely linked if not characterized by transfers. We shall deal with the role of public agents in more detail in Chapter 14 and continue here with the consideration of specific kinds of transfers.

Land Development

This is an example of what is currently called the free rider situation. When an area is provided by public financing with public or merit resources such as roads, sanitation, sewerage, water and energy supply etc. owners of land benefit 'without cause' from big increases in the sales prices of their lots. The current concensus is that this implicit or virtual PIT in their favor must be offset by any kind of taxation, i.e. by a PIT or a PNIT in the opposite sense. Development taxes serve this purpose. The agents taxed are innocent of the increase in the potential price of their possession which can be only materialized if they sell what they own. One can compare this 'free rider' event to the surpluses in the elementary exchange shown in Chapter 9.

Financing Public Goods in Rich and Poor Countries.

This on a local scale is the spatial public policy and on a global scale is what is understood under the heading of international aid.

The problem cannot be analyzed without an extensive consideration of PITs and PNITs. A poor region requires more expenses for providing indispensable public goods such as roads, education, health care, water supply, law and order services etc. But its capacity for financing them by any kind of taxation, for instance by PITs on its consumption or by internal PNITs is either unsufficient or lacking. So external PNITs or, in some cases PITs (i.e. improving its terms of trade) are necessary. This is what is called aid and/or price regulation. Within a given country the same kind of policy utilizes central government subsidies and/or price regulation.

A rich region has also a strong demand for public goods. But their financing can be either (a) in part transferred to the private sector, for instance education or health care and thus cease to require PITs or PNITs and become exchanges or (b) be financed relatively easily by all kinds of taxation. In both cases, as has already been shown, the terms of trade which include PITs play a role in this spatial equalization of the burden of social costs. When further examined the process is the natural dynamic variation of relative productivities of human societies in the spatial dimension. It is not the relative wealth, a static concept that should govern 'aid' or 'trade' but the dynamic concept of distribution, in the sense of probability distribution of relative productivities. This distribution is evolutive and changes not only by transfers of 'values', i.e. of the VA, but mainly by changes in the minds of people and also by their migrations, not only spatial but also between sectors of activities.

Tolls

Tolls are important kinds of transfers of course mixed up with exchanges. The problem here is that the 'sellers' of resources carrying tolls cannot measure or even quantify their utility to them or their cost. The classic case is the zero marginal cost of an available seat on a train or on a plane, of crossing a bridge, etc. The case of increasing returns to scale is more complex. Even more complex is the case of production processes which deliver in a single flow a number of different products.

Many theories, starting with that of Dupuit (1844) tried to solve the problem of the prices that should be charged in all these situations. It is today widely assumed that the pricing must be such that (a) demand is balanced with possible supply, for example in preventing a traffic jam on a bridge. In this role one could dispute the character of a PIT for such a toll and consider that the 'buyer' of the resource, the car driver, exchanges the disutility of payment he makes against the utility of crossing the bridge without delay. He buys time. And (b) in the case of increasing returns to scale and/or of multiple production when marginal costs cannot be a yardstick for pricing, the PITs or 'tolls' must cover fixed costs. This requirement is also valid in case (a) the difference being that the marginal cost in (a) is zero while it can be of any amount in (b). The PITs in both cases must be computed so as to cover the repayment of loans, which often are a great part of the fixed costs. In multiple production the marginal costs of each product can in general be estimated and are a criterion of choices of relative pricing, although demand is mostly more important.

A good yet complex example of tolls as PITs is the pricing policy of utilities where both the above arguments apply. For instance electricity is priced cheaply at night to further its use and the utilization of the generating capacities, while it is expensive during peak periods in order to 'erase' such 'peaks'. At the same time the total revenue of the utility company must cover the fixed costs incurred (they are mainly financial in most situations) for the construction of production facilities, of course in excess of current costs of all kinds. But when utilities try to justify high peak tariffs by the argument that peaks force them to operate old inefficient plants of high marginal cost, they stumble on a contradiction: these facilities are already fully written off and bear no fixed costs other than maintenance, so the total cost of the current produced is normally quite low.

In conclusion tolls are transfers which are also a generalized exchange. In such an exchange neither of the criteria examined in Chapter 9 are essential; the problem of the creation of VA comes in forefront. This problem is also in close relation to the existence of PNITs.

Value added only exists when receipts exceed outlays. Only in such a state can incomes be distributed (the wages being included in this distribution and excluded from outlays) and savings created. But very often if not always (a) the credit economy allows this constraint for a time, at least for several periods, to be relaxed and (b) the public agents who normally participate in the distribution of VA can allow 'tax expenditures' which means that they renounce in part or in total their part in the distribution or pay straight PNITs in order to allow other parts to be distributed, while VA does not really exist. This situation is what Janoš Kornaï calls the 'soft budget constraint' formulated by him [2] as a state when the VA distributed is not submitted to the hard obligation of balancing outlays and revenue. I would call the situation an artificial or external creation of VA by PITs or PNITs. One can add to these practices the neglect to inscribe in the accounts the depreciation allowance representing the input of capital, of course only possible if it is not illegal.

PITs and PNITs also play a great role in the creation of savings. We shall discuss this in more detail later.

In conclusion, transfers are a large part of all processes in human activities. The very existence, the very tissue of a society is not so much expressed on the economic level by 'trade' as by 'aid' i.e. by all kinds of transfers.

REFERENCES

[1] Bernard, G., Price Included Transfers in Market and in Planned Economies, Proceedings of the 33rd Congress of the International Institute of Public Finance, September 1977, Cujas, Paris, pp. 173–190.
[2] Kornaï, J., The Soft Budget Constraint, *Kyklos* **39**, 1986, Fasc. 1, pp. 3–30.

CHAPTER 11

PRODUCTION AND VALUE ADDED

In this chapter as elsewhere in this book the word production will not only mean a positive output of goods and services but also 'negative' outputs of pollution and waste as well as two more abstract concepts, the promiscuity and the proximity on which we shall forward some ideas in Chapter 13.

This real activity is translated into monetary terms by a second kind of output, namely of the value added (VA).

In our approach, as already stated in the preceding chapter, VA is defined as a positive PIT in a period of time, measured by the difference between the scalar products of vectors of real output by its price and of real input by its price. Value added is a nominal flow of wealth expressed in money. It is only when VAs created or 'produced' (we prefer the first verb) are compared for successive periods of time that price variations matter, for instance a price deflator is introduced.

The existence of PITs, i.e. of the VA means that prices do not necessarily express relative scarcities, contrary to usual opinions. For instance energy is well priced even if not scarce and/or its different forms are off the mark as regards their prices in relation to their relative scarcities. This is due to the existence of large PITs in these prices.

In this chapter we shall consider only static or synchronic situations so only nominal creation of VA will be dealt with.

As stated in Chapter 10, in the abstract state of general economic equilibrium formalized by the Pareto–Walras–Debreu model the PIT is nil so no VA exists in the economy. The VA exists only in the states of disequilibria in the formal sense. In fact its existence expresses progress.

Of course the VA created, defined by us as a PIT, can be modified by PNITs existing within the economy such as subsidies or the weak budget constraint of J. Kornaï. We shall show this in greater detail in Chapter 14.

The distribution of VA and its effects have been and are the main subject of current economics. Substantial mathematical and literary treaties exist on the relations between profits and wages, on business taxation, on investment and employment and on the role of finance and credit in the process of distributing VA.

We take a different approach. Firstly the creation of VA is essentially the result of (a) the use of abilities of agents, expressing the state of knowledge (technology, organization, management, education, training etc.) materialized in real vectors of input and output and (b) the 'division of labour' within the economy, expressed in prices, whatever their origin, on markets and/or by any regulation.

(a) is individual or collective and pertains to physical cooperation between agents. (b) is essentially a social or collective process.

Secondly the distribution of VA is a set of PNITs, an essentially social process expressing not only the economic system but the whole of the tissue of society. One can state, and we come to this point in more detail in Chapter 14, that society as a collective agent can be defined by three subsets of choices: firstly in the distribution of VA into different incomes and into saving, secondly in the use of these parts accruing to income bearers, to primary savings, (a part of private finance) and to political bodies (a part of public finance) and thirdly a subset of a different kind, that of political relations between the governing and the governed, between the élite and the people at large. We discussed the general link between polity and economy in Chapter 3.

Of course the three subsets are closely interrelated with numerous and complex feedbacks inherent to the existence of society as a system in its formal meaning. A systemic model should be built in order to research the statics and dynamics of these systems. It is not within the purpose nor within the ability of this author, or in his opinion for any single person to take on the task. I shall restrict my effort to an attempt at further definitions of 'principia' of the creation and of the distribution of VA and of the use of the parts of it by their bearers.

To repeat, to recapitulate and to develop the above:

Value Added (VA) is created by a Price Included Transfer (PIT) which can only exist if the monetary receipts obtained from the sale of output exceed the monetary outlays for the purchase of the input necessary for the realization of the output. We are not concerned here with the technology of production that is with physico-chemical processes which enable productive agents to transform inputs into outputs. Moreover, by a pure convention, we do not bother about the very close relations between the technological choices within these processes, the economic data and processes and the organization of the collective productive agent, including human relations, for instance employment, that is the activity of people within the collective agent. The sales prices of output and procurement prices of input of course closely depend, inter alia, on technology and on the organization of production but we only consider here the immediate origin of the existence of VA.

The existence being assumed of VA, it is distributed by a partition into two main parts: (a) the incomes accruing to all agents entitled to such a distribution and (b) the saving of the productive agent who creates the VA.

The first part (a), of incomes, is again divided into three subparts:

(a_1) Compensation for the participation of the subset of agents who are active within the productive collective agent. This subpart is in current theory the 'cost of labour' or of this 'factor of production' and represents the income of 'wage and salary earners' a micro and macro concept most important in such economic theories.

(a_2) Incomes that are distributed to other agents who are entitled to it. This title is mainly but not exclusively a part of the right of ownership of the productive agent as such and results in dividends to shareholders in the West and in revenue for the public budget in the East. The manner in which this subpart of distributed income is defined includes the concept of profit on which most usual economic theories are built. Profit is in fact a quite fuzzy concept as it commonly includes elements of costs and also elements of the second main part of the distribution of VA, the saving. The more or less conventional definition of profit bears, for instance in the marxist theory, ethical and moral aspects, which are rather strange to an objective analysis.

We shall try to clarify the nature of these two incomes obtained from the existing VA and especially to purify them of all political and ethical influence or pollution.

(a₃) Income accruing to public bodies by virtue of laws, budgets and regulations. This income is what is called taxes in current language, but in our model it also includes the negative distributions of the VA quite common in present societies. Aids, subsidies, tax expenditures etc. are all negative distributions of VA. In particular they enable the productive agents to continue to distribute the sub-parts (a_1) and (a_2) and also to finance part b of the distribution of VA even if this VA does not exist (i.e. the substraction between receipts and outlays is negative). So the net subpart (a_3) can be positive or negative. The rules by which the gross positive and negative elements of (a_3) are determined are quite complicated and are a part of economics called public finance. The positive elements of (a_3) result from the rates and the rules of: (i) taxes on profits such as the corporate income tax, (ii) all taxes on other monetary flows such as the European VAT (Value Added Tax), set on a slightly different definition from our VA, and (iii) social contributions, usually assessed on subpart (a_1), etc. The profit tax includes in its rules some elements of part (b), the saving. The negative elements of (a_3), which as mentioned above are investment aids, subsidies, tax expenditures etc. often depend on subparts (a_1) and (a_2) and also on part (b).

The three subparts of (a) are distinct PNITs.

The second main part (b) of the distribution of VA created by the activity of the productive agent is his saving. Contrary to the first part (a) which leaves the agent as PNITs this part is in the period retained within the agent, under two subdivisions:

(b₁) is the depreciation allowance which is deemed to represent the wear and tear of the equipment in operation during the period. This is a monetary amount defined by more or less arbitrary rules set for economic, technological and fiscal grounds. It should normally anticipate not only the wear and tear of the existing equipment but also its forecasted obsolescence due to technological progress, financial circumstances such as inflation and other arguments of the write off of the means of production. As it is, this subpart (b_1) of the total saving of the firm is at the end of the period a free financial capital at the disposal of management as is any kind of savings.

(b_2) is the remainder of the saving in the period, often mixed up with the 'profit' or with the net cash flow. In the model of ownership of a firm by its shareholders this subpart increases the net worth of the firm or the wealth of the owners. This is the reason for including this subpart in the concept of profit.

In a rather peculiar way, justified by the ancient but still often valid definition of accounts, parts (a_1) and (b_1) are both considered as costs and are not subject to profit taxes while subparts (a_2) and (b_2) are tax liable. On the contrary, when VAT is on the books, (a_1), (a_2), that part of (a_3) that is not VAT, (b_1) and (b_2) are all tax liable by definition.

We see that the participation of public bodies in the distribution of VA closely depends on all parts of this distribution and on the sets of choices, of constraints on choices and of criteria of choices which govern this distribution.

As is normal in all human activities the beneficiaries of the distribution of VA are in competition if not in conflict as each of them wants his part to be as large as possible. Economists have written many books on the subject of this conflict. K. Marx built his theory of labour value of production on it. The arguments in the competition, in the conflict or in the quarrel are manifold. The most important ones pertain to the two big chunks of the distribution, incomes and saving.

Firstly let us consider the subpart (a_1). It is currently called the volume of wages or the compensation of the 'labour factor of production'. When labour is is considered as a good on a market its sellers (i.e. people) of course want to exchange it, in accordance to our analysis in Chapter 9, so as to obtain the greatest utility and the buyers (i.e. the productive agents) have the same objective. Many arguments are put forward in this transaction. The marginalist school, by means of macroeconomic reasoning on equilibria, asserts that (a_1) or, more precisely, its 'price' (i.e. the wage rate which is (a_1) divided by the 'amount of work' necessary for obtaining the product), must be proportional to 'labour productivity' which is the amount of this product divided by the 'amount of work'. This reasoning is most conventional, very difficult to quantify and in our opinion at least is nothing else but an argument in the transaction and/or in the choice of the volume of the subpart (a_1) in the VA distribution.

The marxist theory in its present version says that the 'value' of the product is measured by the 'abstract socially needed work' for its realization. When measured in 'exchange value' subpart (a_1) or, as above, the wage rate obtained on a *perfect labour market* exploits the sellers of work who get less than the real value, the difference being the 'capitalist profit'.

Interpreting the marxist theory with our analysis of the VA distribution we immediately stumble upon a discrepancy with the present state in our societies. This is easy to show by asking the question: what would VA distribution be in the absence of 'exploitation'? Would parts (a_2), (a_3) and (b_2) be reduced to zero? Then the state would raise no taxes on production and productive agents would not save. Or would only no 'unearned income' (a_2) be distributed? This subpart of the VA distribution is never more than a few percentage points of the total VA and so 'exploitation' would persist.

Of course, as we wrote elsewhere, if the sole choice makers for the VA distribution were either the State or the owners of the productive agents, this distribution could be, as it was in Marx' time and is today in some economies, unfair and wrong 'wage earners' by excessive distribution of other incomes, excessive saving and/or taxes. The present reality is not as gloomy.

To sum up the above: 'Profit' as well as 'labour market' shall not be considered in a correct analysis of VA distribution. In the present reality subpart a_1 is in all economic systems governed by social rules. While for us remaining a PNIT it is the result of exchanges between sellers and buyers depending, or not, on markets exchanges not of work but of people with their abilities, behaviours and performances. In many countries the social rules prevail and (a_1) is rigid within the VA distribution, sometimes even up to the point where political bodies intervene to maintain it when the VA ceases to exist.

Secondly the agents entitled to subpart (a_2) also put forward many arguments. No exchange takes place here in the sense of the content of Chapter 9. It is argued (a) that dividends are necessary in order to attract external savings when these are needed to finance the activity of the firm (b) they are necessary for the correct evaluation of the value of shares on financial markets when these exist (the stock exchanges) and (c) in any case the share owners are in all equity entitled to some income. This argument is valid in all economic systems and is completed by stating that subpart (a_2) accrues to agents who save a significant proportion of it and thus contribute to the creation of total social saving necessary for the financing of the social investment, a fundamental ingredient of growth.

Thirdly subpart (b_1) of the VA distribution is the depreciation allowance. It is necessary if the net worth of the productive agent is not to be consumed by bad management. This argument for maintaining the productive stock of equipment in its full capacity is also valid in all economic systems. As mentioned above this part of the total saving b of the firm remains within its accounts.

Fourthly the subpart (b_2) of the total or gross saving (b), called net saving, is a part of the 'profit' of the owners of the firm. Naturally they want it to be as large as possible. Besides this criterion which is often rather less prominent, the net saving is necessary for financing investment. Remaining within the firm it dispenses from such financing by taking up loans or selling equity and thus sparing the costs of these choices.

There is a school of thought which rejects the concept of saving by productive agents. The line of reasoning is as follows: since any 'retained profit' increases the net worth of the productive agent and since this agent is the property of its shareholders which are households all saving is ultimately a household saving. This reasoning is perhaps to a degree correct in an entirely privately owned economy, which is an asymptotic model. In models which endeavour to represent a less distant reality the reasoning is of little value. Firstly the fact is that shareholders are most often not people nor households but other productive agents and also, to a great extent, the two other subtypes of collective agents, financial institutions and public bodies. So the reasoning is far fetched if not false. Secondly, as we have tried to show in this book economics is the study of five sets of agents, of resources, of choices, of constraints on choices and of criteria of choices. Within the last three sets some of their elements may be legal provisions and processes such as ownership rights. But economic choices of all kinds of agents while taking care of these elements are mainly if not exclusively concerned with management. In our problem management is legally and techno-logically required to put aside subpart (b_1) of the gross saving which does not increase the net worth. Further one of the decisions currently to be taken concerns this gross saving and its use for purchases either of real essentially productive assets or of financial assets as we shall see in detail in Chapters 13 and 14. In this current life of firms shares are titles to dividends and also lottery tickets for speculative 'capital gains' or losses on stock exchanges and nothing more. Only if shares are bundled into significant parts of the total share capital does their possesion imply actual control of the man-agement of the firm. This control is outside of our concern.

Finally the State, by establishing the rules of its participation in the VA distribution, rules that consist of fiscal laws and regu-lations, also wants to maximize the amount of revenue from this source. The corporate fiscality is limited by the importance of the VA created and the rights of other participants in its distribution. In planned economies of public ownership of means of production parts (a_2), (a_3) and (b) accrue in principle to the public budgets and serve to plan and finance all investment. The State's share is thus in principle a lion's share of the VA distribution although this principle is progressively forgotten and the overall partition of the VA does not differ much from the one achieved in market economies of private ownership of productive agents.

In conclusion the distribution of VA expresses the social compro-mise in the economic sphere achieved by a rather complicated process vastly differing from what economists write when they build neat models in which firms maximize their profits (what are they?) and wage earners their utility.

We will continue this chapter by analyzing how the technological progress bears on the creation and distribution of VA.

Let us assume that the VA created increases due to this progress which makes the output increase for a given input or the input decrease for a given output. It should be reminded that VA is a nominal monetary amount in a period, in other terms a monetary flow in a discrete measure (it could be idealized as a continuous function of time).

The question arises of how this increase in productivity can be distributed or assigned to the various parts of the VA creation and distribution. We have found twelve different possible choices for this apportioning of the increase but others are may be available.

Firstly as regards VA creation:

1. Prices of output can be lowered. This choice has been and remains the prime-mover of the immense technical, economic, social and political progress of the presently developed countries for the last two centuries. Rendered possible by techniques of mass production and distribution of identical products of good and even excellent uniform quality it has fostered, nay created, the consumption and use of these products by everybody. This economic revolution originated in the United States in the XIXth century, is continuing in our time, in all acitivities, primarily in agriculture and in manufacturing then in energy, transportation, communication, distribution and today in data processing and all personal and collective services.

The low real prices have not only been commanded but have also been limited by markets and the degree of competition on these markets. Monopolies, while only seldom perfect, allowed to dispense with giving buyers the benefit of the increase in productivity. In planned economies where prices are administered increases in productivity may not have benefited consumers. The same could have occured for public or merit goods in market economies.

2. Prices of input can be raised. This would benefit the suppliers. It does not happen often although it is current when production is vertically integrated. High productivity stages can transfer by this choice a part of the increase of VA to the less productive upstream stages or by measure N° 1 to downstream stages, by lowering output prices. The first occurs for instance when raw material extraction is of a lower productivity that the transformation processes, the second if the final distribution does not match the previous stages.

The costs incurred by fighting pollution, disposing of waste, protecting the environment (in other terms 'buying' real negative production) are equivalent to measure N°2 as they raise the prices of input. This utilization of the increase in productivity is a social progress as well.

One can secondly allocate the increase in VA created to the parts of its distribution. Thus:

3. One can increase the distributed 'profits', the subpart (a_2). This is the current result of technological progress and serves as a main if not unique criterion, called 'profit maximization', of the choices of the productive agent.

4. One can increase the saving of the firm, subpart (b_2), it being assumed that subpart (b_1) is governed by technological and fiscal criteria. In current theory and practice the distinction between measures 3 and 4 is considered of small importance since both accrue to the owners of the firm, be they private or public agents. In fact 'profits' are currently defined as a sum of the distributed (a_2) and retained (b_2) subparts. The distinction, however, is essential. Distributed profits (measure 3, (a_2)) are a part of the creation of incomes. They are PNITs that leave the firm and their economic role is quite different from that of subpart (b_2). This subpart of the distribution, together with the subpart (b_1) is the main weapon in the hands of management in the task of developing capacities and efficiency of operations of the firm in the interests of all participants in the VA distribution, customers and suppliers included. Moreover in medium and big businesses which are managed by professionals and not by owners the distributed profits (a_2) are more and more considered as nothing more than fixed costs of capital and one of the tools of financial management.

5. One can increase part (a_1) of the distribution, the income allocated to the direct participants in the activity of the firm, it being understood here that their complement does not change (neither hire nor fire).

This is the current doctrine expressed by the thesis that wage increases must be proportional to gains in labour productivity defined by the real output per unit of work, generally an hour. The thesis states further that if wages increase beyond this threshold cost push inflation occurs directly and demand pull inflation eventually results from the excess of purchasing power distributed since this excess is not balanced by the corresponding increase in supply. The thesis is proved by a macroeconomic marginalist reasoning in which labour is a merchandise whose supply and demand balances on the labour market. The reasoning proves a theorem stating that the equilibrium wage rate must be equal to marginal labour productivity.

Besides the point that the definition of labour productivity is a very difficult proposition, the reality of the existence of short- and long-term unemployment and of the great variety of the efforts and qualities of activities of agents in 'work' renders the whole picture much less than convincing.

Even less convincing is the marxist theory which links part (a_1) of the VA to the 'labour value' of the output. It tries to prove that if on a perfect labour market (i.e. where labour is a merchandise) the absolute power of choice of the VA distribution is vested exclusively with the owners of production capacities, the wage rates decrease to the level of subsistence of the workers. This means that parts (a_2) and (b) are maximized beyond reasonable limits thus leading to a final collapse of the process caused by the fatal decrease of the 'rate of profit', the ratio of the flow (a_2) + (b) to the stock of capital. By the way the dimension of this ratio is the inverse of time which is a rather awkward parameter . . . Moreover the model neglects subparts (a_3) in this reasoning and has some difficulty with subpart (b_1).

Our approach differs widely from these theories. The distribution of the VA among parts (a) and (b) and among their subparts (a_1), (a_2), (a_3), (b_1), (b_2) results from the choices of the productive agents and of agents elements of these collective agents. Each of them follows their three different sets of possible choices, of constraints on these choices and of criteria of choices. The cardinals of *all* these sets are high. The processes are complicated and can be considered as an important part of the social and political life where conflicts are resolved through manifold procedures such as negotiations, strikes, arbitration, legal suits, etc. In our opinion the economic evolution depends on this whole process resulting in the whole of the VA distribution and not only in a part of it, for instance (a_1) or (a_2) + (b) as is asserted by current theories. It also obviously depends on economic dynamics, on transfers of 'values' in time. A part of Chapter 12 and some of Chapter 14 are devoted to this last point.

6. The increase in VA created due to an increase in productivity can accrue to the State (to central or local governments). This effect

is automatic if the tax rates remain constant, especially if VAT is on the books as this tax is, as its name says, assessed on the VA and thus increases almost proportionally to the increase in productivity. Other tax revenue depends on the VA distribution for instance the corporate income tax on the allocations to measures 3 and 4, the social contributions on those to measure 5. Local taxes are in general less dependent on the VA created while sales taxes and excises are assessed on output prices etc. One can hold that if the managers of public budgets favor an increase in productivity for reasons of revenue their fiscal interest in general does not favor lower prices, i.e. measures 1 and 2 as both compensate the increase in physical productivity by lowering the nominal VA created. So, in general, the government has no fiscal interest to fight inflation by increases in physical productivity obtained by technological progress.

7. As a part of the increment in VA distribution due to an increment in productivity one can consider the payment of interests on loans which allowed this increase by financing investments.

8. One can also consider as such a part payments due to patent and know how owners. This could be justified when the purchase of such immaterial rights is the direct cause of the improvement in productivity.

We have not yet finished with the consideration of the distribution of VA or more precisely of its increment due to an increase in productivity.

9. The technological progress, for instance robotization, which is the main cause of an increase in VA has in most cases the effect of diminishing the need for active participation of members of the productive agent mainly of individuals 'working' within the organization. This results in the possibility of decreasing subpart (a_1) of the distribution by firing unnecessary people.

The increase in productivity results in an increase of other parts of the distribution over and above of what would be possible if subpart (a_1) has not decreased.

This effect is the mainstay of the current management science and of business practices. It is also at the bottom of most theories of growth be they neoclassical or marxist. The technological progress seems to lead to excessive 'non-earned' distributed incomes (subparts (a_2) and (a_3)), to excessive saving (part (b)) and to unemployment. Marx and Keynes built their macromodels on these choices.

Our analysis endeavours to show that the current sets of choices and of criteria of choices, mainly consisting in the maximization of the subsum (a_2) + (a_3) + (b) of the VA distribution, are not mandatory amd unavoidable. We submit that it is possible to adopt choices 10, 11 and 12 below.

10. Diminish the time of presence of the participants in the activity without diminishing their number or their incomes. They will spend this income by enjoying more free time. If nevertheless the VA created increases, as is quite possible, other parts of the VA distribution will increase.

11. Diminish the intensity of their activity by slowing down the rate of this activity. While measure 10 increases the 'quality of life' outside the productive activity this last measure improves the quality of life at work, under the same restriction as above of a constant number of participants and of their incomes. Here again the VA may increase.

12. Contrary to the usual tendency to produce with more equipment and less personnel it is possible to change the processes and achieve a high overall productivity with *more* people, that is, increase (a_1) not by increasing individual incomes but by increasing the number of their beneficiaries. The main distribution of VA can be considered as a partition in two: the compensation for the presence and 'work' of people, the subpart (a_1) and the compensation for the use of equipment subpart (b_1) (and (a_2)?) There does not seem to exist an unavoidable obstacle to either increasing (b_1) which is the current practice or (a_1) which is a more unorthodox choice but more and more necessary as the technological requirement of (b_1) increases less that the productivity of equipment in our electronic age.

It seems that these last tendencies are at present more and more in the forefront. Three known proposals show in a more or less explicit way that the problem is one of our time.

A. In the United States in 1984, Martin L. Weitzman, professor at the Massachussets Institute of Technology published a book 'The Share Economy' [1] which deals mainly with subpart (a_1) of the VA, the wages. He writes: 'The wage variant of capitalism is essentially a poorly designed system possessing some very undesirable tendencies toward inflation and unemployment. A profit sharing economy on the other hand has a natural inclination toward sustained, non-inflationary market oriented full employment . . . the wage system, like the gold standard simply represents a foolish way of organizing an economic society'.

Weitzman shows that our measures 10, 11 and 12 are reasonable and possible if we abandon the principle of labour as a good on a market bought and sold, an element of the cost of production. He implicitly shows the great inconsistency of the current economic 'science'. As we explicited: *labour cannot be at the same time a cost and a part of the value added.*

What is the 'profit-sharing economy' Weitzman proposes?

It is (a) to consider, as we propose, the activity of people within the firm as a title to a part of VA created and not as a good sold to the firm at a price called wages and (b) to link (a_1) to other subparts of the VA distribution instead of being, in 'wage capitalism', a cost linked to something called 'labour productivity'. Weitzman's is a rather primitive rule of the game. The VA distribution as we have tried to show must result from a much more refined model including its creation and, as will be dealt with in the following chapters, the economic dynamics and the activity of public agents. This model must not be micro as in Weitzman's proposal but macroeconomic.

B. In the Federal Republic of Germany in 1977 H. J. Baumann, chairman of the Degussa Corp. published an article on 'Job Certainty Against Income Uncertainty' [2] (my translation from the German) where he quotes the proposal of professors P. Steinbrenner and W. Engels [3]. Baumann deals extensively with VA creation and distribution. His approach is somewhat different from ours and is in our opinion incomplete (see the appendix to this chapter). But he draws from his exposé a proposal which is similar to Weitzman (and by 7 years anterior; Engels, whom Baumann quotes and follows proposed his 'partnership' system in 1972 . . .)

As Weitzman, Baumann proposess that the activity of people in firms shall not be a good sold and bought, a cost, but a title to a part of the VA. He justifies his stand by stating that in the present 'capitalist' system the income risk of the owners of businesses coexists with the job risk of the employees. The former cannot be fired but their incomes are at risk and even their wealth can be lost if the business fails. The latter have a guaranteed often fixed income but only as long as they have a job. The situation is not well balanced. We would say in our language that the disutilities of uncertainty of the two parties are different. Baumann's proposal is to follow the suggestion of Steinbrenner and Engels and consider a productive agent as a collective body (we say a collective agent) all of whose members are partners and as such active in this firm as long as it exists, so cannot be fired. But all these partners bear the income risk according to the results of the activity. In our language this means that all participants in the activity have a title to the distribution of the VA and that no part of this distribution is a cost of production. Neither Baumann nor Engels propose, as Weitzman does, a rule of VA distribution by a link between its parts. Engels' proposal is in fact more refined. He writes: 'Karl Marx asserted that workers are compelled to sell themselves to capitalists. Today the exchange is reversed, workers no longer sell themselves to capitalists but buy themselves their capitalists'. This saying can be translated into our language by stating that *all* agents active in a business are equal partners and finance their activity by outside savings and their firm's savings as well, as we have shown. Engels moreover thinks that a firm organized along such lines (i.e. being a partnership of all people and agents active in it) can and mostly will hire short term young and unexperienced workers who, contrary to the partners, will only temporarily cooperate, in fact land a temporary risky job. They will eventually stabilize their career by becoming partners in some firm.

This is an old story stemming from the medieval structures of artisan guildes. We can make the same remark as we did about Weitzman's proposal: besides these microsystems macroeconomics, essentially dynamic, has to be considered in a global model aggregating such microstructures especially with regard to the equilibria of demand and supply, of savings and investment of the financial economy at large and, more generally, of the stability of the overall system.

C. The third proposal which in a sense concurs with our views comes from the USSR. Professor G. Popov of Moscow University published in 1984 a paper called 'Global Accounting of the Main

Stage of Economics' [4] (my translation from the Russian).

He defines his 'global accounting' by three principles: (a) the right to choose 'orders', in our language the liberty to sell to customers. The firm shall be free to accept or refuse contracts of sale. Prices of these contracts – this is explicitly stated in the article – while determined by a centrally established unique rule shall be defined by demand and supply. Of course such prices cannot be independent of a socialist centralized overall plan, writes the author; (b) in our language the second principle concerns the VA distribution. The author insists in his soviet jargon, not only on 'funds' of a budget, but also on financing investment and public expenditure, on the distribution of incomes, on the conditions of the existence of VA only if revenue exceeds costs in a production cell (chain link in his parlance). Literally he writes for instance: 'higher income (i.e. VA) means higher receipts for the center'. I shall translate this sentence by: 'if the VA created increases, its part $(a_2) + (a_3) + (b)$ which accrues to the "center" will increase'. (c) the third principle concerns part (a_1) of the VA distribution, what in the soviet terminology is called the wage fund. Here comes a striking analogy to the share economy of Weitzman or the partnership of Engels. Popov in his country's layout proposes to consider subparts $(a_2) + (a_3) + (b)$ mandatory and subpart (a_1) as a remainder of the total VA when this sum is substracted. Contrary to fixed wages the incomes distributed to workers will be flexible over a certain subsistence minimum and depend on the creation of total VA.

Popov's article shows that totalitarian tendencies were still strong in his country at the time of its writing. Maybe this has somewhat changed since. In any case professor Popov manifests a clear consciousness of the reality of the creation and of the distribution of VA. His is, of course, only an academic exercise but such are also those of Weitzman and Engels. All three correctly analyze the problem and go largely beyond the current assumptions of wages as costs and as main parameters of equilibria while 'profits' are deemed to be the best tools of growth.

It is worthwhile mentioning here the numerous laws and regulations in France and Germany which tend to introduce 'participation' and 'comanagement'. These setups have not been justified by the three more theoretical proposals quoted here. One can mention too, in conclusion, the reference [5] where professor Ichiishi writes: 'the present paper deviates from the traditional value theory by postulating that labour is not marketed. Wages are not therefore prices which are determined in markets by the law of supply and demand. Each economic agent participates in a production unit as a labourer and wage is a reward he earns by that participation'.

REFERENCES

[1] Weitzman, Martin L., *The Share Economy. Conquering Stagflation*, Harvard University Press, 1984.
[2] Baumann, Dr. H. J., Arbeitsplatzsicherheit gegen Einkommensrisiko? *List Forum*, Band 9 (1977/78) Heft 3, Oktober 1977.
[3] Engels, Prof. Dr. W., Kompetenz und Verantwortung, *Die Zeit*, 13.10.1972.
[4] Popov Prof. Dr. G. H., Polnyj Chosraschot Osnovnovo Zvena Ekonomiki, *EKO* (7), 1984.
[5] Ichiishi, Tatsuro, Coalition Structure in a Labor Managed Market Economy, *Econometrica* **45** (2), March 1977.

THE CREATION AND THE DISTRIBUTION OF VALUE ADDED IN ONE PERIOD OF TIME

A. Creation of VA

Let q_s be the vector of products (the output),

p_s the vector of their prices,

q_f the vector of factors (the input),

p_f the vector of their prices,

y the value added

r $= p_s q_s$ is the revenue or turnover,

a $= p_f q_f$ is the expense or the cost of procurement,

y $= r - a.$ (1)

B. Distribution of VA

Let c be the credit $= dD \gtreqless 0$, $c > 0$ taking loans, $c < 0$ repaying loans,

D the debt,

i the interest payments on the debt,

$w = a_1$ of the text = volume of wages and salaries,

$d = a_2$ other incomes distributed, mainly dividends,

k the financial depreciation allowance,

$$\text{either } k \text{ or } k' = b_1$$

k' real capital wear and obsolescence

b_2 the retained 'profits'

S the saving. $S = k + b_2 = b_1 + b_2 = b$ (2)

W gross worth

c_1 positive variation of net bank account and cash

c_2 sales of shares in the period

$c = c_1 + c_2$

$e = e_1 + e_2$

e_1 current subsidies

e_2 capital subsidies

I real investment in the period

$t_1 = h_1 (y - I)$ the VAT

$t_2 = h_2 w$ social contributions and wage taxes, if any exist
$t_3 = h_3 (d + b_2)$ the corporate income tax
$t_4 = h_4 W$ the property and similar taxes
$T = t_1 + t_2 + t_3 + t_4 = a_3$ the total fiscal burden $\qquad$ (3)

One has:

$$
\begin{aligned}
y = r - a \qquad & \text{VA creation} \\
= w + d + k + b_2 + T & \qquad\qquad\qquad\qquad (1) \\
= w + T + d + S \qquad & \text{VA distribution} \qquad\quad (4)
\end{aligned}
$$

The net 'profit' is

$$p = d + b_2 \qquad\qquad (5)$$

Writing (1):

$$r = y + a \qquad\qquad (1')$$

expresses the current balance of receipts and outlays, the virtual outlay of gross saving S being included. Equalities (1) to (5) represent the current monetary flows in the period.

Two other flows interfere:

(a) the firm has a twofold debt: the loan debt D_1 and the equity debt D_2. The total debt $D = D_1 + D_2$ is a monetary negative stock. D_1 is net of claims, D_2 net of external equity holdings. D varies in the period by $c = dD$; i is paid on D_1, d on D_2.
(b) the firm transfers to public budgets

$$F = T - e \qquad\qquad (6)$$

Now the current financial balance is

$$r + e + c = a + y \qquad\qquad (1'')$$

so that the VA distributed can be increased by $e + c$ (if this sum is positive) The net worth at the end of the period is

$$W_{t+1} = W_t - D_t + b_2 + (k - k') - c - e_2 \qquad\qquad (7)$$

or

$$W_{t+1} = W_t - D_t + S - k' - c - e_2 \qquad\qquad (7')$$

and if $k = k'$:

$$W_{t+1} = W_t - D_t + b_2 - c - e_2 \tag{7''}$$

One can analyze the following choice criteria of management:

1. Short Term Profit Maximization

The maximand is (5): $p = d + b_2$.
From (1'') and (4) one obtains:

$$
\begin{aligned}
p = d + b_2 &= y - w - T - k \\
&= r + e + c - a - w - T - k \\
&= r + c - a - w - F - k
\end{aligned}
\tag{5'}
$$

In this case the management tries to maximize production and its prices. These two choices are constrained by the market and/or by regulations and by the production capacity. Further the management tries to

- obtain the maximum of credits
- pay the lowest prices for the procurement and enhance the productivity of the production process.
- pay the smallest wages possible
- depreciate as little as possible
- avoid as far as possible paying the taxes while obtaining maximum subsidies and tax expenditures

But taking up credit implies future payments of interest and this decreases the net worth; if $k < k'$ the net worth also decreases by not compensating for wear and obsolescence of the equipment.

This is the model for 'crude capitalism'. In present reality w is rather rigid. So bad business can result in situations where $k = 0$, $b = 0$. The worth of the firm is thrown away by an exaggerated VA distribution. And in all circumstances, even if business is better, there remains the conflict between the desire for immediately disposable income and the safeguard of productive capacity.

2. Long Term Private Firm Management

Both p and dW are maximands, constrained by laws and regulations mainly consisting of procedures, contracts and obligations pertaining to labour relations, to accounting methods, to assessment of taxes. So, besides (5) or (5′)

$$z = b_2 + (k - k') - c - e_2 \qquad \text{max!} \tag{8}$$

The management tries in this case to

- maximize the saving S
- minimize the equipment's tear and wear
- decrease the indebtness
- prefer current government subsidies to share capital

k is governed by fiscal laws; here the maximization of p also leads to 'capitalist exploitation'.

3. 'Social' or Union Management

An additional maximand is w. One has from (5″):

$$w = y + c - F - k - p \tag{9}$$

p has to be minimized, F and k, y and c are to be maximized. Here the compensation for capital and the saving is to be as low as possible; net worth is dilapidated. This case can occur in mixed welfare state economies, especially in badly managed nationalized firms. Subsidies e are welcome as well as tax expenditures decreasing F.

4. VA Maximization

This is nowadays a popular management criterion of choice in planified economies and in some western countries when governed by socialists.

The criterion is socially noxious as maximizing

$$y = r + e + c - a \qquad \text{(from (1″))} \tag{10}$$

means selling at high prices by monopoly practices, begging for subsidies and credit and exploiting suppliers. This is typically the management of public monopolies if they are not strictly regulated. Their net worth decreases by $c + e_2$, assuming (this is often a

dubious assumption) that the saving $S = b_2 + k$ remains at the
necessary level. The choice is contrary to the social general benefit.

5.   Weitzman's Share Economy and Engels' Partnership Managements

They propose in essence to enhance the flexibility of the main three
components of the VA distribution:

- the wage fund w
- the other distributed incomes d
- the saving S

which as shown also influence the fourth component, T.

To obtain this increase in flexibility they both refuse to consider w
as a cost. This, in our opinion, is a consistent position while the
current one is inconsistent. They as well as this author put w on the
same level as all other components of the VA distribution. Due to
historical ownership criteria current economics blurs the picture by
shifting a part of the VA distribution, (the workers income w) into
costs often also considering T as a cost and integrating $S + d$ into a
'gross profit', all greatly irrational assumptions. Thus even if they do
not explicitly propose it, Weitzman and Engels dismiss the criterion
of profit by melting its components into the whole of the VA
distribution.

Popov, unable to dispense his research from the soviet dogmas,
verbally privileges that part of VA accruing to the State (to the
Plan) by rigidifying $k + b_2 + d + T + i$, leaving only w as a possible maximand. But implicitly he reasons correctly, as do his
Western colleagues about the overall VA distribution and the
possible choices for its parts. He spells out the critical opinion that
work as a title to this distribution must depend on the creation of VA.

Some remarks are in order as a conclusion of this more detailed
analysis of the creation and of the distribution of VA.

1. The distinction between costs and parts of the VA distribution
is in marginal cases more or less a convenience. Interest payments
on debts and, for some authors (e.g. Baumann in [2]), some taxes

are considered as costs. The extreme thesis, however, assuming that taxes are expenses for the supply of public goods, is difficult to accept. Firstly taxes finance not only these goods but also transfers and many other budgetary outlays which do not benefit taxpayers and secondly public budgets are also financed by other revenue, for instance the personal income tax.

2. It is clear from our presentation that 'profit' is a very fuzzy concept stemming from the historical role of the owners of businesses. If of course owners are the sole choice makers the VA distribution will be biased in their favor. This is only natural but is mostly not the present reality. In our opinion all theories based on rates of profits, all macro policies such as enhancing profits in order to kindle on investment or equating wages to the marginal productivity of labour etc. are only alibis or arguments in negotiations to resolve conflicts naturally arising in the VA distribution and *not* economic data. The same is true of opposite arguments presented by·unions about the possibilities of increasing the share of w in this distribution. And most of these arguments lead to the demand to increase output prices without consideration for outside constraints and the well being of buyers of the product.

3. In general, the use of rates of profit or rates of wages defined as ratios between some parts of the VA distribution, which are all flows, to the stock of capital is an awkward method since the dimension of such rates is the inverse of time, while the dimension of the standard capital/output ratio is time. Only if the year is taken by a general consensus as a unit of time can such ratios be of any utility. In an age of instant communication and ultra high speed of data processing this unit is quite anachronistic.

In our opinion the only valid ratios are the percentages of the parts of the VA in its total. Such percentages are available although their value suffers from incorrect definitions of the VA and of its parts. It is thus estimated that the 'labour compensation' oscillates between 65 and 70 % of Y and the 'gross cash flow before taxes' is the complement, with some additional small positions. For a different definition of VA and probably defining w as being only direct income the following percentages were estimated for France in 1984:

Wages	51 %
The State	29 %
Shareholders	4 %
Debt Payments	6 %
Investment	10 %

This partition seems to be sensible: 50 % of the VA goes to the incomes of active members of the firms, 30 % to the State and 20 % to the 'capital'.

CHAPTER 12

SPACE AND TIME IN HUMAN ACTIVITY

This chapter and the following two: Chapter 13 on relations between agents and Chapter 14 on economic processes propose a conclusion to our effort. Chapters 12 and 13 touch upon the two fundamental paradigms of space and time and of the power of choice for all kinds of agents: individuals, firms, associations, local and central sovereign governments. Chapter 14 briefly discusses, without formalization, the intricate system of human societies and their activity. Economic principles and models, such as the passage from micro to macroeconomics, are a small part of the overall systemic model. Although it will be difficult to achieve, it is possible that in a near future such a model will be built, integrating economics into a globality of psychology, politics, power and the biosphere.

As with any activity the economic activity exists and evolves within spacetime. For the purpose of our study of the principles of economics, and in contrast to physics, it is superflous to refine our understanding of what space and time are. Neither the relativity theory nor quantum mechanics with their very sophisticated and up to now controversial problems of spacetime are of any use here. We can limit our understanding to the vulgar three dimensions of space and a steady oriented flow of time from the past through the present to the future and consider each of these two objects separately.

In Chapter 8 which dealt with money and prices we touched upon the concept of scarcity as distinct from value and from utility. Resources that were initially abundant can become scarce, they can also evolve in the opposite sense. Economic growth can be defined as the progressive abundance of resources that were initially scarce. As we have shown in the preceding chapter when discussing the N° 1 effect of an increase in productivity on the VA distribution this evolution has been expressed in history in the decreasing prices of progressively more abundant goods and services.

Such is not the case for space and time. Their scarcity is at most constant and in general increases. For the dimension of time the statement seems to be really final; for the dimension of space one can dream of a future in which humanity will populate the Universe or at least the solar system.

SECTION 1. SPACE

Space can for our purpose be split into a two-dimensional roughly spherical surface of the Earth, supplemented by the third dimension of height or depth, the whole being the biosphere where man appeared and now lives. Since the beginning of this century man's activity has extended in altitude, first to the atmosphere and now, for some thirty years, within the vicinity of our planet. One can hope that in the next century our activity, but not our habitat, will extend to the solar system. So, a three-dimensional space is now at beginning of its economic use.

The practically two-dimensional biosphere on the surface of the Earth has to be divided into sea and land, and land into habitable, arable and hostile areas. Modern technology progressively blurs out this last partition which, however, subsists. Thus man lives and is active within a limited space, to simplify within a limited area of land. And his activity impinges on the natural evolution of the biosphere.

For the purpose of this book it is sufficient to consider three kinds of effects of this fact. Of course all three are closely linked.

1. the direct scarcity of geometric space
2. the effect of human activity on the biosphere
3. the proximity and the promiscuity effects.

1.1. The scarcity of land can be defined globally by the ratio of human population to the available area of land, called the population density. It results from demography. The human population has quantitatively exploded for some 250 years now. Until quite recently its increment was hyperexponential: the world population rate of increase was equal to 0.3 per cent in 1650 corresponding to doubling it every 250 years and 2.1 per cent in 1970 corresponding to doubling it every 33 years. This evolution could not of course continue. Due to many causes among them the overall development and new techniques of birth control, the second derivative of the temporal population function is now reversed in sign. In 1983 the rate was 1.7 per cent corresponding to doubling every 41 years and it is expected to reach zero by the end of the first century of the next millennium. It is anticipated that the present world population of about 5 billion will stabilize sometime around 2100 at the level of about 10 to 11 billion people.

Thus globally per each square kilometer of emerged land the number of humans living on Earth increased from 7 in 1800 to 32 at present and is predicted to be 70 in 2100.

Of course global rates and ratios are a very crude description of the problem. Conditions vary enormously on Earth. India, China, some smaller European, Latin American and South-East Asian countries are very densely populated and in consequence the scarcity of the land is high there. The two superpowers, the USA and the USSR have plenty of available land. Other countries lie between these two extremes. The rates of population increase are also very variable; they are under control in many societies. In some highly developed societies they are even already negative, as in Germany, but in others they remain at high levels, for instance in Africa and Latin America.

Moreover even at equal global demography in a country other parameters are of importance.

Firstly it is the age pyramid which specifies the active population it its middle and the two consumer but not producer extreme parts of the young being raised and educated and the old being in our societies provided with pensions. In this respect the fairly recent progress of medical science had very profound economic and other effects, many of them in opposite directions. On one side modern health care, extended to all in many societies, increased the mean life span and decreased infant mortality, increasing the importance of the extreme parts of population pyramids. Biology and biogenetics, a part of the overall technological progress on the other hand offered new possibilities for a comprehensive and effective birth control which provided an efficient tool for controlling population increases. But the fine-tuning of these policies is difficult and impinges on ethical and religious choice criteria; its financing by welfare economics changed the economic choices of all kinds of agents.

Secondly the urbanization process is quite diverse. Cities still grow in young societies, in some cases explosively, for example in Mexico or Lagos. They start to decay in older countries, mainly due to modern technologies of transport and communication. In all cases land scarcity is incomparably different in urban and rural areas, both as geometric space and for productive uses. Productivity rents are the main factor in the country while scarcity rents and development costs are more important in cities.

Thirdly and naturally a society lives in a given geographic space in which the easily used land area varies largely. In Japan the ratio is low as well as in the African Sahel where the desert advances. The contrary is the lot of the two superpowers.

It is not the purpose of this book to discuss any further the relation of demography to space and time scarcities. It seems worthwhile to have briefly mentioned its economic importance to which we shall return in the two final chapters. What is of interest here is the impact of the relative land scarcity depending on overall and local demography and landscape on land prices or land opportunity costs. The land price as any price proceeds from three distinct sources each of which generates a part of the price: the productivity rent (see Chapter 10), the scarcity rent (Chapter 8) and the depreciation allowance, an incorrect label here since this item is the compensation during the time of the use of land of the costs of its transformation from the primitive 'wild' state to the one adapted for this use. Such costs disappeared in most of our present societies a long time ago. They pop up again in the local, microeconomic cases of land development schemes discussed in Chapter 10 on transfers.

Two remarks are in order here. Firstly we have just used the word 'time' with reference to scarcities. There is much more to it, as Section 2 of this chapter will show. Secondly there are other spatial scarcities closely connected with time, beyond allowances for land development just mentioned. Section 1.3 of this chapter is devoted to this subject.

1.2. Human activity induces a second kind of spatial scarcity, different from but linked to the directly geometric just discussed. Our activity depletes non-renewable primary natural resources and creates thermal, chemical, radiation and material waste pollutions of the biosphere, globally reducing its original availability. Nicholas

Georgescu-Roegen aptly defined human material activity, the subject of economics, as an input flow from Nature and an output flow of waste. The material activity is a dissipative process which increases the entropy of the biosphere. Erwin Schrödinger thought that 'economies are dissipative processes maintaining themselves by consuming low entropy'.

These models would of course only correspond to reality if the biosphere were a closed system. It is not so by far; the biosphere originated in the distant past and continues to evolve with the steady inflow of solar energy. The Sun's energy in particular successfully counteracts many kinds of human pollution, directly by its vehicle, the electromagnetic radiation of different frequencies and mainly indirectly by the very peculiar life processes which create negentropy. Nevertheless many human activities have irreversible effects unsuccessfully fought by the incoming solar energy or by life processes.

Such is the depletion by man of primary fossil resources of the Earth's crust, of the oceans and of the atmosphere. The last two are vastly beyond any conceivable human needs but the land resources seem to be more limited at least within the limits of their possible recovery. For centuries economists have shown that the increasing scarcity of non-renewable resources irreversibly transformed by our technology, such as some metal ores, coal, oil, gas will increase not only their price, i.e. the rents or PITs but also and necessarily their real cost, the necessary real inputs for their recovery. This means that such resources are mostly not physically scarce in relation to human needs but are increasingly difficult, that is expensive, to find and to recover. This difficulty or cost is however essentially a problem of availability of energy, at present not yet resolved since the transformation of fossil sources into its convenient forms is a relatively costly process which moreover generates high levels of thermal, chemical and waste pollution. Technology forecasters seem to anticipate that the solution will be in view, when fusion energy is available.

Long term effects of these pollutions and the countereffects of the Sun on them are still subjects of controversy. What is on the contrary now considered to be dangerous for our future with a high probability is the impact of human activity and human applications of knowledge on the life processes existing on Earth. Their natural evolution is a very delicately balanced process. At present the genetic stock i.e. the great variability of species and, within the species, of genuses is at risk. The great polymorphism of Nature is being attacked by the extensive use of land for agricultural and other activities, obtained by deforestation. It is attacked by the modern technologies of animal and vegetal breeding and even by the creation of artificial life forms with unknown side effects. It will perhaps be attacked by increased intensities of noxious frequencies of the incoming electromagnetic spectre and by the existence, since the middle of this century, of man made sources of such radiations on Earth.

1.3. A third kind of spatial scarcity (and also temporal which we shall discuss in Section 2) is more directly man made, a social phenomenon. I call it the dialectic between proximity and promiscuity, or between proximity and congestion or overcrowding.

What is proximity? It is an abundance of resources and of possibilities, the immediate availability of all material and spiritual goods and services, of extended exchanges and trades of all kinds. The cities have been and are spaces where proximity acts. Nowadays the instantaneous diffusion of information and of culture by means of manifold tools such as inexpensive books, newspapers and magazines, the electromagnetic broadcasting of speech and pictures, the greatly improved techniques of mass distribution of consumer and other products, the convenience and abundance of individual and collective systems of transport and of communication have lessened the importance of cities as tools of proximity.

What is promiscuity? It is the scarcity of silence and solitude, which are valuable 'goods' for many individuals; it is congestion, traffic jams, queueing up, waiting, noise, the inconveniences of crowds, the difficult and slow travel, the pollution of air and water, the destruction of Nature, to sum up the scarcity of space and time and also of beauty and comfort.

It follows that the dialectic of proximity and promiscuity is a dialectic of scarcity and abundance which is a most primary occurrence in economics. Urban life is not the only one to be affected by this dialectic. It acts in all relations between people, between agents and between them and the outside world.

Certain resources are of natural origin and it is naturally assumed that since they do not cost, they should not be paid for, although they are of great utility and even necessary for life: fresh and pure air, wild nature, pure water, free roads, etc.

The example of roads, already discussed in Chapter 8 on prices and tolls illustrates well our dialectic. If the traffic is fluent, the proximity is enhanced and promiscuity absent; on a jammed road the promiscuity is high, the proximity is scarce and the toll is its price. Solitude is a very abundant 'good' in the desert and does not cost anything there, while it can be quite expensive elsewhere.

When any of these resources becomes accessible to every one (that is more abundant) by means of our advanced technological civilization, promiscuity is enhanced and proximity becomes a scarce good. Pure air, non polluted water, solitude, silence, the beauty of the surroundings then become costly and high prices are paid by those who can afford it: owners of country houses in our affluent societies, the rich and the powerful in their palaces in countries where the bulk of people live like ants in their noisy slums or, blessed by 'progress', in high rise apartment blocks . . . Enjoying proximity without suffering from promiscuity has at all times been the privelege of the powerful and of the rich. To live in promiscuity often without suffering from it but without using the boons of proximity has been and remains the fate of the poor who are unable to pay the tolls of the scarcity of these blessings.

Such tolls are not yet fully understood. They play the same role that prices of resources played at one time. Food and energy are abundant in developed countries and are affordable by the great majority, but not by all. Elsewhere food and man made slaves moved by energy remain scarce. Globally this is still the case for a great part of the Earth's population.

An ideal society would be one where the proximity gifts are available to every one without promiscuity destroying them. The perception of the danger of the population explosion on the spaceship Earth, naturally resource- and space-bounded, stems from the consciousness of this dialectic.

On our beaches and our roads in summer, in the slums of the cities, and for the humanity living in varieties of concentration camps the vices of promiscuity overwhelm the virtues of proximity.

In more economic terms 'free' resources are public goods as long as they remain free which means that they do not follow the principle of exclusion. When however they begin to be scarce by promiscuity or pollution they change into private goods: fresh air in a country house, fishing rights on a stream, picking up mushrooms, a ski slope . . . Most leisure resources were more or less public a century ago. Today there are expensive private goods in our societies like safaris in Africa . . .

In our developed societies the car, the telephone and the television are fairly new devices (the oldest is barely 100 years old!) which bring proximity everywhere, even far from the urban concentrations of people and far from possible promiscuities. But the use of the first two of these tools creates new spatial scarcities due to congestion and waiting, generating in turn a scarcity of time. This happens if the capabilities of roads and of telephone exchanges are unsufficient, if road and telephone tolls, regulation and police are ineffective . . . The abundance of proximity can dialectically induce promiscuity, a special kind of scarcity, and a high price of such scarce resources. The enormous potential market unabated in all societies of automobiles and of telecommunication is a proof that in our present era of technological civilization and universal education the need and desire of proximity without promiscuity is a powerful economic factor.

SECTION 2. TIME

2.0. Economics, as any other human activity, is a dynamic process which evolves in time. This economic 'factor' has the special quality of being unidimensional, homogeneous and thus in principle easy to quantify and to measure. Man is the only animal who started doing this at the beginning of his existence, at first looking upward at the sun, the moon and the stars and acquiring the knowledge of their apparent periodic movement, from which he established later the units of time that are still operational. The direct measurement of time using these units is however a rather recent activity whose stages punctuate the global progress of knowledge and in particular of applications of time measuring to fine arts (such as music), technology and economics. The pendulum, the spiral spring and escape ratchet, now in extensive use for some twenty years the immense revolution of the applications of the piezoelectric effect of quartz crystals and, for more precise measures, of the properties of the electromagnetic field by atoms and nuclei are such stages which progressively changed the perception by people at large, by active economic agents in particular, and of course by scientists of what time is. For the prehistoric man and for most people up to the end of the XVIIIth century time was nothing but day and night, then seasons, years, hours for some, and minutes for a few. Many of us, for instance radio and TV professionals, financiers etc. now live with seconds, athletes live in 10^{-2} seconds, electronic engineers in 10^{-12} to 10^{-15} seconds, physicists in their theories at 10^{-45} seconds after the Big Bang while on the other end of the scale astronomers and cosmologists deal with 10^{12} light years. . .

Due to this progress the perception and measure of time (the latter remaining in fact always the same, the frequency of a periodic phenomenon) progressively changed from 'circular' as some philosophers label low frequency events such as seasons to an unidimensional oriented continuous flow which seems to be a physical reality. As is known its standard unit is since a few years the velocity of photons in vacuum. Although, according to quantum mechanics, photons are simultaneously particles and waves, i.e. periodic events and besides represent spatial probabilities no one has yet proposed quanta of time.

All this is physical time which is, of course, of importance for economic activities as are climates and seasons. For agents in their activities and in their choices in particular (not only in economic ones) there exist two other 'times': for individuals the physiological and subjectively psychological durations and for all agents, individual and collective, the social time. While one can perfectly label the physical time as being abundant, more precisely so for human horizons, and extending without limits uniformly and unbounded in the past and in the future, the two other times can and must be integrated into the sets of possible choices, of constraints on these choices and of criteria of choices, and are by definition 'scarce'.

We mentioned in Chapter 1 and in Section 1 of the present chapter the demography of agents, their birth, life and death. This demography is obviously in close connection to physiological, psy-

chological and social kinds of time. We shall now deal in more detail
with this fact and start our approach with the consideration of
people, the individual agents.

2.1. Time of course plays a considerable role in the choices of
individual agents. One has only to think about the limited (i.e.
scarce) daily, weekly, seasonally, yearly and life availability of time
for people. Further, the productivity for individual agents of the use
of time in work, leisure, entertainment, culture, fitness, vacations,
communication, etc. at different periods of life is of utmost importance. Finally, the discounting of the future, its anticipations such as
education and learning, saving and investment, retirement and
pensions play a big role in the choices of people.

The use by a person of the 24 hours in a day is constrained by the
physiological needs of sleep, hygiene, eating and other natural
functions, by family care etc. The remaining time available, in the
mean slightly above half of the total, has to be divided into economic, social and personal activities such as work, transport, social
functions etc. The economic activity commonly called work is
currently considered as resulting for the person in the income he or
she can obtain. Other activities, which are called 'leisure', in fact fill
out the time the person chooses to allocate for his or her needs and
desires, essentially 'consuming' not only this time but also a part of
the obtained income, its other parts satisfying mandatory needs
which constrain the total available time. One currently finds in
treatises on economics the assertion that the disutility of work is
compensated by the utility of income received in exchange. In other
terms people sell their labour or work activity and its price is for
instance an hourly wage.

Even if the assertion were true it would only pertain to a fraction
of active adults, the salaried employees. In fact activities which
justify or entitle people to receive incomes are infinitely diverse so
that it is very complicated if not impossible to formalize or
adequately specify the assertion. A convenient and simple idea
would be to state that people do not sell their 'work' but their time.
The diversity of the kinds of work in a unit of time would be
somewhat concealed but not eliminated. The marxist theory when
confronted with this difficulty attempts to stick to the idea of work

as a scarce commodity sold on markets by reducing the diversity of activities into a unidimensional concept of 'abstract', labour, which is not really very convincing.

Our approach is different and rather straightforward. What is called work, that is a productive activity of a kind which suits an active person, his qualifications and his psychology, tastes and abilities, can be and is in numerous occurrences resented by this person as a nuisance, a bad use of his or her available and scarce time of the day, the week, the season, the year, the life. But this is not always and even rarely so. Be it God or be it Nature, man has been endowed with brains, with some muscular strength for males and with skilful hands. In consequence, one could say physiologically, he or she draws a satisfaction from using these gifts which are always available, although in variable proportions, in all persons. The great majority of normal individuals need to 'work' and thus to accomplish themselves not only in exchange for income but also as one of the aims of their existence.

A. Koestler studies the 'act of creation' in detail which he connects with laughter, another specifically human attribute. Other scholars write about the dignity of work, of self accomplishment etc. We state that the utility of working is often positive; its disutility was and often remains the effect of the 'absurd link' as Weitzman writes, between receiving income without which it is impossible in our societies to live and the effort and the physiological stress naturally accompanying any kind of productive or creative activity.

All the above is currently found in labour economics and sociology. Management consultants call the systems that enhance the positive utility of productive activity 'motivation techniques'. It is however clear that since a day has 24 hours, a week 7 days, a year 365 days . . . and all people are mortal . . . for *all* individual agents time is a scarce 'commodity' and as such must have a price. It is clear too that trade-offs between different allocations of the available time are essentially subjective and different for each and every person. This variability increases or decreases the price of time of work and even makes it negative, although mostly remaining positive. In other terms the individual active person can perform the elementary exchange of his or her time for the received income. For the productive agents who create the VA – they can be the person just mentioned – the part of the distribution of this VA accruing to this person is *not* a purchase of some amount of his labour but results from a deed to this PNIT, a deed created by the activity of the agent and making up his or her income.

We negate by this proposition the adequacy of all closed economic models found in the literature, the most prominent being those of K. Marx and John von Neumann. In these models mere living makes the person a productive agent consuming inputs and producing an output called work. So such a productive agent must create a VA which is distributed between his savings and the society since by definition all his or her consumption is 'input'. Maybe one of the parts of such VA distribution is the person's happiness or joy . . . But how can such a part of the VA be quantified?

While the approach by closed models may nevertheless seem to be consistent on a microlevel (its morals accepted) it is not consistent on a macrolevel: (a) It is contradictory to the national accounts logic where labour, a factor of production, is part of the VA created, the GDP, while only the VA created by active individuals, that is the difference between their output, labour, and their inputs, the private consumption, should be counted. Thus this private consumption (or only its subsistence component?) should be subtracted from the GDP. And, (b) moreover and more importantly, in our and not only our principled opinion the finality of any micro or macro activity is *not only* to produce. So this approach is not correct on the fundamental grounds of our understanding of what we are and what we do.

To summarize the above, we state that economy is *not* by essence joyless. It becomes joyless only if people desiring and able to be productive are not allowed to be it because of the vices of the macroeconomic and social system. This is the drama of unemployment, in the economic terms of our analysis, of a waste of individually and socially available productive time. There is a stark contradiction in such a system. It considers work as a merchandise sold in the market for the price of the wages, the direct consequence of this proposition being that without such sales no income can be obtained. And it does not allow many individuals to operate this sale but nevertheless allocates to them some subsistence income. The whole setup, again quoting Weitzman, is absurd. We shall discuss this subject in more detail in Chapter 14.

If we now consider the activities of individual agents in longer units of time: weeks, months and years, the above applies with some small changes. Once the time necessary for chores e.g., house cleaning, repairs etc. is deducted, people partition their total available time into work (including the duration of transport if necessary) and 'vacation' or other 'free' or voluntary activities. This trade-off creates a 'price' of work, corresponding to the income obtained by it. The same analysis as previously made for the daily partition of time and of the positive and negative utilities in this elementary exchange is valid here. Thus 'leisure' can cease to have a positive utility if it lasts too long while work can increase this utility. Unemployment considered as an excessive leisure is a case in point independently of the loss of income.

It is more interesting to consider the lifespan of people and the scarcities in its partition. The active life, i.e. that part of life span of people during which they are productive, decreases in developed societies in absolute terms as well as in relation to the total duration of their existence, which on the contrary increases. So problems of financing education at the beginning of life and of providing income at its other end become acute. These are PNITs so intense in our societies. They can be freely chosen by their beneficiaries and as such are the free saving of households. The partition of incomes into spending and saving is concomitant to the partition of the available life time into the three main activities of education, work and retirement. Saving for individual agents is closely linked with their anticipations and/or predictions about their future. One can further link these behaviours as relative to the future to a criterion of choice proper to human nature, the one of games of chance, the pleasure of gambling or on the contrary the aversion to risk, in more scientific terms, the valuation of uncertainty. We shall not discuss this important economic fact here. It is the concern of a particular theory of utility in uncertainty. It has many similarities to the problems of time availability and scarcity.

The partition of the life span of individuals is also a social fact closely controlled by laws and regulations. For instance the compulsory school age (5 to 16 years . . .) and the mandatory retirement age are social constraints on personal choices. This is an example of situations in which 'scarcities' do not appear on markets and do not result in tolls or prices but in public or private time and resource transfers.

At the conclusion of this section on time scarcities of individual agents it is worthwhile mentioning how some modern and very recent technologies have allowed to spare daily, weekly, yearly and life limited time of people and in the end increase their sets of choices. Such are transport, communication, information and data processing availabilities, the personal work and leisure facilities provided by the automobile, the jet airliner, the telephone, all applications of electronics in DP, PCs, TV, HiFi etc., the many older household appliances, housing controls such as automatic tempe-rature controls etc. All these devices are time sparing that is they decrease the time scarcities. This has been and is particularly so for women. These equipments are investments in productivity when used in 'productive' activities but are not currently considered as such when used by people. This is incorrect and we do not follow the common usage. In all circumstances these tools reduce the time necessary for any activity, productive or not and, as already men-tioned, increase the time available for all of us for more freedom of choice.

2.2. Time scarcity for collective agents. The demography of collec-tive agents also exists as we have shown in Chapter 1. These agents are born, live and some of them die. Their demography is however fundamentally different from the demography of individual agents who are living creatures subject to the physicochemistry of this domain of Nature. In particular people disappear within a relatively short time interval. Collective agents are social creatures (that is entirely man made) and their life span is subject to human choices. Firms can and often do disappear,* or they may exist for even a few centuries. Associations and religious groups can be either short-lived or on the contrary in the economic horizon eternal as for instance the roman catholic church which is now two thousand years old. Public bodies are in principle, in human History, immortal and in its reality States practically never disappear voluntarily. This

'*) The infant mortality of firms is high, much higher than it is for humans.'

happens by external violence although internal decay does contribute. More can be found on this point in Spengler and Toynbee.

Daily, weekly, yearly time availability has a different impact on the activity of collective agents than on the activity of people. Some activities but not all are not pursued at night, others are continuous, others still are seasonal and differ according to some yearly seasons or even longer periods. The time scarcity intervenes in all these circumstances in variable ways. This diversity essentially depends on the particularities of the technologies of the production processes.

Life time availability is also different for collective agents. Their main concern is to remain 'alive', i.e. active. This is of course also the concern of people but it depends less on their economic choices. Collective agents (in which, to repeat, we include in this respect individual productive agents) stay alive as long as they create VA, although credit and other transfers for private firms, associations, local governments and States relaxes this constraint. For the last category of collective agents, the sovereign States, this constraint is even more relaxed by their capacity to issue money. Many collective agents, especially the public bodies do not disappear even if their VA creation is intensely negative. We experience this situation by what is called the debt crisis of international finance.

The main economic task of time management by collective agents concerns their expectations, i.e. their savings and their gross and net investment and globally their economic choices, policies and planning. In these activities physical but also human, i.e. subjective parameters play a role, the whole picture being pervaded by the essential reality of uncertainty and of time scarcity.

Here we can only list these parameters with very short comments.

– For the present time scarcity acts in a similar way as time partition by people. What is called economic management or activity organization is an allocation of the available time of people and of equipment in order to achieve planned results. In economic terms criteria of choices are attempted to be satisfied, for instance the optimal creation and distribution of the VA.

– For choices of the future, by definition made at present, agents also operate, as explained in detail in Chapter 6, on sets of possible choices, of constraints on these choices and of criteria of choices. But here the first two sets are forecasts and are relative to the time horizon, i.e. to the assumed duration of planned activities, in discrete terms the set of future periods of time. Within this horizon time scarcities are expressed by technological forecasts, the financial time discount and monetary and fiscal illusions or their antinomic rational expectations.

Let us here dwell only on financial time discounting. It is in a sense a reduction of the dimensionality of the sets of choices and of constraints on choices, the dimesions being here the number of points in time, the future dates whose set is the time horizon. To each of the elements of this necessarily bounded set one can link an attribute such as the VA created, the real production, a market share, new products, any part of the VA distribution such as profits.

The set of any of these attributes in the future within the time horizon is of the dimension of this horizon. In the most simple model the cardinal of such temporal sets is reduced to 1 by means of a discount or actualization rate. The device proceeds from the assumption that future results lose more and more of their present utility or disutility as they recede further into the future. The discount rate, mostly discrete and annual but in some theoretical models continuous, expresses by its measure 'a' this marginal 'scarcity' of the future. As a increases from zero to ∞ the 'value' of the future decreases. Thus $a = 0$ expresses a criterion of choice when the future has the same value as the present. This could mean a perfect abundance of time: present choices of the future increase infinitely in value so what happens now loses in relative importance as the time horizon lengthens. This is an unrealistic, an asymptotic situation in which no time scarcity exists. $a = \infty$ on the contrary denies any value to the future. Choices are made without any consideration of what will happen and the time scarcity is maximal. This state is also unrealistic today as it represents the behaviours of primitive agents, people and societies, and of all animals with the exception of man, squirrels and perhaps a few other species.

Between the two limits the scale of a represents actual behaviours and time scarcities. In financial terms the rates a are compared to (i) real and nominal economic growth rates e and $e + f$ (where f is the rate of inflation) (ii) real and nominal monetary market interest rates i and $i - f$, (iii) the 'internal return rate' r and (iv) the rate of alternate profit p . . .

2.3. Finally time is the essential factor of economic growth as it is by definition in all dynamic processes. One could in this domain consider relative scarcities of time. For instance the growth of knowledge, called in its applications 'technological progress rate' often exceeds the rate of social and political development and induces stresses and tensions, which are results of such descrepancies in temporal evolutions. Stagnant societies subjected to external influences and shocks, such as imported products, methods and morals, can lag in applications of these carriers of knowledge. Lags, discrepancies or even discontinuities of this kind induce tolls of disequilibria such as unemployment, indebtedness and often violence.

One can summarize the contents of this chapter by stating that space and/or time scarcities induce two consequences which are also a means of compensating the scarcities.

1. Scarcities induce tolls or rents which are PITs accruing to agents who hold title to scarce resources. By the mechanism of elementary exchange these PITs decrease the demand for scarce resources and so decrease their scarcity. This is the general case on markets of commercial resources as for instance in transport and communication, or in road and telephone networks. In almost all these cases the supply, i.e. the capacity of producing and offering the scarce resource can be increased, very often thanks to PITs arising from tolls and allowing the necessary investments to be financed.

But in some situations this evolution is impossible. The scarcity is final, physical. This is the case in the scarcity of time for the activity and life of all agents. The scarcity of land in a city or in a country cannot be increased beyond at most a very small amount. The scarcity of the electromagnetic spectre or of the number of satellite stations on the unique geostationery orbit cannot be changed by any means. It is only their use that can be improved.

In such situations tolls could be and are applied, for instance by means of land prices when land is scarce. The resulting PITs cannot be significantly used, however, for increasing the supply of the scarce resource and thus to fight its scarcity. This saving is transferred elsewhere. In most of these cases, for instance in radioelectric activities and in part in transport, communication and land use the tolls and PITs are replaced by rationing, i.e. regulation and public distribution of the scarce resource. This is a different story, that of public choices, to which we essentially devote the next chapter.

2. The second and most common consequence of spatial and/or temporal scarcities is their equivalence to measure N°2 of Chapter 11, by which the PITs generated by the scarcity are transferred to upstream stages of activities, thus decreasing the VA created in the considered stage. This transfer is or should be the consequence of a pollution or of promiscuity. Public choices are often necessary to regulate the process.

CHAPTER 13

RELATIONS BETWEEN AGENTS

We come back by a partial and in our opinion useful repetition of what has been written in previous chapters. We have analyzed the five fundamental sets of agents, resources, possible choices, constraints on choices and criteria of choices; further we have discussed the concepts of value, of labour and of utility, the essence of money, transfers, elementary exchange, value added creation and distribution and time and space. We shall now deal with the following subsets of the set of relations between agents:

- how the VA is distributed,
- the specific characters and operation of public, i.e. political agents within the domain of economics,
- the behaviours and choices of individual agents in their private activities,
- the saving and the investment in microeconomics,
- the financial and monetary economy,
- the other types of relations between agents.

SECTION 1. THE VA DISTRIBUTION

This is the main economic process. In current economics it is treated in a way for the reader of this text should appear as insufficient. In this current approach the analysis of the VA distribution is almost entirely restricted to the consideration of a 'profit' accruing to agents who decide themselves and only themselves how to maximize it by optimizing the management of the productive agent, account being taken of the necessary but minimized costs of production which include a purchase of labour on its market.

In historical perspective the reasons for such a model of relations between agents in the distribution of VA are quite apparent. In the past an entrepreneur hired capital (often his own) and labour, received permission from the sovereign, paid for these three factors and reaped a profit which was the difference between all his outlays to all other agents and what he collected by the sale of his produc-

153

tion. He, mostly a person, was the absolute owner of the products
sold so the scheme was legally correct. Nobody besides himself
cared about what he did with his profit, whether he spent it on
gambling or on his needs and desires or saved it.

Today's legal, fiscal and even moral picture is quite different.
Marx was in fact the first and Keynes the second of the great
thinkers who started to care about what happened to 'profits' and to
the rest of the VA distribution, in particular distributed incomes
and productive savings. Marx called these 'accumulation'. Neither
Keynes nor Marx clearly distinguished between the productive
saving, a monetary amount generated by the VA distribution and
retained within the firm, and investment or 'accumulation', an
exchange of the *total of all savings*, of which the productive saving is
a part, for real capital. In his concept of constant capital Marx even
confused this particular exchange with current exchanges for ex-
pendable inputs, which are costs. And both, Marx and Keynes,
often confused savings with other components of the gross profit,
such as dividends or taxes.

This statement is of course not a critique of the immense contribution of Marx and Keynes to economics. In their times they
achieved great advances in the understanding of economic activity.
But nowadays their continuing influence is an obstacle to the understanding of the present circumstances and of possible anticipations
of what the future will be. The proposals of Weitzman, Baumann
and Popov deal exclusively with that part of VA distribution called
wages and only propose to link it by a more flexible rule to profits
without a precise definition of this last item. They do not propose an
overall analysis of the rules which govern the relations between
agents leading to an assessment on an equal footing of *all* parts of
the VA distribution.

Such an analysis is a rather involved matter. We will try to sketch
it here in words while a very coarse formal model will be presented
in Chapter 14.

We recall from the appendix to Chapter 11 that the VA, a
nominal monetary flow, or an amount in a period, is partitioned into
five major parts, which are all PNITs:

- w the labour compensation,
- d the other distributed incomes, mainly dividends including or

excluding interest payments,
- k the depreciation allowance $= b_1$,
- b_2 the retained profits or the productive net saving,
- T the transfer to the public agents, i.e. the fiscal burden $= t_1 + t_2 + t_3 + t_4$, where t_3 is the corporate income tax and t_1, t_2, t_4 other taxes on business,
- the total productive saving $S = b_1 + b_2$,
- the gross profit $B_g = d + k + b_2 = d + S$ and the net profit $B_n = d + b_2$,
- the gross cash flow before taxes in its general acception $d + b + T$.

Alternatively $t_1 + t_2 + t_4$ are considered as costs and excluded while t_3 is included in the gross cash flow before taxes which becomes $k + b_2 + d + t_3$ and the corresponding net cash flow $b_2 + d + t_3$. The total distributed income is $D = w + d + T$.

This VA distribution is discussed today on meetings of boards of directors or similar bodies on which sit not only the representatives of shareholders, i.e. of owners of the firm but also those of executives and of employees in general. Moreover in many firms some directors represent unions, consumers and public bodies such as city councils, state and federal administrations. Even if these last categories of agents are not official members of deciding bodies their influence on choices is never negligible, the more so as fiscal rules largely condition the whole of the VA distribution.

Contractual, legal, traditional, customary and sheer force arguments are put forward in the discussion as well as material, market, human, financial and other necessities often backed by considerations of the results of current economic theory such as the links between the marginal labour productivity and the level of wages or, more directly, the danger of inflation. The final VA distribution is the fruit of all this complex activity.

Here are some additional remarks to the above and to the appendix to Chapter 11:

(a) The total of the expense for compensation for the activity of all members of the productive agent is at present more than half the total VA distributed. Its partition is a complicated secondary process in which the composition of the work force plays a role. A 'hightech' activity will result in a high proportion of high salaries while in an assembly plant manned by less skilled people many incomes of smaller unit volume can nevertheless result in an even greater total volume of this part of the VA distribution. The problem is further blurred within the global compensation of executives where fringe benefits are mixed with activity compensation, dividends and other distributed incomes as well as savings. Market considerations, for instance competition for highly competent people further distort the pattern and complicate the process, while high unemployment can act in an opposite sense.

(b) Dividends in today's developed market economies often acquire the same character as interest payments and can be and sometimes are considered as costs. They differ only from other distributed incomes and from interest payments by their direct and legal dependence on the specific part of the VA distribution called profit and by their assessment rules as an amount per share linking this subpart of the VA distribution to the equity capital. Quite often dividends seem to be the most flexible part of the distribution. Their linkage to the wage level which seems to be the essence of some proposals such as the one of Weitzman is precisely destined to enhance the flexibility of wage volumes that are currently rather rigid. In fact dividends are only a small part of the total VA and acquire more and more the sole quality of a premium influencing the price of shares on stock exchanges. It is a fact of life that, in general, agents who collect dividends save a greater part of their total income than other agents in particular the wage earners. But a bulk of dividends accrues to collective agents and enters directly the financial market, thus creating direct saving. The marxist and neo-classical models which assume that wage earners do not save while only the other distributed incomes create the total of the macrosaving are unrealistic and should be abandoned for the explanations of our present developed economies. All agents, individual and collective, do save in variable proportions of their income or their VA created. As previously shown the current model stems from the assumption that the productive saving (and the depreciation allowance) is owned by the shareholders. This is true in the legal sense but is certainly quite off the mark as regards the choices of the use of this saving in which the 'owners' have very little say.

(c) The depreciation allowance depends on the fiscal rules and on the capital intensity of the productive process. While legally rigid it is often in hard times fixed below the correct compensation for equipment wear and obsolescence. It is a part of the productive saving and as such often considered as a residue after all other parts of the VA distribution have been allocated. When the VA created is substantial the depreciation allowance is often limited by fiscal rules. This limitation is due to the most common tax structure by which in the assessment of corporate income tax the depreciation allowance is considered as a deductible cost. The rationale for the rule is that both compensations, for labour, as represented by wages and for capital as represented by the depreciation volume, are outlays for the two production factors and should be considered as costs. As we have already shown, the rationale is inconsistent. Either both 'costs of production factors' are not included in the VA created or both should be included and *not* considered as costs. For the assessment of Value Added Tax (VAT) which is on the books in Europe, this last option is used while in all accounts and economic models the wages are costs. As a marginal remark, it seems strange that when in a period some equipment is purchased its price which has nothing to do with VA creation and distribution is deducted from the VA on which the VAT is assessed. The entire setup is arbitrary and irrational.

Our description shows the conventional character of the concept of value added. Some marginal items can be shifted between this concept and the concept of factor input costs. But, to repeat, the two main production factors, the activities of equipment, currently called the real capital and of people, currently called labour, must be appraised in a consistent way. They are both the source of the VA and should participate equally in its distribution.

(d) The conflict called class struggle by marxists is produced by the natural opposition of interests in the VA distribution and is of course a reality. We endeavour to propose a clear and, as far as possible, objective picture of this reality. For this and other reasons we also disconnect both capital and labour compensation from their productivities and/or from their macroeconomic roles in consumption and in investment. This proposal is founded on the simple fact that neither the first part of the VA distribution, w, when aggregated does not represent the total consumer demand nor the second part, k adds up to the total aggregate called the saving in the period.

And, in our opinion, productivities are only arguments in the negotiations concerning the overall VA distribution.

(e) The saving of the productive agent $S = b$ is a part of the VA distribution which remains within the choices of this agent (remains on the books of the firm). In current economics this is often compared to the required outlays for capital purchases in the period. A rate of 'selffinancing' is computed as the ratio of these two monetary amounts. This is largely an inconsistent practice. Being only a part of the total macro aggregate called saving in an economy, this productive saving S enters in market economies on the financial market and in planned economies into the public budget. The distinction is marginal and pertains only to the elements of the sets of agents who will decide on the use of savings and obviously to their sets of choices and of criteria of choices. For instance the criterion of a market interest rate operates only in market economies.

Quite often the gross profit B_g is compared to investment outlays by projecting this part of VA distribution into the future and discounting the resulting 'rates of return' in order to choose between alternative uses of savings. It is obvious from our approach that this reasoning is inadequate since (i) the dividends d are incomes of other agents who, in part, do not save them and (ii) investment choices are closely dependent on macroeconomic data of the financial part of the economy, either market or publicly controlled. Thus neither the gross profit B_g nor its part, the savings S of the productive agent can directly influence real investment choices, besides the traditional but often unrealistic considerations of ownership.

(f) The part of the VA distribution accruing to public agents is a PNIT. It is assessed by numerous and often intricate rules which result, as estimated in Chapter 11, in some 30 per cent of the VA created in our developed countries. As for almost all monetary flows discussed here, this part is only a fraction of the total public revenue. Some of this part is called direct taxation such as the profit tax, some is called indirect taxation such as sales taxes or the VAT, some are lump taxes such as the local property 'rates' etc. We shall not enter into a more detailed consideration of this part of the VA distribution as it is treated in Section 2 hereafter but only stress that while the rules of assessment are established by a political process the resulting PNITs, i.e. the tax liabilities closely depend on all choices for the VA distribution. These last choices are not made by political processes such as a majority vote but, as shown above, by negotiations, consensus or force. The reason for this situation is that a distribution of wealth cannot be laid on a minority by a majority or vice versa but must be accepted by all or else will result from violence. In fact the VA distribution historically and most often at present expresses the will of a minority laid on a majority so that it directly opposes the democratic principle of a majority vote accepted by a minority. This is so not only for historical, traditional or ownership reasons. It is necessary if the choices of productive agents are to take sufficient care of the future as compared to the present. The interface between political and economic choice processes represented by the three different sets of choices, of constraints on choices and of criteria of choices we have distinguished in this book has been and remains one of the fundamental building stones of societies.

A few words must be written here on individual productive agents (craftsmen, lawyers, doctors, farmers, writers and artists etc.) Their behaviours as producers are rather complicated since they are mixed with their consumer status and choices. If some of them succeed in dichotomizing their overall economic activity, others are unable to achieve it. In this last case their VA created is divided by them in two main parts, one is retained by the agent and in turn partitioned into his consumption and his private saving and the other is transferred to the State as taxes.

It is well known that inflation exacerbates the 'fight' for the VA distribution which, in turn, enhances inflation. The distributed nominal incomes in inflation decrease in real or purchasing value while their relative increase in the, by definition nominal, VA distribution tends during inflation to increase when compensated for this decrease in purchasing power. Since at the same time the factor prices increase, the nominal VA creation can only be maintained or increased if the prices of output are increased. The fight for the VA distribution is a great cause of inflation, and also its effect. Such an effect has been observed in oil consuming economies when crude oil

prices skyrocketed between 1974 and 1980. The part of the VA
accruing to labour remained rigid so the savings decreased dramati-
cally and investment suffered while inflation soared.

A different kind of fight for the VA distribution is indirect,
through the channel of its public part, T. It pertains essentially to
relations between agents but also to the macroeconomic problem of
financing public goods and, more generally, indirect incomes in
welfare societies. We shall discuss this more fully in Section 2.

In this section we have tried to dissociate the reality of the VA
distribution from the value judgments on forces and arguments
which lead to this distribution: ethics, violence, lust for power,
greed, etc. and also of apparently rational arguments of marginal
productivities and necessities of preserving the future. We try to
stick to this standpoint.

One can present the reality of the VA distribution in different
terms, as a non-zero sum game of five players: distributed incomes,
saving, State, buyers of products and sellers of factors which includes an internal zerosum subgame of two players, dividends and
wages, and an external zerosum subgame between consumption and
investment. Any expert in game theory knows how difficult it is to
analyze such a system.

SECTION 2. THE PUBLIC AGENTS

Besides their genuine political role public agents are in our opinion
productive agents who create and distribute VA. The VA created
by public agents differs only in its origin from the one created by
other privately or publicly owned productive agents. The revenue of
public agents is not predominantly obtained by exchange that is
through the sale of products. Its source is mainly but not exclusively
PNITs from other public and private productive or consuming
collective and individual agents. These PNITs are called fiscal
and/or customs revenue. The revenue is completed by proceeds
from the sale of goods and services. Total budget receipts also
include the distributed incomes a_2 of the publicly owned productive
agents. As defined, the VA created by public bodies is equal to the
difference between the revenue and the outlays for the procurement
of goods and services and is distributed as any other VA created into

distributed incomes and savings, both being PNITs accruing to other agents.

There are however some differences between this activity and the 'ordinary' VA creation and distribution. The first and most common difference is that public bodies often do not create a positive VA and are not able to create available savings. In many circumstances the VA of public bodies has been negative which means that their revenue was smaller than their outlays. To be able to distribute incomes and transfers or even consume public bodies must in such occurrence receive PNITs other than the current revenue. These PNITs are the credit and are also provided by issuing money. This last capability is available today only to sovereign States while in history many kinds of 'private' money existed. Moreover since the financial economy is a unique interlocking system it is trivial that credit in general also creates money. It is also well known that, since Keynes, negative VA is often considered as a virtue of public agents while in the medium and long term it kills ordinary productive agents.

One can dispute the difference we assume between tax revenue considered of the same 'virtue' as proceeds of sales for ordinary productive agents while this virtue is refused for other PNITs used to create the necessary VA such as sales of bonds, bank credit, or the issue of money which are all PNITs, as are taxes. In our opinion the fiscal revenue differs essentially from other PNITs by the fact that it results from political decisions and does not infer any liability for the public agent other than its responsibility before the citizens, in general in Parliament, for a thrifty management of public funds. All other PNITs create such liabilities with the exception of the issue of money. This last source of positive VA is, as is well known, a concealed taxation.

Let us recall that all productive agents and individual consumers also supplement their VA creation and/or incomes by taking up credit and thus incurring debt. But none of these agents can in our present economies use the PNITs of the nature of taxes, with the exception of racketeers. All non public agents normally boost their VA creation by means of PITs as is described in Chapter 11.

Another difference between public and ordinary agents resides in the absence in the former's VA distribution of the subpart (d) of 'other distribute incomes' or dividends. Public agents being in essence political bodies cannot distribute such incomes. This is however only a convention of the modern polity. When kings and other rulers considered their realms as their private property they had title to great 'private' incomes, parts of the VA distribution of such societies.

It is further a rare feature of public bodies to set aside a part of their VA distribution as a depreciation allowance for instance for roads, bridges, armaments, monuments, city streets paving and sewerage etc. The subpart (b_1) of the appendix to Chapter 11 does not exist. The subpart (b_2), the saving does exist in principle as the 'below the line' part of public budgets. Public budgets ignore the concept of profit while in fact their wealth or 'net worth' increases with their savings. The whole picture is very fuzzy within the elaborate theory and practice of public finance and budget management. The fundamental reason for this state of affairs is the almost permanent existence of public deficits and also the 'sovereign' character of public choices.

A final particularity of public finance, in our understanding an euphemism for the creation and distribution of VA, is the great part played by other PNITs in the VA distribution. Even when public budgets do borrow funds, at the same time they lend and give away contributions to other budgets, to the VA creation of other agents and/or to the incomes of agents, including the individual consumers. They utilize this activity as a tool of economic policy while being credit institutions. We shall deal with this last category of agents in Section 5 of this chapter.

One finds in the literature a distinction between two kinds of transfers (whether straight donations or loans) by public agents. Financing public goods and services is, in this approach, a first kind of transfer while creating indirect incomes is a second kind. The first is deemed to be a cost and the second one to be a part of the public VA distribution.

We shall not adopt this explanation. Public goods are a real output without an inflow of money as is the case for private goods sales. In the absence of this inflow of money the VA is created by revenue, essentially from fiscal sources from which the outlays for real public inputs is deducted. The VA created is distributed by direct and indirect incomes the latter for instance by supplying without charge all kinds of private goods.

The distinction between the two kinds of transfers attributed to Walther Eucken is in fact the distinction between VA creation and distribution. Of course such distinctions are, in their essence, conventional. In a more precise analysis of the problem care must be taken of direct and indirect scarcities, for instance congestions, creating the necessity for rents and tolls. These 'prices' may change the conventions that is the distinction between the VA creation and distribution.

In conclusion the economic activity of public agents is not very different from the activity of other productive agents while nevertheless not exactly the same. The essential difference resides in the sets of choices, constraints on choices and criteria of choices. For public agents the general welfare, law and order, power etc. play a significant role. As already noted, public agents ignore the concept of profit and do not maximize any direct microeconomic aggregate. Their criteria of choices are essentially either macroeconomic or extraeconomic.

In particular the conflict between agents entitled to the parts of the VA distribution is in general not resolved by means of equal negotiation and/or force but by political decisions within public budgetary procedures in the executive and legislative branches of government. For instance it is difficult to consider the salaries of public servants as the result of a claim to a part of the distribution of the public VA. One must substitute for such a title a more customary one of compensation for services rendered not to their employer but to the community at large. Unions, for instance the teachers' unions not only play on such arguments but also on comparisons of their incomes to those of other categories, as do all unions of wage earners. The concept of Weitzman's share economy or of the other proposals of increased flexibility of wages, as mentioned in Chapter 11 is void of significance for public agents. It is a considerable difficulty for the implementation of such proposals.

On a more general level it is obvious that political procedures, i.e. the activity of government, influence the activity of all agents. Public budgets, central bank policies, prices and tariffs, monetary and real consumption and investment of public bodies, the regulation of

energy, of transport and communication are essential macroeconomic data and variables. In this particular relation between
the public agent called government and all other agents the government's activity is 'instrumental'. In all other aspects its activity is in
our opinion microeconomic as it is for all other kinds of agents,
public or private. The government's 'instrumental' activity is on the
contrary macroeconomic and for this reason it will be further
discussed in Chapter 14.

SECTION 3.   PRIVATE INDIVIDUAL CONSUMER AGENTS

In current economics this category of agents is called households,
including one person units. Their economic activity consists in our
approach firstly of receiving incomes which are PNITs and to which
they have title (a) by virtue of their activity in all kinds of productive
agents, (b) by their wealth, in our societies mainly represented by
financial instruments or deeds such as bonds, shares, certificates of
deposit, current accounts, cash and also by titles to land, to housing
and to other property, (c) by straight subsidies from public agents
such as education grants, etc. (d) by titles to pensions, social
security benefits etc. and (e), last but not least, by taking up
'consumer credit' i.e. borrowing.

Some comments are in order on each of these titles to income.

(a) The activity in all kinds of productive agents is not, according
to our approach as developed in previous Chapters, a sale of labour
on a market. It is in general a title to a part of VA created by these
productive agents within the whole of production and exchange in
an economy. The entitled agent can be a member of the household,
the male head of a family in its traditional shape or, at present, just
any of its members whether male or female. The entitled agent can
be a stock exchange speculator whose income depends on his risky
operations. The bulk of consumer households however draw their
main income from the participation in VA distribution of productive collective agents, which income is currently called wages or
salaries.

(b) the 'other distributed incomes' d of our picture in Chapter 11
and in the first section of the present chapter is the main source of

this kind of household incomes. We assume here for simplicity's sake, although the assumption is not that far from reality, that interest payments of all kinds of debts is included in d. All kinds of rents stemming from real property are also included as stated. British economists call this part of household incomes 'unearned incomes'.

The subpart, d of the VA distribution, accrues only in part either to households or to public agents. These transfers are PNITS between all kinds of agents and in their bulk between productive agents. They create an important part of the global saving of the economy, as already stated before.

(c) In modern welfare societies households are entitled to straight state subsidies such as education grants, family aids etc. They are by nature selective negative taxes. One must distinguish these PNITs from the set of negative PITs such as social security payments, medicare, free travel, subsidized transit fares, free education etc. The zero price of some of these free resources can and for consistency's sake must be considered as negative PITs equal in theory to their price in the optimal state of the economy.

(d) Pensions may be included either in the other distributed incomes d from productive agents if they are purely financial PNITs from private sources such as insurance companies or be considered as straight subsidies, see (c) above.

(e) The last category of 'incomes' in a period of time consisting in taking up consumer credit is an additional monetary inflow.

Some of these incomes are common, accruing to a great majority of households while other categories are more selective: education grants for the young, family aids for younger women, pensions to old people, rents to land and houseowners etc. We shall not enter into a detailed consideration of these differences.

The second main economic activity of households is to dispose of their total income. They partition it into several parts. The first part of this partition are taxes: income tax, property tax and other fiscality labelled direct taxes. These are PNITs accruing to the public agents. We include all personal social security and other contributions as we have done for the 'employer's' part of such contributions in our analysis of the VA distribution.

The second part of the income distribution is called private saving in current economics. In contrast to this economics we remain consistent with the concept of saving of productive agents by defining a total household saving. For productive agents the part of VA distribution called saving is the sum of the depreciation allowance and 'retained profits' $S = b_1 + b_2$ and is currently spent on the purchase of the means of production. Households only rarely depreciate their 'means of production', with perhaps the exception of housing, but they too spend a part of their savings for purchases of such 'means of production', in current economics called durable consumer goods, for instance cars, appliances, furniture etc. All these outlays are included in that part of income distribution called saving. In consequence we shall take exception to the inclusion of this part of the use of incomes of households into the macro-economic aggregate of consumption. In a way that is quite analogous to the analysis of the VA distribution by productive agents in our view households use a part of their savings for direct investment in equipments which allow their members to enjoy an activity of high productivity, whether in compensation for a part of their income or for leisure or for any other choice for the partition of their available time. Only the remainder of their total saving enters the financial and monetary markets through purchases of financial property such as shares, bonds, saving accounts, life insurance or more directly by checking accounts or straight cash.

Of course agents that are active in finance are only interested in this remainder so they call it, (and economists wrongly agree) the saving of households. This saving as any other saving is a PNIT in time and can and will in a future period be a part of the income of the household.

Thirdly the remaining income is really spent in the period for the current necessities of life: food, transport, leisure, travels, entertainment, social functions etc. Only this part of the total income should be called consumption, by excluding all 'durables'. Of course the distinction is mostly difficult and must be the result of a convention. But this is true too for many 'investment goods' in business activity.

One could be even more consistent and represent the management of the income by households as VA creation and distribution. This approach would be as follows, although it would be even more at variance from the usual economics than our position above. We propose it only as a variant.

In this light the last third part of the utilization of income would be the 'cost' of the existence and of the activity of the household. The VA would be the rest of the income in the same sense that the sum of distributed incomes and savings is for other agents.

The agents called households are in one respect distinct from other types of agents. Their VA distribution and in some respects their VA creation too, is assumed to be the result of choices whose main criterion is the utility of utilizations of the available time and, as specifically regards their income distribution, the utility of real resources obtained and of their financial savings (cash holdings included). In current microeconomics households maximize the vector of non-additive utilities under the constraint of available income and in current macroeconomics aggregate their choices into propensities to save and for liquidity. In our approach there remains only the propensity to save, as cash holdings, i.e. liquid assets are a part of the total saving of the household.

It is generally assumed that compulsory negative PNITs by households, as are taxes, are not counted and the only budget constraint is the disposable income. We do not concur and assume that households maximize their subjective utility in which monetary holdings create a positive money utility while tax payments create a negative utility. One could include in this model the positive utilities provided by real resources that are created by the availability of public goods offsetting in an always non-additive mode the negative money utility of tax payments. Our approach would be an improvement on the current theory of optimal direct taxation which directly and additively compares the direct taxes paid by households to public goods financing, without considering the revenue stemming from other agents or the utilization by households of only some, but not all, public goods.

Through the use of the concept of utility households themselves resolve the conflicts arising from their VA distribution. Such conflicts exist in the life of real households; they are families of several individuals expressing conflicting needs and desires more generally possessing different behaviours. The conflicts are resolved either by consensus after negotiations, in the present parlance in a convivial way, or by the will and choices of the family head. By this last remark we see the strong similarity to what happens concerning the VA distribution in productive agents with many thousands of participants when this distribution is decided upon by the person of the owner of the business or by a board of directors and results from protracted negotiations and discussions within this board and by many other types of agents.

One last remark is in order here. The distinction between individual agents as 'people' mainly consuming, i.e. driven by needs, desires, happiness, beliefs, all this included in the concept of utility and all other kinds of agents, collective and individual, productive, private or public, all more or less rational, is essential. The dichotomy is of course artificial and even fictitious. It is a great difficulty when dealing with economic principles, but is it necessary at least in our approach. The dichotomy does not infringe on the philosophical, ethical or political prominence of the person as the ultimate goal of human activity.

SECTION 4.   SAVING AND INVESTMENT IN MICROECONOMICS

This section will be short since the essential features of the concepts of saving and investment are macroeconomic. We shall only consolidate what has been written on the subject in previous chapters and previous sections of this chapter in order to show the main distinction between direct investment of their saving by all types of agents and the rest of these savings entering the financial side of the economy and creating the world of finance.

As for all economic activities the creation of financial savings is the result of choices made by the agents. Among the arguments or criteria of these choices are the utility of money, the interest rate, the possibility of borrowing and lending, etc. Keynes consolidated these criteria into the propensity to save and the preference for liquidity, for us both pertaining to the financial saving and discriminating only between its different tools.

The productive agents create within their VA distribution a saving consisting of the sum S of the depreciation allowance b_1 and the 'retained profit' b_2. This saving can either be directly invested by the agent himself in real resources by purchasing and installing means of production or be 'sold' or 'invested' on financial markets by buying bonds or shares of other agents, lending or conserving cash etc. A part of this last monetary saving is in reality a tool of production, i.e. the necessary positive balance of current financial liquid operations, a balance that is equivalent to stocks of raw materials and of semi-finished supplies as well as finished products within the processes of production.

The public agents seldom create their own positive savings but rather borrow them from other agents. This financial operation is currently called financing public deficits or in short deficit financing. But public agents do heavily invest their own or borrowed savings into collective infrastructures of all kinds. They seldom include into their VA distribution the item of depreciation allowance which would often be fictitious when their own savings are nil or negative. This state is of course only conventional since it assumes that the 'earned income' of the public agents is restricted to fiscal revenue while any 'unearned' public income stems from issuing money or borrowing.

Households are, as shown in Section 3, the sole type of agents who solve their problem of VA distribution (of their income less current 'subsistance' expenses) by 'maximizing their utility under the budget constraint', this last being precisely the VA created. Their free saving is what we call within the VA distribution the saving S less all direct investment in durables and housing. What Keynes called propensities to consume was the explanation of the choices essentially made by households for the partition of the available VA, equal to the disposable income less the subsistence consumption for all other expenses in current real resources called in current economics discretionary or de luxe resources mixed up with investments in durable and in housing, which are parts of the saving.

For all financial investments Keynes defined their criterion as the propensity to save. These investments are in fact only a part of savings, either spent on the purchase of financial assets or by virtue of the preference for liquidity held in cash (or in current bank accounts) Post-Keynesian economists such as Pigou or Patinkin refined the representation of choices of households for their VA distribution by their model of the real balance effect. None of these economists clearly distinguished between the sets of choices and of the criteria of choices of different kinds of agents or between the specific kinds of savings and of their utilizations. This is what we have tried to present here.

As previously stated, real investments are financed, in plain language bought, in part directly by means of the own savings of the agents who make such exchanges. This is common occurrence for households who often do not bother about the involved computation of the profitability of an investment or compare such a profitability to an interest rate. When a household buys a car or a house it does not generally quantify the increase in productivity of its members resulting from the use of this equipment. Even when fiscal rules allow taxpayers to deduct a 'depreciation allowance' for such investments in the assessment of their income tax liability, the criteria of choices between these investments and a purchase of financial assets or of keeping income in cash are not common practice. Such comparisons, quite usual in business, are most often a marginal criterion when compared to the personal utility of the possession and use of the equipment that are bought. When productive agents directly invest a part of their saving S in real resources, then contrary to households they take care in most cases of a set of criteria of choices between such decisions and a financial investment in, for instance, bonds or shares of other agents, private or public. These financial investments must contribute to the VA creation. The set of criteria of choices includes four quite common items: (a) the rate of return, a ratio of the future VA creation (or of a part of it, the 'profit') to the cost of equipment, (b) very often the comparison with alternative equity or loan financing of the real investment, (c) fiscal rules for tax assessment and (d) the market interest rate or the return on financial investment.

SECTION 5.   FINANCIAL AND MONETARY ECONOMY

This section deals with relations between financial agents and between these agents and other kinds of agents. Finance is an activity purpose of which is trivially not to deal in real resources but in money and in other representations of 'value' labelled and measured in money, such as bank accounts, shares and bonds, insurance contracts, factoring, financing trade and public budgets and, in our view, primarily the creation and distribution of VA. All these representations of value, in older times materialized by bullion, then by written and printed texts and pictures on paper are today mostly only bytes in computer memories supplemented by listings and documents produced by computer outlets. Financial operations are today instantaneous, global and continuous in time. They build what some authors call the world-economy.

The financial capital is a prominent resource in developed market economies. While less important it plays also a role in planned economies. This immaterial resource is created by the real economic activity before being able to represent it. As we have shown, agents create the saving whose different streams flow into the sea of capital operated upon by financial agents. And since money is the universal medium of the economic activity all kinds of agents are more or less 'financial'. We do however understand under the label of 'financial' those elements of the set of agents which are exclusively active in finance. As stated above we do not distinguish in their essence cash or liquid financial assets from other kinds of saving, that is from financial capital but of course assume that the manifold species of this capital possess various qualities and functions.

It is necessary to define the manner in which financial agents create and distribute VA it being assumed that in their specific capacity they do indeed create and distribute it. We remain here in microeconomics while the resource dealt with by financial agents, 'capital', is by essence macroeconomic and will be examined in Chapter 14.

Financial agents are the ones who buy and sell savings or 'capital' or 'IOUs' or 'credit'. When any agent opens a bank account, the bank 'buys' an input 'sold' by the agent and paid for by the interest paid by the bank (often this monetary price or cost of the input for the bank is nil and is represented by real services rendered by the bank). When a family buys a mortgage or insurance the savings bank or the insurance company sells to this family the savings of other people or agents which it has previously bought from them. When a corporation makes a share or bond issue or when the Treasury sells and buys bonds on the open market, these are transactions in the existing saving created by all kinds of agents.

Thus the output of financial agents is a sale of savings for an amount of money resulting from prices which mostly are the interests received and also all other monetary inflows such as the speculative or capital gains. The VA created is, by definition, the nominal flow of the difference between the monetary inflow in compensation for output and the monetary outflow in compensation for input, to which difference all PNITs are algebraically added. This VA is divided, in the same way as is done by other productive agents into distributed incomes such as wages, dividends, taxes etc., and savings which combine with all other savings to sum up into the macroeconomic aggregate of saving or financial capital, the direct real investment of financial agents not entering the markets.

This description can easily be applied to any and all intricate financial operations such as the exchanges between currencies or against monetary gold, to any kind of investment in the financial sense of the word and, of course, to the entire activities of banking, insurance and thrift institutions.

SECTION 6.   OTHER TYPES OF RELATIONS BETWEEN AGENTS

Up to this point we have considered the relations between agents within the economic sphere of exchanges, of VA creation and distribution and of all kinds of transfers. It seems appropriate to conclude this chapter with a brief description of a more general realm of relations expressed not exclusively, or even not at all, in economic data but remaining in close connection with economics.

We find in the literature the analysis of a first kind of such relations under the label of the couple principal-agent. The word agent has in this case a different meaning from the one we have adopted in this book. Consequently it is necessary to very briefly analyze this couple. We understand the relation principal-agent to be a situation in which the agent surrenders to the principal some subsets of his sets of choices, of constraints on choices and of criteria of choices. The principal has his choice horizon enlarged and the agent restrained. This can be the case in economic as in any other sets of choices. The relation principal-agent exists between the governing and the governed, between public and private agents (between the Administration and the firms, associations and citizens), between dominating and dominated productive agents (price leading and price taking firms), etc. . . . .

A second more general type of relations worth mentioning is the couple of competence and authority. It is a very real dialectic in economics as in all realms of social activities.

The question is: Does competence confer the capacity to decide, to make choices? If the answer is yes, line organization structures or such relations as those between principals and agents are preferable: the superiors know better than the subordinates and those who know decide.

For centuries the military were the first to be, by the sheer binary result of their choices, victory or defeat, compelled to study and to codify the relations between agents and have learned the inadequacy if not the dangers of such a setup. They separated the task of the commander who decides from the task of his staff who know.

The necessity of separating the competence from the authority is at present more acute because, among other advances in knowledge, of the intrusion of mathematics and more recently of electronic data storage and processing in economic as well as in most other activities. There are now agents who weigh and measure facts and arguments and understand techniques and there are those who, without wholly understanding what the first ones do, choose. These last agents are currently called decision makers and are provided by the first, who may be called consultants, with the 'science' or 'theory' of decision which in our opinion is not science but an art as it has always been.

This setup is adequate for a simple reason. Authority must be accepted by those to whom it addresses. The acceptance is a cultural event in which the sacred: traditions, birth, property, faiths and beliefs etc. play a big role. Even if the rational, called competence, is not the quality of the commander but is inspired by his advisers, it is taken as such by the agents who accept his authority. In different terms the competence can be defined as the subset of rationality within the set of criteria of choice of the decision maker. The complementary subset of this set is by large not void; its elements are today often called charisma. . .

Once the separation between competence and authority has been made, two structural social choices remain open:

– One can centralize everything, including decisions, in a measure unknown before our time because that was impossible in the absence of modern means of storing, processing and communicating all data, criteria and choices. On the political level, democracy becomes absurd in this hypothesis: the parliaments are ignorant and hence powerless in the presence of an omniscient hence powerful administration. This tendency is apparent in many countries. It is counteracted without much success by hiring staffers who are opposed to regular officials. In economics this type of relations between agents exists in planned economies with the known result of generic inefficiency.

– One can establish a network or a system of staff-line connections by committees or otherwise within or without the organizations, in the society or in its economic sphere. The main feature of such systemic setups of relations between agents is the existence of numerous and intense feedbacks imbedded into the system. The consistency of the great number of more or less independent choices and decisions at the different strata of the system, resulting from the difference between competence and authority is maintained by the staff connections or in other terms by a hierarchy of agents who know parallel to a hierarchy of agents who choose. The market economic theory asserts that prices are the tool that can alone fulfill the task, within their action. We doubt it.

In any case we are now living the development of electronic tools consisting of computer networks which will eventually enormously increase the efficiency of this second principle. But this will only be so if the decision makers remain outside the setup. If not, networks will kill activity by the sheer weight of new routines. The October 1987 crash on New York Stock Exchange is a case in point.

It is natural to apply our remarks to the overall social activity. The dialectic of competence and authority can be transposed into the dialectic élite-people, formally the mapping of the set élite into the set people. I have dealt with this relation elsewhere besides mentioning it in this book. Assuming that the society is democratic which means following Lincoln's principle of government of the people by the people for the people, the reality is that the people or its representatives are decision makers who 'do not know', that is, are not sufficiently competent in modern science, technology, economics, sociology etc. The élite 'knows' or is defined as knowing. Hence the dialectic we have tried to describe. It is a macroeconomic effect. On the microscale one can cite the rational expectations theory as an example of our dialectic.

CHAPTER 14

ECONOMIC PROCESSES

This is the final chapter of the book. We consolidate our results by the use of the 'building blocks' we have previously proposed: the sets of agents, of resources, of choices, of constraints on choices, of criteria of choices, the concepts of value, of utility, of money, of time and space, the elementary exchange, the PITs and PNITs, the VA creation and distribution and the relations between agents. We shall now present a coarse macroeconomic model of economic processes.

This presentation is divided into four sections:
– Section 1. Definitions and notations,
– Section 2. Presentation of the model,
– Section 3. Aggregation,
– Section 4. Dynamic interpretation and discussion of the model.

SECTION 1. DEFINITIONS AND NOTATIONS OF THE MODEL

Four aggregates are the vertices of the graph G (see Chapter 4), as shown in Figure 14.1:

a representation of the households called the 'HOUSEHOLD'
a representation of the productive agents called the 'FIRM'
a representation of the public agents called the 'STATE'
a representation of the financial agents called the 'BANK'

The transition from the real sets of agents, for each of its types, to the representative AGENT, i.e. the aggregation process will be considered in Section 3 together with the problems of aggregation of flows and in particular of the VA.

The flows are the arcs that connect the vertices. They are PNITs in an interval of time (a period) in the discrete approach or functions of time at time t expressed in money in the continuous approach. We use the discrete mode in the first three sections and the continuous one in the last section on dynamics.

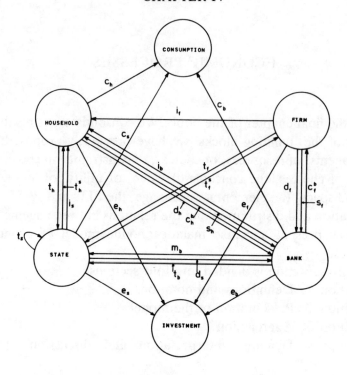

Figure 14.1.

An essential point will be developed hereafter namely that some of these PNITs come from or go to other periods or time points.

A second part of the model concerns the VA creation. The main but not the only, 'powerplant' of this creation (or production but this word will not be used) is located within the FIRM. The three other AGENTS also create it. As shown in Chapter 11 the VA is the result of exchanges between agents of real resources against money, generating PITs which constitute the VA.

Of course the production of real resources by means of technology and organization is a prominent economic process. Current economics deals extensively with this process by building production functions, studying the substituability and the complementarity of factors, representing the technological progress etc. Further current economics analyzes in detail the price formation (i.e. the exchange of real resources against money) and considers consumption and investment functions in the private and in the public sectors, the demand and supply functions, the elasticities, the wage and profit rates etc.

As already stated we shall deal only with some parts of this discipline while of course not neglecting the relation between the VA creation and distribution and the real production system. This system is a social process combining the applied sciences of Nature *and* people with economic data on scarcities and costs together with the essence of relations between agents as described in the preceding chapters. We shall not analyze the production system further, other than stressing again that while agents do create and distribute VA, the 'labour', i.e. the productive activity of people is only one of the titles to this distribution but is *not* a factor of production.

It is necessary to let appear a binary partition in the model dividing the set of real resources into consumption and investment. This partition is quite arbitrary for many goods and services; it is only a convenience. We assume by definition that the real investment is the subset of real resources exchanged in the period for savings and that consumption is the subset of real resources exchanged in the period for the rest of the current incomes available in the period. The qualification 'in the period' does not apply in the same way to investment and to consumption and is not applicable to the production of real resources exchanged. Only the VA created exclusively concerns the period.

A third part of the model would be the outside world. We shall only marginally deal with it. By definition the VA created in this realm is not our concern. We shall assume that the subsets of real resources which we have defined as consumption and (real) investment within the economy considered include all resources available for exchange, whether produced in the economy or imported and shall not directly consider real resources produced within the economy and exported. These assumptions allow us to reduce the relations between the economy considered and the outside world to financial flows between the four AGENTS and the outside. They are made for simplicity's sake and are conventional.

We have now to proceed with the specification of the model

before establishing in the next section the identities and relations between the variables.

Firstly we have to define precisely the four representative AGENTS.

1. The FIRM represents the productive sector whether public or private, individual or collective. This means that it aggregates all agents who produce and trade in real goods and services whether they are public institutions, firms of private or public ownership, individual professionals, farmers, craftsmen etc. While of course dealing in finance the FIRM is distinct from the BANK as this last AGENT is defined here. The same is true of the HOUSE-HOLD and of the STATE.

2. The HOUSEHOLD represents the sector of people, families, associations, clubs, churches etc. who consume, save and pay taxes. The HOUSEHOLD can distribute incomes for housing rents and domestic services. If this is the case, rents are considered as current spending and the compensation for domestic services is assumed to remain within the representative AGENT so it does not appear. People who are productive agents are fictitiously split up into a part belonging to the HOUSEHOLD and a part belonging to the FIRM.

3. The BANK is the part of the productive sector which trades exclusively in money and other financial assets such as stocks, bonds, options and futures etc. It includes the part of government which manages its purely financial tasks, in particular the activity of the Central Bank, the money issue, government securities, Treasury notes etc. The BANK is the AGENT who manages the credit, including the creation of money within the banking activity. The BANK also includes the insurance industry.

4. The STATE is the AGENT who has a double role. It manages the public budgets and is the decision maker in social, political and economic policies.

1. The FIRM creates the primary value added: VA_f^p equal to sales of the product minus purchases of inputs. This is by definition a PIT. The 'enlarged' VA_f^e of the FIRM is the sum of this PIT and of two PNITs: the subsidies from the STATE t_f^s and the net credit from the BANK c_f^b.

The FIRM distributes the enlarged VA into PNITs which are:

- the income distributed to the HOUSEHOLD which is the sum of wages, salaries, dividends, interests etc., i_f
- the taxes, dividends and interests to the STATE, t_f
- the financial investment or saving or purchases of assets to the BANK, s_f
- the dividends and interests to the BANK, d_f
- the cost of real investment, e_f

2. The HOUSEHOLD creates its primary VA:VA_h^p which is equal to its incomes from the three other AGENTS minus its current consumption as defined. Its enlarged VA_h^e is the sum of this first total PNIT, of the net consumer and mortgage credit c_h^b from the BANK and of the net subsidies of all kinds from the STATE, t_h^s.

The HOUSEHOLD distibutes its enlarged VA_h^e into PNITs which are:

- taxes t_h to the STATE
- its financial saving or investment or purchase of financial assets s_h to the BANK
- the cost of its real investment in durables, housing etc. as defined, e_h
- interest to the BANK, d_h

3. The BANK creates its primary VA_b^p equal to the difference between the proceeds of sales, which are the receipts of dividends, interests and capital gains, and the outlays which are interests paid for deposits and the BANK's consumption. Its enlarged VA_b^e is the sum of the primary VA_b^p and of all PNITs received which for the BANK are *not* the interests and dividends received, which are included in its primary VA_b^p but all savings received i.e. the sales of assets and the balance of current deposits of the HOUSEHOLD, the FIRM and the STATE.

The financial saving of the BANK remains within this AGENT and does not appear. It has in part a peculiar origin stemming from the phenomenon of risk pooling currently called the bank transformation of credit. The current deposits redeemable on sight create by their statistic a disposable 'saving' as they are almost never simultaneously claimed. This allows the banks to offset in a safe measure its distributed credit, even on long term, against the balance of current deposits. The risk pooling creates a similar effect within the insurance industry since the perception of uncertainty is mostly subjective for the insurance buyers while it is mostly objective and different for the insurance sellers. This effect is integrated however into the purchases and sales of insurance and appears within the primary VA_b^p of the BANK.

4. The STATE's primary created VA_s^p is assumed to be the sum of its fiscal revenue from the other AGENTS and from itself and of the proceeds of the sales of goods and services when included in the public budgets, minus all its outlays for current inputs defined as the STATE's consumption. If the STATE's sales are not included in the budget, for instance the receipts for entry tickets for parks, they shall appear within the FIRM. The same convention is applied to dividends and interests received. If not included in the budget, they belong to the BANK.

The STATE's enlarged VA_s^e is the sum of the primary VA_s^p and of the deficit financing m_b, by money issue and/or by credit from the BANK. As stated above, the sales of government securities and other open market operations belong to the BANK, the activity of the Treasury included.

The STATE's VA distribution consists of:

- taxes paid to itself t_s
- incomes distributed to the HOUSEHOLD i_s (the wages of government employees)
- subsidies to the HOUSEHOLD $t_s^h = t_h^s$ (medicare, the poor, family allowances etc.)
- subsidies to the FIRM $t_s^f = t_f^s$
- the cost of the STATE's real investment e_s. Its parts are transport, communication, urban and similar infrastructures, when publicly financed, buildings, monuments and shrines, armaments but not current military expenditures nor most of public goods and services, all included in the consumption of the STATE.
- interest payments to the BANK d_s

A comment on saving and investment is in order here to clarify our presentation of the model.

1. The FIRM's saving in a narrow sense is, as previously stated, the sum of the depreciation allowance on its capital and of 'retained

profits'. Marx and his followers have called this part of the VA distribution with dividends and interests added, the share of the 'capitalists' in the distribution and have labelled it 'exploitation'. Our model being essentially descriptive does not adopt this value judgment. But we do agree that in a sense the sum of the depreciation and of retained profits is, on a macroscale, a 'forced' saving if we define as 'free' saving the result of the personal voluntary partition by people of their incomes into consumption and such a saving.

The total saving of the FIRM is a part of its enlarged VA_f^e equal to the sum of its cash holdings, of its financial investment in assets, transferred to the BANK, s_f and of the cost of its real investment e_f. Quite often a great part of this real investment is financed by external credit coming from the BANK, (c_f^b) as loan or equity and from the STATE as subsidies (t_f^s). It is assumed here, as is mostly the case in real life, that the HOUSEHOLD invests in assets exclusively through the BANK.

2. The HOUSEHOLD creates a saving from its enlarged VA and voluntarily transfers part of it to the BANK. This is called the financial investment by the HOUSEHOLD consisting in purchases of stocks and bonds, in deposits on current accounts etc. We include holdings in cash in the financial investment. This investment is a loan by the HOUSEHOLD, explicitly contracted, except the last item, which is also a loan made to society in its whole but felt as implicit. The same is true of the FIRM as regards its financial investment. As regards holdings in cash, reference to Chapter 8, Section 1 should be of some utility.

The remainder of the total saving of the HOUSEHOLD, its real investment e_h, does not appear in financial operations and thus does not interest people active in finance for which the 'private saving' is currently assumed to be only the financial saving as just defined. By the way, in current economics the 'private saving' does include expenses on housing but excludes for instance purchases of furniture. This is to us is an inconsistency due to the legal difference between mobile and fixed real assets. The transactions in land property are a special case and will not be considered in this book. The HOUSEHOLD seldom allows in its saving for depreciation on its real investments.

3. The BANK's essential task is to manage the savings of the

other three AGENTS. As stated it also creates its own enlarged VA_b^e and a part of the distribution of this VA is the BANK's direct real investment. The other part of its total saving is the BANK's financial investment which is considered in our model as remaining within this AGENT and added to other such investments.

4. The STATE acts in its material activity in a way similar to that of the FIRM even if its management methods differ. In the social and political sphere on the contrary the STATE acts more like a HOUSEHOLD. The saving of the STATE is even more 'forced' than the saving of the FIRM as its sources is fiscal revenue and deficit financing. Both are mandatory transfers of resources from the rest of the economy.

The BANK and the STATE are the main levers by which societies, while being governed by political institutions, control the economy. What is currently called the budgetary or, incorrectly, the financial policy is the playground of the STATE with intense links to the BANK, the FIRM and the HOUSEHOLD. What is currently called monetary and should properly be called financial policy is the playground of the BANK with the same or other intense links to the other three AGENTS.

Our model endeavours to 'paint' a dynamic reality. All saving, all credit and all investment are dynamic processes. This means that these PNITs are not only transfers between the four AGENTS within the considered period but are also temporal transfers between the past, the present and the future of all these AGENTS. For instance the financial savings of the FIRM and of the HOUSE-HOLD, in the considered period, are PNITs to the future while the deficit financing, a PNIT from the BANK to the STATE is a PNIT from the future to the present, etc. We shall use this point later on.

We integrate the fifth 'AGENT', the outside world, within the FIRM as regards exchanges in real resources and within the BANK for financial operations. The fact is that these last operations today largely exceed those of current trade and that the BANK is today almost wholly integrated into a 'world-economy', a global network of continuous and instantaneous operations. We cannot give more detailed consideration to the important subject of world-economy which would require a separate book and we conclude this section by a remark on the main differences between market and planned economies. Firstly, in the latter the STATE and the BANK are blended into one AGENT. The second difference is that prices and quantities are not chosen by real agents but are planned by this unique AGENT, the STATE, moreover owning the FIRM. In the reality of planned economies the differences tend to wither but remain in doctrines and teachings.

SECTION 2. PRESENTATION OF THE MODEL

We refer to Figure 14.1.

Firstly we shall write equalities of flows for each AGENT and secondly we shall try to distinguish the instrumental relations between some of these flows. The policy or behavioral variables in these relations govern the evolution in time of our static model. This part of our study will essentially be contained in Section 4.

1.. The FIRM

One has:

$$\text{VA}_f^e = \text{VA}_f^p + t_f^s + c_f^b = i_f + t_f + d_f + s_f + e_f \tag{14.1}$$

The incomes i_f distributed by the FIRM are here the 'earned' incomes w. We assume what all unearned incomes transit through the BANK. In our model d is included in the flow d_f from the FIRM to the BANK.

The total tax burden on the FIRM t_f is, as shown in the appendix to Chapter 11, a sum of different taxations. With some simplifications and in our present notations, we can state

$$t_f = t_1 + t_2 + t_3 + t_4$$

where:

$t_1 = h_1(\text{VA}_f^p - e_f)$	is the VAT,
$t_2 = h_2 w$	is the social contribution and the wage tax if any exists,
$t_3 = h_3(d + s)$	is the corporate income tax,
$t_4 = h_4 W$	is the property tax.

The volume of t_f is closely dependent on the choices of the FIRM within the whole of its management. The STATE chooses only the tax rates h_1, h_2, h_3, h_4. s is the fiscal saving of the FIRM as defined in Chapter 11. It is here:

$$s = s_f + e_f - c_f^b - t_f^s - b_1$$

The balance sheet saving $s + b_1$ is equal to the sum of financial and real investment minus subsidies and bank credit received; b_1 is the depreciation allowance and W the property tax assessment wealth.

d_f is the loan and equity burden of the FIRM and flows to the BANK. As stated above, the HOUSEHOLD does not lend to the FIRM nor does directly buy its stock but does so exclusively through the BANK.

s_f is the financial investment of the FIRM. In real life this item's volume depends on comparisons between the market real interest rates and the possible VA_f^p creation. Quite often the bulk of the FIRM's financial needs are covered by external credit. This means that the FIRM's own saving s_f is nil or negative in a narrow sense. But as we include in s_f all repayments in the period of the principal of debts, it will be positive for most personal firms and can also be considered so for the FIRM.

e_f is, as stated above, the outlay in the period for all real investment for production factors which will contribute to the VA creation in several future periods.

On the instrumental level the variables of (14.1) have the following roles:

- The VA_f^p is the result of production and price policies and of other choices of the FIRM. It expresses the purpose of the activity. It is widely accepted that VA_f^p should be positive; if not, the FIRM shall in the long term cease to exist.
- t_f^s is the expression of the STATE's economic policy. If t_f^s exist it means that the society, for any reason within its set of social choices, allows the FIRM to remain active even if its VA_f^p becomes negative, by exception to the rule just stated. On the macrolevel t_f^s exists and is rather important in most economies.
- c_f^b expresses the normal relation between the FIRM and the BANK. The latter's role in the economy is to collect the savings of all agents and to make them 'work', i.e. contribute to the VA creation by supplying credit to the FIRM.

- i_f, according to the assumption at the beginning of this section, is the 'labour cost' of usual economics which reasons on the equality:

$$(VA_f^e - i_f) = (VA_f^p - i_f) + t_f^s + c_f^b = t_f + d_f + s_f + e_f \quad (14.1)'$$

and establishes relations between production and price policies VA_f^p, the profit $(d_f + s_f)$ and the investment e_f; moreover relations are established between these flows and a stock called the capital or productive equipment.

We propose to put all variables in (14.1)', 'except the VA_f^p on an equal footing and build a new model of their relations. For the purpose of a comparison with usual theories, let us simplify (14.1)' by assuming $s_f = 0$ and $c_f^b = e_f$, obtaining:

$$VA_f^p = i_f + d_f + (t_f - t_f^s) = I_H + I_B + T \quad (14.1)''$$

The value added created by the FIRM is the sum of incomes distributed to the HOUSEHOLD and to the BANK and of the mandatory net transfer to the STATE. The current theories are built on this equality: I_H are the wages, I_B the profits and T the net participation of the STATE. The unique choice criterion of the FIRM is to maximize I_B.

In our view, and contrary to these theories, the actual partition of the VA is not the result of the simple choice of maximizing I_B but of a contract after negotiations and/or of trade–offs between many criteria of all four AGENTS, generating a sensible partition into the three flows specified in the right hand side of (14.1)''.

2.   The HOUSEHOLD

When restricted to economics the choices for the HOUSEHOLD are expressed in the equalities:

$$VA_h^e = VA_h^p + c_h^b + t_h^s = i_f + i_b + i_s -$$
$$C_h + c_h^b + t_h^s = d_h + t_h + s_h + e_h \quad (14.2)$$

- the total income $I = i_f + i_b + i_s$ is a flow in the period from the other three AGENTS
- the consumption C_h represents in our model only the outlays for current goods and services consumed within the period, i.e. delivering *no* services or satisfactions after its end.

- c_h^b is the net credit to the HOUSEHOLD within the period.
- t_h^s is the total of subsidies received from public bodies. It includes all welfare payments, social security and family aids etc.
- d_h are the interest payments of the HOUSEHOLD to the BANK.
- t_h is the total of taxes paid by the HOUSEHOLD essentially the income and property taxes.
- s_h is the financial investment of the HOUSEHOLD.
- e_h is its total real investment, most of it in durables and housing.

These flows differ in their nature.

- On a macroscale the income I has been decided upon in the VA distribution of the three other AGENTS. One can assume it to be exogenous, while on a microscale each of its components depends on the behaviour of the AGENT receiving any of them.
- t_h^s and t_h result from exogeneous choices of the STATE as regards the rules of their assessment. On the microscale their actual flows also depend on the behaviours and choices of the HOUSEHOLD; on the macrolevel the statistics of these two PNITs are elements of the STATE's economic and social policies.
- the total saving and the investments of the HOUSEHOLD are obviously not only dependent on the propensity to save, i.e. of the marginal or mean ratio s_h/I, as is currently assumed but result from choices of the HOUSEHOLD on the partition of flows on which it is capable of deciding upon. The HOUSE-HOLD chooses in the period:

> its consumption C_h
> its new credit c_h^b
> its financial investment s_h
> its real investment e_h

While C_h and e_h bring immediate utility or satisfaction, c_h^b and s_h are financial choices where such parameters as the interest rate and the maturity terms play a role. One can assume for illustration, as we have done for the FIRM, $c_h^b = e_h$ so that (14.2) can be written as:

$$I + t_h^s = C_h + d_h + t_h + s_h \qquad (14.2)'$$

If I, t_h^s, t_h, d_h are exogenous in the period the remaining choice set is C_h, s_h. This is the historic case of the choice by income bearers between consumption and saving on which many economic theories have been built. Our model shows that in real life the sets of choices, constraints on choices and criteria of choices are larger.

3. The BANK

The equalities expressing the BANK's activity can be written as:

$$VA_b^e = VA_b^p + s_f + s_h = t_b + m_b + i_b + c_b^h + c_b^f + e_b \qquad (14.3)$$

and

$$VA_b^p = d_f + d_h + d_s - C_b$$

One can assume that the items t_b, i_b, e_b, C_b are exogenous. The main 'factor' of the BANK's activity is the collected saving $s_f + s_h$ and its main 'product' the credit $m_b + c_b^h + c_b^f$. If $s_f + s_h$ is invariable any increase in m_b decreases the sum $c_b^h + c_b^f$. This is the expression of the crowding-out effect produced in a period by public deficits. As stressed above, s_f is limited in our economies so the essential 'production factor' of the BANK's activity is the financial investment of the HOUSEHOLD. In usual economics this is called 'private saving'. We have precisely defined what it is. Intense promotion is current in order to enhance this important economic parameter. The constraint on the BANK's activity can be written as:

$$s_f + s_h + D = [C_b + t_b + i_b + e_b + m_b] + (c_b^h + c_b^f) \qquad (14.3)'$$

where

$$D = d_f + d_h + d_s$$

It follows that for a given level of the BANK's activity and of the STATE's deficit in a period (the square bracket), the intensity of the transformation of savings into credits depends on (a) the thrift of the HOUSEHOLD, (b) the importance of the profits of the

FIRM and (c) the exact repayment of debts by the three other AGENTS. Item (b) is generated by a high PIT, i.e. a high VA creation, for instance by price cartels within the FIRM. This picture, a slight discrepancy to what has been previously proposed, is however a good representation of the world-economy BANK AGENT in recent years.

4.   The STATE

Its equalities are

$$VA_s^e = VA_s^p + m_b = t_s + i_s + t_h^s + t_f^s + e_s + d_s \qquad (14.4)$$

and

$$VA_s^p = t_h + t_f + t_b + t_s - C_s = T - C_s$$

The sales of goods and services are neglected or transferred to the FIRM. T is the total fiscal revenue, C_s the public consumption.

This shows a discrepancy from the usual national accounts which use the equality

$$VA_s^p = i_s$$

We shall not analyze this difference while of course considering our approach to be consistent. The STATE's VA creation consists of its fiscal revenue minus its consumption as is defined for any VA creation and as we have proposed above. The VA_s^e is distributed as incomes and subsidies and as the total investment cost. The 'deficit financing', i.e. the main PNIT between the STATE and the BANK includes the STATE's financial saving if any since m_b is the net deficit financing.

The STATE, as explained above, is the carrier of the social utility, i.e. in the language used here it carries the three sets of social possible choices, social constraints on these choices and social criteria of choices. Its economic tools of action are the fiscal policy symbolized by $T = \Sigma t$ and the budgetary or expense policy consisting in choices of its consumption and of all PNITs such as t_h^s and $t_f^s t_h^s$ is the social policy of the STATE, i.e. all transfers to the HOUSEHOLD for ethical, demographic or solidarity criteria. t_f^s is the economic policy of the STATE which, together with t_f (the fiscality on the FIRM) and t_h (the fiscality on the HOUSEHOLD) endeavours to influence the sectors of production and of consumption in view of an overall balance in trade, of price stability and of full employment. This policy also uses the public consumption C_s and the public investment e_s both of which are moreover main tools for the fulfillment of the goals of the STATE as regards prestige and power, besides supplying society with the necessary public goods and public infrastructure, including security, law and order. The investment e_s could be divided into productive and unproductive. This last quality is not the same for the STATE as for the FIRM.

To conclude this section here are some additional comments:

1. Our model completes the description of Chapter 4. It is less literary although not as mathematical as usual models are in micro and macroeconomics.

2. The HOUSEHOLD and the STATE are by definition spatially defined AGENTS. The HOUSEHOLD represents real consuming and saving individuals, families and associations living in a specified territory bounded by international frontiers. The STATE which represents all public bodies: elementary communities, local and regional governments and central Government is also defined within a given territory on which all these bodies are competent.

The FIRM and the BANK are on the contrary more temporal than spatial. Both are nowadays elements of the world-economy, transgressing spatial boundaries. It is a mostly artificial assumption to consider these two AGENTS within a given space in a given period of time. Such assumption is, however, unavoidable if we want to build a static economic model.

3. We deem it necessary to recall that the influence of technology and organization which is currently expressed by production functions is in our approach imbedded into the VA creation where it expresses the efficiency of the economic process. The exchange of factors and products within the FIRM and the exchange of products between the FIRM and the other three AGENTS is outside our model. We leave aside the theories of prices, the input-output analysis and most of the usual micro and macroeconomics. In Section 4 on dynamics we shall only consider the price variations between periods, aggregated in a GDP deflator or a CPI. We devote Section 3 to a more detailed study of the VA creation and aggregation.

4. Consumption C and real investment, e, are aggregated exchanges of monetary flows for real flows (amounts of resources in the period). The two categories C and e only differ, as has already been recalled, in the fact that consumption is 'consumed' as exchange and satisfaction of needs and desires *within the period* (or at a given point of time) while investment if it results by definition from the exchange in the period and is measured by the monetary outlay for investment goods in the period, will satisfy the needs and desires in several periods, including or not the present one. If we consider the aggregated VA in the period (the GDP currently denoted Y) one cannot write, as is currently done, $Y = C + I$ in constant prices since the financial operations within the economy and with the outside world distort the picture. Measuring the GDP in 'real terms', i.e. deflating the monetary VA total by a price index, is a fictitious if not false dynamic operation since the monetary VA total in a period is different from the monetary total $C + I$.

5. Those who control the BANK naturally wish to increase the share of the aggregated VA (of the GDP) which transits through this AGENT. For instance, and as an example, they are opposed to the type of management of pension funds by which resources are directly transferred from active adults to inactive pensioners. They prefer the processes of saving by active adults whose proceeds will make up the future pension outlays. The transfer is essentially the same in the two methods, i.e. a temporal PNIT. But in the first method the financial resources cannot be 'invested' that is flow through the BANK since in a period the contributions to pension funds by active adults serve to pay out pensions to inactive seniors. It is obvious that such a system leads to a decrease in the volume of available saving in a period.

The same remark could be made as regards the STATE. Any decrease in the fiscal revenue decreases the volume of available finance under the control of this AGENT.

One can state that the activities of the BANK and of the STATE result in an increase in the scope of the sets of constraints on choices of the FIRM and of the HOUSEHOLD and a corresponding decrease in the scope of the sets of constraints on choices of the BANK and of the STATE.

6. The aggregate AGENT called the STATE is the only one of

the four that creates its VA by a mandatory PNIT from other agents. Taxes have existed for eons and their existence is justified by the unique quality of the STATE to be the carrier of the social set of choices, as distinct from the sets of choices of other agents. Now the existence of this compulsion leads in our complex societies to a replica of the child play of sheriffs and thiefs: the former who are the revenue collectors try to catch the latter, the taxpayers and the latter try to avoid being caught and to pay . . . This play gives birth to an underground economy which of course is not represented in most economic models, including ours.

7. A small remark is finally to be made: our model does not account for the existence of stocks of real resources or for their financing and their valuation in the accounts of the FIRM. This does not accord with standard accounting procedures.

SECTION 3. AGGREGATION

The aggregation concerns

(a) the nature of representative AGENTS: the FIRM, the HOUSEHOLD, the BANK, the STATE and the outside world.

(b) the aggregation of monetary flows circulating between the four AGENTS.

(c) the real aggregates CONSUMPTION and INVESTMENT.

(d) the aggregation of the VA created in the economy into a global representation of the wealth created in a given period of time within this economy and usually called the gross domestic product GDP denoted by Y.

(a) The Nature of Representative AGENTS

As previously stated we adopt the convenient assumption that AGENTS are fuzzy sets of real economic agents active in the period. These sets possess manifold inclusions of subsets and their elements can belong to more than one set. The picture of a multi-dimensional Russian doll aptly illustrates the situation. People can be elements of the set HOUSEHOLD *and* of the set FIRM; people can simultaneously be active as consumers and as creators of the PIT which generates VA by exchanging money against real resources. Other people, for instance the young and the old, are elements of only the HOUSEHOLD and not of the FIRM.

The FIRM in its bulk is the set of real collective agents commonly called firms. To be precise, firms in our understanding are not production sites but legal and financial 'moral' persons. These two possible characters of the concept of firm are blended in small firms but are mostly distinct in medium and big productive collective agents. The case of multinationals, i.e. of such agents active in several economies, i.e. elements of several sets called the FIRM, is special and will not be dealt with in detail.

A model is by definition a simplified representation of the reality. Thus we have to simplify the concept of the FIRM by adopting the two following definitions:

1. The FIRM is the set of productive agents each of which receives and delivers within the economy and in a given period of time the monetary flows shown on Figure 14.1. The definition is similar to the one of money: money is what money does . . .

2. The FIRM is the set of productive agents who exchange real resources for money. The definition is injective but not bijective as other agents exchange as well.

In our understanding definition (1) excludes from the concept of the FIRM the intermediary trade consisting in the activity of its elements buying current inputs and selling all outputs. By an inconvenient but necessary exception to this rule the activity of the elements of the FIRM consisting in buying real investment is included.

In its present state the model as defined by (1) also neglects the relations of the elements of the FIRM with the outside world in the realm of real resources and in that of monetary flows. For instance we do not bother about the origin of real investment, whether it is of domestic or foreign origin.

Definition (1) settles the problem of multiple facilities constituting a firm. While within an economy it consolidates a firm into its center which deals with monetary flows, it excludes from its concept all its activities outside the economy. The problems of ownership and of wealth are not considered here.

The definition (2) includes within the FIRM the commercial

activities of the STATE such as the State postal service. This activity is in our aggregation an element of the FIRM.

The case of the BANK is grosso modo similar. As stated, definition (1) applies to a part of its activity while definition (2) has to be worded as

(2') The BANK is the set of agents who deal exclusively in finance. Tautologically the BANK includes all the banking activities of the STATE. The specificity of the BANK, as compared to the FIRM and in some aspects to the STATE is that its links to the outside world are so tight and so intense that it is difficult to apply to it definition (1) in all its rigour. For instance its flows of incoming savings (i.e. of the financial capital available) and of outflowing credits (i.e. of public and private loans and of purchases of stocks and securities) are at present global. One could propose limiting these flows to the national currency and excluding all deals in foreign exchange. This proposal would perhaps have been correct some fifty years ago but it is unrealistic in the present situation with the existence of powerful 'xenocurrency' markets dealing in a world money.

We now have to consider the STATE. This AGENT is the one which the multidimensional fuzzy Russian doll describes at best. It is not a set of equiimportant elements as is grosso modo the HOUSEHOLD nor the set of legally equal productive agents as is the FIRM. It is a pyramid of social structures with widely dispersed choice sets, in other terms of widely dispersed degrees of freedom. These structures are not economic but political. Their economic role is only important as a means of achieving social and political goals; it is not as primary a rule as it is for the FIRM or the BANK. In a sense, economics while very important is somewhat on the margin for both the STATE and the HOUSEHOLD, both governed by the criterion of utility.

As stated above we exclude from the STATE's activity its primary banking activity, usually concentrated in the Central Bank and in the Treasury. It is assumed that the management of the budget remains within the STATE and is not the Treasury's task but is that of some other agency of the executive branch.

A controversial matter about the aggregate STATE is found in the literature. Two schools are in presence. One assumes or asserts that one can aggregate the three sets of choices, constraints on choices and criteria of choices of all real agents into social or collective sets of these arguments. A second school denies this possibility and assumes an exogenous existence of the three sets for a society. Such sets deem to stem not only from material and rational realms of activity but also, as is the case for real elementary agents, from the realm of the sacred including beliefs, symbols, and traditions, what is called, in short, the culture of society.

The question arises: which representative AGENT operates on social choice and criteria sets? The answer seems for us straightforward. We have included in the set of agents the public agents and in the set of the four representative AGENTS the STATE. This is in our view the only AGENT carrying the social set of choices and considering the social set of criteria of choices. The other three AGENTS are deprived of this capacity; neither the HOUSEHOLD, or the FIRM or the BANK has social goals and available social choices. They represent elementary agents without aggregating their sets of choices. Thus the STATE is the AGENT less different from elementary agents than the three other AGENTS as regards the availability of the three sets governing choices.

(b) The Aggregation of Monetary Flows

As represented in Figure 14.1 this does not require a comment. It is currently obtained by the techniques of national accounts. Differences in classifications and some other details would merit a refined analysis which we skip here.

(c) The Aggregates of CONSUMPTION and INVESTMENT

In Figure 14.1 these are monetary flows representing aggregates of real resources which are sets of enormous variety and cardinality in quantities, qualities and prices of goods and services produced and exchanged in an economy within a given period of time. The powerful dimensionality reducer of money allows us to operate in this manner. The partition into two flows of *consumption* and *investment* is a necessary convenience, no more.

As already stated the usual production, price, market, input-output, growth and development theories deal mostly with the economics of real resources. In this book on principles we skip this part of the discipline since one has to limit the scope of a study.

(d) The Aggregation of the Value Added Is a Problem

As mainly analyzed here and in Chapter 11 the VA created by agents seems to present many double counts. We shall now try to eliminate these double counts and also clarify the entire picture as far as is possible.

It seems that only the primary VA shall be included in the aggregation since all the enlargements are PNITs between the four AGENTS and, in consequence, are counted twice. This opinion must be largely qualified. Many of the PNITs concerned can be considered as originating in the preceding periods of time or as flowing into periods following the period considered. Even if in some cases, as we shall see, this assumption seems to be unrealistic, it is very convenient. It allows us to obtain a consistent static (synchronic) definition of the GDP which otherwise would be very complicated to assess in a non-dynamic formalization.

A convenient way to see the issue is to write the equalities (14.—) together:

(14.1) $\mathrm{VA}_f^e = \mathrm{VA}_f^p + t_f^s + c_f^b = i_f + t_f + d_f + s_f + e_f$

(14.2) $\mathrm{VA}_h^e = i_f + i_s + i_b - C_h + c_h^b + t_h^s = d_h + t_h + s_h + e_h$

(14.3) $\mathrm{VA}_b^e = d_f + d_h + d_s - C_b + s_f + s_h = t_b + m_b + i_b +$
$\qquad\qquad c_b^h + c_b^f + e_b$

(14.4) $\mathrm{VA}_s^e = T - C_s + m_b = i_s + t_h^s + t_f^s + e_s + d_s + t_s$

to which it is necessary to add:

(14.5) $C = C_h + C_b + C_s$

(14.6) $I = e_f + e_h + e_b + e_s$

We have explicated in these equalities only the FIRM's VA_f^p as it is the only one in our model created by PITs, the VA of other agents being due to PNITs.

The FIRM's enlarged VA_f^e consists of the primary VA_f^p plus transfers from the STATE (subsidies) and from the BANK (credit and possible equity raised in the period). We shall assume that these two transfers have their origin in the preceding period and count this entire enlarged VA in the aggregate $Y = $ GDP. By similar procedures for other agents we can write the following reduced equalities where the PNITs in the period are eliminated:

$$(14.1)^r \quad VA_f^e = VA_f^p + t_f^s + c_f^b = i_f + t_f + d_f + s + e_f$$
$$(14.2)^r \quad VA_h^e = c_h^b + t_h^s - C_h = t_h + e_h + s_h$$
$$(14.3)^r \quad VA_b^e = d_h + d_s - C_b = t_b + i_b + c_b^h + c_b^f + e_b$$
$$(14.4)^r \quad VA_s^e = m_b - C_s = i_s + t_h^s + t_f^s + e_s$$

With equalities (14.5) and (14.6) we obtain: $Y = $ GDP $= $ VA is equal as created to:

(A) the primary VA created in the FIRM +
    transfers from the STATE (from preceding periods) +
    bank credit from the BANK (from preceding periods) +
    interest payments from the HOUSEHOLD and the
    STATE to the BANK +
    the deficit financing from the BANK to the STATE,

and $Y = $ GDP $= $ VA is equal as distributed to

(B) the incomes distributed to the HOUSEHOLD +
    the transfers from the STATE (to the following
    periods) +
    the bank credit from the BANK (to the following
    periods) +
    the savings of the FIRM and of the HOUSEHOLD +
    the interest payments from the FIRM to the BANK.

One can of course adopt different assumptions with regards to the dynamics of the GDP. Ours is only an illustration.

While for the sake of consistent presentation we included the consumption of the BANK in Figure 14.1 in fact we explicated in this diagram only the consumptions of the HOUSEHOLD and the STATE. These two consumptions are parts of the two ultimate economic goals in the period, that is in the synchronic approach. The first satisfies the needs and desires of people and contributes to their happiness. The second consumption satisfies the needs and desires of societies as expressed in the choices of governments. These choices and the very existence of governments is the result of the political activity which we do not consider here.

Consumption is not the only ultimate goal of economic activity. The investment e_h of the HOUSEHOLD satisfies the diachronic personal needs and desires while the other three components of total investment play the same role with regard to economic, social and political diachronic needs and desires. For instance, part of the investment of the STATE satisfies the desire and need of the society to assert its prestige, its power and its influence in this world as well as to promote and enhance its cultural specificity. The remainder of the STATE, FIRM and BANK investments develop the future capacities of the economy destined to serve the people.

A question could be raised as to how the equalities written in this chapter could represent an optimal state of the economy. This point has already been touched upon in Chapter 11. Our approach does not maximize any parameter and the assumptions of Walras-Pareto are not applicable within the model. In the Walras-Pareto optimal state of perfect equilibrium the optimal price vector corresponds to the absence of PITs while the process of proving the existence of this state assumes the absence of PNITs.

Let us assume however the existence of an optimal state in our model, without proving it, that is without deleting from it all PNITs. The condition that all PITs shall disappear is fulfilled by writing $VA_f = 0$ for all firms; they sell 'at cost' (the labour not being a cost) As in the Walras-Pareto proof, we reason in macroeconomics and write over equalities by deleting VA_f^p.

This variant of our model represents an economy in which the FIRM sells rigourously at cost. It follows that the incomes, the taxes, the savings of all agents are elements of PNITs between them. The real resources consumed and invested are bought for a part of these transfers. Such an economy seems to require a very high fiscality and very high public saving that is a very high degree of centralization under the control of the BANK and of the STATE of all available or created wealth. Such an economy seems to be very inefficient and not at all optimal.

SECTION 4. DYNAMIC INTERPRETATION AND DISCUSSION OF THE MODEL

We touched upon dynamics in the preceding section when we examined the VA aggregation. We shall now look more closely into what happens in successive periods of time and, at variance with the remainder of this chapter, by a continuous approach. We shall consider growth, inflation and employment. We shall not deal with development since it pertains predominantly to extra-economic social, political and cultural processes.

The FIRM represents the productive economy so it is mainly concerned with the subject. Contrary to its usual treatment where only productive economy behaviours are analyzed we have explicated the fact that all four AGENTS, the FIRM, the HOUSEHOLD, the BANK and the STATE employ people, distribute incomes and save. Also contrary to the usual economics we do not connect distributed incomes to employment, i.e. to the activity of active adult individuals.

We propose to formalize an obvious link between (i) the employment E, (ii) the gross domestic product GDP denoted Y, i.e. the total VA created and aggregated as shown in Section 3 above, (iii) the stock of equipment (real capital) present in the period K and the load factor of the economy l in a general heterogeneous relation

$$F(E_t, Y_t, K_t, l_t) = 0$$

It is immediate that

$$K_t = K_{t-1} + I_t - D_t$$

where I_t is the gross real investment at time t and D_t the real wear and tear of the equipment and not the depreciation allowance as defined above. The term l is correctly expressed by the ratio of actual Y to a potential $Y°$ which would be obtained by the maximum possible economic activity. l is often assumed to be equal to the ratio of the utilization of the capacities of K_t but is in fact a more complex parameter implying employment, organization, a stable currency, law and order etc. The problem of estimating l is the main econometric and statistical difficulty but by far not the only one.

We can write F with E as a dependent variable:

$$E_t = f(Y_t, K_t, l_t)$$

The specification of F and/or of f is a second econometric problem as found among other problems in many macromodels of the literature. We shall not grapple here with this enormous effort.

Following Okun's Law we state that $\partial E/\partial Y$ is in general positive: the employment rises with economic growth. It would be better to use the form F and write its total differential as:

$$\frac{\partial F}{\partial E} dE + \frac{\partial F}{\partial Y} dY + \frac{\partial F}{\partial K} dK + \frac{\partial F}{\partial l} dl = 0$$

and then study these variations. If employment rises with Y for instance, Y is an increasing function of E, K and l. F can be considered as expressing the numerous feedbacks imbedded into economic dynamics. A more general relation could be written as:

$$\mathcal{F}\,(E, K, Y, p, B, l) = 0$$

where p is the price index and B the external net balance.

Professor Okun estimated the elasticity of employment with respect to the product to be 1/3 in the United States: a 3 per cent increase in Y increased employment by 1 per cent of the active population. He did not really estimate F and assumed the increase in Y due to an increase in l to be possible in the short term. One can doubt that this is so for all arguments of the variation of l.

The whole of F should be submitted to econometric specification. In particular the partial derivative of f, $\partial E/\partial K$ is of great interest. It can be positive or negative. The problem has been discussed on a microlevel in Chapter 11. On a macrolevel one can state heuristically that capacity increasing investments increase employment while productivity enhancing investments decrease it within a certain time (on short and medium term). The econometric problem is quite difficult since the data discriminating the two types of investment are seldom available and, besides, the distinction between capacity or productivity investments is artificial: productivity investments most often increase capacities and capacity investments almost always increase productivity since any new purchase of equipment follows the technological progress.

The variable Y in the relation F is the result of the activity of all four AGENTS. So it would be correct for any analysis of growth to consider all these AGENTS and not, as is usual, only the FIRM. If we explicit Y in F by writing

$$Y = g\,(E, K, l)$$

g will be increasing in all three arguments. One must also assume that Y increases with the increasing skills of people, resulting from education, training and motivation and with improved technologies of activities resulting from applications of the scientific and applied progress not only in the material means of production but also in such applications for the organization and behaviours of people. These influences which change g, depend on what is called the culture of society, its 'development'.

The GDP, i.e. the aggregated VA, is only created if markets for the production exist so that the positive PITs defining the VA can be obtained. This condition concerns the relation between VA creation and distribution. It is formulated for instance in the Keynesian theory of multipliers and of effective demand. The relation has been concisely but very partially formulated by Helmut Schmidt who stated that 'profits (i.e. savings) of today make investments of tomorrow and employment the day after'. We see from our presentation (which is by far not a precise analysis) that this strict causality must be qualified. The whole of the economic processes, not only saving and investment has to be considered. As regards the real investment, much depends on whether this investment is productive or for public goods or unproductive by outlays for prestige and power or war . . .We shall not go any further on the subject and only propose some remarks.

Consider the two transfers from the STATE: to the FIRM t_f^s and to the HOUSEHOLD t_h^s and their sum t^s as a function of time.

If we assume, as is proposed in Section 3 that the t^s which contributes to Y created in the period originates in the preceding period and is now denoted t_c^s (in the past) while the t^s distributed in the period will contribute to Y in the following period (t_d^s in the future) the net impact of t^s in the period will be $t^{ns} = t_c^s - t_d^s$. If t^s is an inceasing function of time, the t^{ns} of the period will be negative. The transfers from the STATE will brake growth.

If we consider the two transfers t_f^s and t_h^s separately and not only their total t^s it will be possible to compensate the negative impact of the welfare increase t_h^s by a decrease of the business transfers t_f^s; if the STATE decreases the welfare outlays it can increase subsidies to business without braking growth . . .

The same reasoning can be applied to the activity of the BANK selling credits c_h^b to the HOUSEHOLD, c_f^b to the FIRM and m_b to the STATE.

All these PNITs change Y and by virtue of the relation F (or f) the employment E. One shall not miss the fact that K not only plays a role in the FIRM but also in the three other AGENTS. For instance the BANK's employment is now sharply declining by its great investment in data storing, data processing and communication equipment while its capacity which is greatly increased acts in the opposite direction. The same is true, to a lesser degree, due to political or traditional influences and to the arguments of the sacred as opposed to those of the rational for the STATE. Even the HOUSEHOLD by an increased use of appliances, of home automation, of leisure equipments etc. (i.e. of increasing its K) changes its contribution to Y.

We consider *inflation* only on a macroscale as measured by a price index. Micro or sectorial variations of prices while contributing to better or worse resource allocation are outside this analysis.

Two kinds of price indices are in use: the Y deflator and the CPI (consumer price index). They differ in their scope and in their evaluation methods. We shall not deal with this part of economics.

Inflation as well as other financial imbalances concern monetary flows; this is not the case for the relations F, f and g just discussed. In our approach inflation is caused by imbalances between separate elements of the VA creation and distribution which are by definition globally equal in a period. These imbalances are expressed by monetary and financial elements (credit and money issue) some of which are exogenous. In usual economics inflation (i.e. the price increase) is caused by an excess of money over real resources available, as expressed in the Cambridge or Fisher equation $\dot{M} + \dot{V} = \dot{P} + \dot{Y}$. Our analysis shows that transfers from the STATE, a dynamic process, can contribute to inflation as do also the transfers from the BANK. The primary VA created by the

FIRM in the period which is the bulk of Y when compared to the sum of incomes and savings plays a great but not very direct role in inflation. One must not neglect other VA creations e.g. the role of transfers and of variations of real stocks, to which must be added the existence of 'leaks' in the overall VA creation and distribution by the real and financial external exchanges. The process is rather complex but can be illustrated by a very simple example: when prices of imported raw materials rise, the PIT which generates the VA decreases so the volume of Y decreases and, for the same distributed VA, prices rise and E decreases.

As regards the specific role of transfers due to their temporal lags, as shown above, inflation exaggerates their impact: if prices rise, the transfers from the past decrease in real terms while the part of Y distributed to the future remains in the period at the same nominal level. If $p_t > p_{t-1}$, t^s_{t-1}: $p_t < t^s_{t-1}$: p_{t-1} while t_t remains the same. So in real terms the inflation decreases the contribution to Y of the transfers from the past. The opposite occurs if the prices fall.

These short remarks on inflation do not by far exhaust the matter. The overall influence of trade imbalances is not explained. The budgetary imbalance (the public deficit, for instance) is, on the contrary accounted for in our presentation, as is easy to see.

We shall conclude this section and the chapter by some loose comments.

1. In our developed economies the distributed incomes are predominant. Such is not the case in the less developed countries (the LDCs) where the saving and the 'profits' play, in general, a greater role in the monetary (perhaps not in the real) VA distribution. These profits are often exported and the economy is bled and does not develop as it could do in this absence of this bleeding. The crucial problem is the problem of how to best use the savings of the HOUSEHOLD and of the FIRM.

2. As already stated in several places in this text the VA distribution influences the production processes, i.e. the VA creation, while generating a special feedback in itself. High distributed incomes (a high ratio of incomes to savings) generates a diachronic evolution of high capital/output ratio. High wages, i.e. high unit time compensation generates the elimination of unqualified activity. In other terms, if the technology allows it, a change in VA distribu-

tion in favor of incomes implies an enhanced use of the technology in order to compensate this tendency. The process creates unemployment. Formally it changes the relation F or f.

3. It seems to be an experimental result that any concentration of savings, i.e. a centralization of investments choices decreases the efficiency of these choices. This is a complex matter however where the kind of production processes, for instance, their high or low capital/output ratio plays a great role. We tackled this point only on a very global level of the scope of choices of different agents and their alienation from individual or small collective to ever bigger collective agents, including the State. We shall only mention here a contradiction when a decentralized use of savings is a public credo coexisting with a high budget deficit. This state of public finances implies a high degree of centralization of the available savings in contradiction with the proclaimed rationale.

4. Our presentation of economic dynamics, especially by the relation F, shows the importance of correct forecasting by the agents. Of course perfect or 'rational' expectations are a dream. It is important however that forecasting be not very difficult. The budgetary and trade balance and stable prices are means which lessen the difficulty of the task. Stable foreign exchange rates also contribute to this end.

5. Flexibility is also a requirement for growth and development. In real life the natural occurence of changes in habits, in knowledge and in procedures is opposed by the equally natural fear of change and of the risk that is implicit in any change. The preference for what exists compared to what can occur is common to people and to their groupings. In a democratic society this reality is an obstacle to the improvement of economic and other processes and to growth. In our model this obstacle is often revealed by the importance of transfers from the STATE to the FIRM intended to maintain obsolete activities which would otherwise create negative VA. Governments are compelled if they want to be reelected to compromise with the aversion to change and to risk at the expense of growth and development.

SUMMARY AND CONCLUSIONS

1. There are five sets of economic objects: of agents, of resources, of choices of agents, of constraints on choices and of criteria of choices. Their analysis is the concern of this book.

2. The activity of people called labour in current economics is not an input but a title to a part of the value added distributed. As such it is not a cost.

3. The value added (VA) is a nominal monetary flow in a period of time, created by a PIT (a Price Included Transfer) corresponding to the difference between the inflow of money compensating for the outflowing real output and the monetary outflow compensating for the inflowing real input. This PIT is supplemented or enlarged by all PNITs (Price Not Included Transfers) whether positive or negative, flowing to and from the agent.

4. Prices, i.e. the ratios of flows of money to flows of resources, appear in elementary exchanges by mechanisms of comparison of marginal utilities of money and of resources exchanged, which are different for the buyers and the sellers. Prices are socialized in economics by secondary processes.

5. It follows from the existence of PITs as the source of prices and as the origin of the value added that prices do not express real relative scarcities and are unsufficient indicators for an efficient resource allocation.

6. The primary VA distribution consists in its partition into two parts, namely incomes and savings. This primary distribution is followed by a secondary partition, into taxes, 'earned' income of active persons and 'unearned' income of other title bearers, savings directly invested into real resources and savings transferred to the financial sector by the financial investment, i.e. purchases of bonds, shares and other 'instruments' as well as deposits into accounts and holding cash.

7. This VA distribution is in all its stages and choices a process of a resolution of conflicts, either between people or between groups. The earned income for instance, currently but not here labelled

'labour cost' has been and remains the essence of the economic fight between owners or managers of businesses, be they private or public and their hired workers. The personal conflicts are often resolved within families; collective conflicts are resolved by negotiations of contracts, by force, power, traditions and usages. 'Rational' arguments in these processes are the subject of the current economic 'science'. It analyzes the VA creation and distribution and endeavours to establish normative rules such as the Ricardian, Marxist, Walrasian, Keynesian, neoclassical, monetarist etc. theories, cited here in chronological order. In the realm of public choices laws regulate the economic activity and establish the rules by which, particularly by means of taxation, the society is a partner in the VA distribution. Public choices are guided by the arguments of law and order, security, general welfare, education and health care etc., by the necessity of procuring other public goods and services and also by reasons of justice, equity, solidarity and ethics and morals, of power and prestige lusts.

8. The VA creation and distribution are the two main socio-economic and political material processes of societies. Which of the two methods used in these processes is the more efficient: of PITs through markets or of PNITs through social choices remains an open issue. It seems that the thesis of Coax in favor of the former is too narrow since the division of labour, more precisely of activities, and the use of equipments require the partition of the VA created into incomes and savings, i.e. the distribution of the VA by means of PNITs.

9. The author takes exception to any normative rules and limits his effort to a description of the resolution of all types of conflicts by means of the three sets of choices, constraints on choices and criteria of choices, all three being in almost every circumstance of a high cardinality. The VA distribution is the result of an intricate process of choices. Any analysis of this process is a catalogue of possibilities and arguments for or against any given distribution. For instance most current models divide incomes and savings into wages and profits and build relations between these two parts and their subparts justifying such relations by parameters of labour productivity, rates of return on the capital, profit maximization, demand and supply, investment and growth, price, balance and em-

ployment equilibria etc. This book does not contain discussions on these arguments.

10. A simplified macroeconomic model is proposed. It consists of four aggregate AGENTS: the HOUSEHOLD, the FIRM, the BANK, and the STATE. A fifth AGENT, the outside world, is mentioned but not really included. The model differs from traditional proposals by two particularities: it integrates the STATE into the set of 'common' agents and does not partition people into for instance workers, landowners, capitalists and entrepreneurs . . . .

The four AGENTS and the two aggregates of real resources: CONSUMPTION and INVESTMENT are the vertices of a graph of monetary flows which are PNITs. The VA is not explicated in this diagram since it is generated by PITs. Its aggregation into the GDP allows to analyze some dynamic properties of economies.

11. A general dynamic relation is proposed between employment, the product, the stock of real capital and its load factor. A relation denoted $F(. . .) = 0$ is specified.

12. A crude analysis of F shows how capacity and productivity investments act on employment and how transfers from the STATE and the BANK influence growth.

13. An important brake on growth consists in socio-economic rigidities. The technological progress combats these rigidities. We show that technology acts as a 'solvent' on the sets of constraints of all agents, making many of its elements disappear. Sociologists have noticed an image of this contemporary tendency in the general relaxation of constraints in fashion, clothing and manners at the end of this century.

14. Equilibrium as a general concept is not applicable to economic reality. Growth is, by definition, contradictory to equilibrium. The theories of golden path and similar try to bypass the contradiction by considering successive static states of equilibria. Real dynamics cannot be represented by such models since this implies the existence of causes of the dynamics of growth, inflation, employment etc. which are the essence of disequilibria.

15. As in most scientific inquiries an apparent paradox arises from the book's approach. It results from the proposed model that in the asymptotic ideal state of optimality in the marginalist model or in the 'zero-exploitation' state of the marxist model the VA

created will be zero: the cost of the input will be equal the price of the output, a zero PIT will be generated. The economic activity of the BANK and of the STATE will be paramount since all distributed income and all saving will transit through these two AGENTS. Such would be the 'pure economy' of Walras.

INDEX

abundance 16, 46, 135, 140
accumulation 154
activity 26
actualization 150
affluence 14, 75
agents x, 1
  abstract 29
  collective 1, 2, 17, 52, 148
  consumer 164
  elementary 1, 17
  individual 49, 144
  productive 159
  public 57, 158, 160
aggregation 67, 175, 191
aggregates 78, 103, 175
age pyramid 137
aid 108
alienation 36, 42
allocation (of resources) 44
armaments 15
Arrow, K. J. 66
artifacts 10
associations 5
atomic bomb 25
attraction 17, 19
auctioneer 99
authority 173

bank 70, 78, 85, 178, 187
  central 70, 83
barter 68, 74, 100
Baumann, H. L. 124, 132, 154
beauty 30, 47, 140
Bernard, G. 67, 110
Big Bang 21, 143
biology 137
biosphere 37, 136, 139

birth control 137
brain 19
Buckingham, E. 61
budget 78
  public 158
  soft constraint 110
bullion 69
buyer 90

Cambridge identity 87, 201
Capital 16, 29, 72
  constant 154
capitalist system 13
capitalists 64, 125
Carnot, S. 21
cashflow 155
causality ix
choices
  sets of possible 30, 76
  – constraints on 30, 76, 77
  – criteria of 30, 44, 76, 78
churches 5, 148
claims 30
class struggle 3, 60, 157
Clerk-Maxwell, J. 61
Coax, J. 205
Cobb-Douglas production
  function 65
cohesion 17
comanagement 126
commodities 76
  commodity prices 82
communication 11, 74
competence 173
competition 31
complementarity 63
computer networks 174
Condorcet, M. J. 66

conservatives   22
constraints   2
costs   80, 83, 139
    marginal   109
    of labour   113
consumer demand theory   49
consumer price index
        (CPI)   189, 201
consumption   12, 14, 16, 76,
    166, 194
contract   4
credit   56, 72, 77, 83, 84, 86
criteria   2
currency   70
    fiducial   70
    scriptural   70

Debreu, G.   45, 82, 83, 111
decision theory   42
deficit, public   87
De Jong, F. J.   61
demand   49, 81, 92
democracy   22, 174
demography   6, 136, 138,
    148
depreciation   56, 114, 156
development   198, 203
dialectic   140, 141
dimension   45
dimensional analysis   61
dimensionality reducers   46
discount rate   150
disequilibria   ix
distribution   32
dividends   55, 113, 117, 156
division of labour   19, 39, 74,
    80, 81, 112
dream   75
Dupuit, J.   109
dynamics   ix, 197

Econometrics   22
economics   ix, 16, 22, 117
    financial   170

planned   183
processes of   175
pure   207
Edgeworth, F. Y.   90, 91
education   144, 147
efficiency   31, 32, 45, 89
Einstein, A.   20, 21
elasticity
    of demand   92, 93, 104
    of substitution   104
electromagnetic spectre   140,
    151
élite   23, 112
employment   198
    full   39
energy   11, 17, 139
Engels, W.   124, 126, 132
entropy   139
equilibrium   ix, 45, 49
    theory   102
ethics   4, 21
Eucken, W.   163
exchange   x, 4, 29, 61
    elementary   34, 90
    cost of   99
exclusion, principle of   13

factor of belonging   2
factor of production   64
faith   42
family   4
feedback   23, 24
fields   17
    attraction   20
    repulsion   20
finance   56, 72, 89, 170
    private   106
    public   106, 114
firm   1, 4, 53, 178, 183
Fisher equality   61, 201
fixed point   91
flexibility   203
flows   62
fluctuations   21

forces   17
forecasting   6
Fourier, Ch.   ix
freedom   36, 75
  economic   39
  cultural   40
free will   36
free rider   107
Freud, S.   ix
Frey, B. S.   22, 23
Froude   45
fuzziness   ix, 2, 29

gamble   75
genetics   137
Georgescu-Roegen, N.   67, 139
Gibbs, J. W.   21
gift   4
gluts   82
goods   12
  capital   27
  consumption   27
  deluxe   14
  discretionary   14
  final   27
  intermediate   27
  merit   12, 13
  private   12, 16, 76
  public   12, 16, 76
  subsistence   14
government   1
graph G   26
  fuzzy   3
growth   198, 206

happiness   36
Hayek, F.   90
Hicks, J.   18
household   1, 4, 52, 57, 59,
    178, 185

Ichiishi, T.   127
illusion   75
incomes   x, 12, 55

indivisibility, principle of   13
inflation   28, 84, 86, 89,
    159, 198, 201
information   11, 16, 74
inputs   5, 7, 54
interest rate   72, 84, 85, 132
insurance   178, 180
investment   14, 16, 54, 64,
    73, 76, 89, 144, 168, 194

justice   21, 22, 31, 32

Kant, I.   35
Kastler, A.   20, 22, 28, 29
Keynes, J. M.   ix, 83, 123,
    154, 161, 168, 169
knowledge   ix, 11, 28, 32,
    112, 151
Koestler, A.   46, 145
Kornai, J.   110, 111
Krelle, W.   xix

labour   16, 29, 34, 45, 46, 49,
    61, 62, 65, 73, 116
  marginal productivity of   121
  division of   19, 39, 74, 80,
    81, 112
Lang, A.   x
leisure   144, 147
Leontieff, W.   26, 27
Lesourne, J.   28
liberals   22
libertarian   7, 80
Lincoln, A.   174
life   139
load factor   198, 199

Mach, E.   45
macroeconomics   18, 29, 48, 58,
    61, 72, 82, 84, 175
Malinowski, B. K.   90
management   54, 118, 120
marketing   64
markets   9, 18, 29, 81, 89

market control 104
Marx, K. 8, 22, 27, 30, 33,
    45, 62, 64, 75, 79, 81, 83,
    115, 123, 125, 146, 154, 181
marxist theory 116, 121
matter 17
Maxwell, J. C. 21
McIntyre 22
Mead, M. 90
medical care 39
Mera, K. 78
metabolism 6
metarationality 21, 25, 28, 58
microeconomics 48, 72, 168
models ix, 18, 88
    closed 7, 146
    descriptive x
    keynesian 83, 200
    marxist 56
    neoclassical 56
    normative x
    open 7
money x, 11, 30, 46, 56,
    61, 68, 135
    central 84
    neutrality of 84, 86
monetarist theory 88
monopoly 31, 119
    bilateral 90
morals 4, 21
Morishima, M. 65, 70, 79
Musgrave, R. & P. 78

nation-states 37
Nash 90, 91
Nature ix, x, 10, 18, 140
negentropy 139
Neumann, J. von 8, 146
Newton, I. 21
non-exclusion 16
non-rivalry 13, 16
nuclear fission 25
nuclear fusion 139

nuclear winter 18
numéraire 68, 69

objective 54
Ohm, G. S. 21
Okun, G. 198
optimum 45
organizations 29
Orwell, G. 42
owners 64
ownership 20, 60
output 5, 7, 54

patents 30
Patinkin, D. 83, 169
Pareto, V. 101, 103, 111, 197
participation 126
peace 31
pensions 144, 165
people 23
person 1
physics ix
Picasso, P. 46
Pigou, A. 169
PIT (price included
    transfer) 32, 82, 101,
    151, 161, 165
Planck, M. 45
planning 6, 27, 31, 89
PNIT (price non-included
    transfer) 32, 101, 160,
    161, 165
Poland 48
policy budgetary 58
    economic 59
    monetary 58
pollution 38, 111
Popov, G. 125, 132, 154
population density 136
poverty 40
power 20, 41, 135, 185, 197
preference for liquidity 168
prices x, 40, 54, 64, 71, 75, 80,
    91, 135, 144

deflator 111
elasticity 92, 104
principal 172
probability 51
product 55, 64, 76
  social 57, 72
  gross domestic (GDP) 190, 200
production 29, 32, 100
  factors of 64
productivity 74, 144
  of labour 121
  marginal 121
profit 53, 56, 64, 72, 74, 113, 116, 120, 133, 154
  maximization 130
  rate of 133
progress ix, 32, 111, 118
promiscuity 16, 20, 111, 136, 140
propensity to save 168
proximity 16, 20, 111, 136, 140
psychology ix, 17, 135

quantum mechanics 135, 143
quarantine 39
Quesnay, F. ix

radiation 139
randomness ix, 20
rational 22, 25, 28
  expectations 25, 88
rationing 152
Rawls, J. 31
reducer of dimensionality 45, 73
regulation 38
relativity theory 135
religion 4, 36
rents land 103
  productivity 103
repulsion 17, 19
resources x, 10, 39

material 10
immaterial 10
Reynolds 45
Ricardo, D. ix, 33, 45, 86
risk 26
risk aversion 47, 147
  love 47, 147
  pooling 179
Rousseau, J. J. ix
Russian doll 2, 191, 193

sacred 22
satiation 54
saving 12, 14, 55, 59, 72, 89, 114, 117, 144, 147, 158, 166, 168
  forced 181
  free 181
Say, J. B. 71
scarcity 16, 30, 46, 63, 80, 89, 111, 135, 140, 142, 148, 151
Schmidt, H. 200
Schrödinger, E. 139
selffinancing 158
seller 90
sex 20
Solari, L. 62
Smith, A. ix, 8, 33, 45, 62
socialist system 13
sociology ix
sovereignty 57
space x, 135, 136
Spengler, A. 149
stability 25
state 1, 8, 55, 57, 64, 118, 121, 148, 178, 188
statistics x
starvation 54
Steinbrenner, P. 124
stocks 62
strategy 54
strike (right to) 40
substituability 63

surplus 91
supply 81, 92
  side theory 88

taboo 38, 40
taxes x, 4, 55, 76, 100, 133
technology 113
Thornton, H. 70, 86
time ix, x, 19, 26, 49, 63, 65,
  85, 135, 142, 148
  physical 143
  physiological 143
  social 143
  discount rate of 150
tolls 108, 141, 142, 151
totalitarian 8, 80, 126
Toynbee, A. 149
trade 100
  terms of 105
transfer x, 4, 29, 57, 72, 82, 100
transport 11
truth 41

uncertainty ix, 20, 27, 42, 44,
  51, 54, 75
underground economy 191
unemployment 28, 89, 123,
  146, 147
urbanization 137
USA 24, 137
USSR 24, 137
utility x, 3, 30, 32, 44, 46, 49,
  53, 61, 63, 65, 71, 73, 76,
  78, 81, 94, 100, 135, 144
  expected 51

marginal 49, 78, 91
  social 3, 52, 188
utilities 109

value 12, 32, 44, 46, 61, 65, 70,
  71, 73, 81, 135
  exchange 33, 79
  judgment 32, 49
  surplus 33
  usage 33, 79
value added x, 4, 7, 12, 32, 55,
  59, 62, 72, 83, 94
  creation of 32, 55, 111
  distribution of 32, 55, 113,
  114
value added tax (VAT) 106,
  114, 157, 158
vertices 3, 26, 31, 175
votes 23

wages 55, 72, 74, 83, 154
  wage rate 133
  equilibrium wage rate 121
workers 64, 125
Walras, L. ix, 30, 63, 81, 101,
  103, 111, 197, 207
waste 111
war 30, 31
wealth 4, 40, 72
Weitzman, M. L. 123, 126, 132,
  147, 154, 156, 163
Wicksell, K. 69
world-economy 20
world outside 177
work 103, 144, 145
Whyte, A. xix

THEORY AND DECISION LIBRARY

SERIES A: PHILOSOPHY AND METHODOLOGY OF THE SOCIAL
SCIENCES

Already published:

Conscience: An Interdisciplinary View
Edited by Gerhard Zecha and Paul Weingartner
ISBN 90–277–2452–0

Cognitive Strategies in Stochastic Thinking
by Roland W. Scholz
ISBN 90–277–2454–7

Comparing Voting Systems
by Hannu Nurmi
ISBN 90–277–2600–0

Evolutionary Theory in Social Science
Edited by Michael Schmid and Franz M. Wuketits
ISBN 90–277–2612–4

The Metaphysics of Liberty
by Frank Forman
ISBN 0–7923–0080–7

Towards a Strategic Management and Decision Technology
by John W. Sutherland
ISBN 0–7923–0245–1

Principia Economica
by Georges Bernard
ISBN 0–7923–0186–2